National Rights,
International Obligations

National Rights, International Obligations

EDITED BY

Simon Caney,
David George,
and Peter Jones

WestviewPress
A Division of HarperCollinsPublishers

Copyright © 1996 by Westview Press, Inc., A Division of HarperCollins Publishers, Inc.

Published in 1996 in the United States of America by Westview Press, Inc., 5500 Central Avenue, Boulder, Colorado 80301-2877, and in the United Kingdom by Westview Press, 12 Hid's Copse Road, Cumnor Hill, Oxford OX2 9JJ

A CIP catalog record for this book is available from the Library of Congress.
ISBN 0-8133-2938-8.—0-8133-2950-7 (pbk.).

The paper used in this publication meets the requirements of the American National Standard for Permanence of Paper for Printed Library Materials Z39.48-1984.

10   9   8   7   6   5   4   3   2   1

Contents

Preface

For many years political philosophers have focused upon the internal arrangements of states to the relative neglect of questions concerning state boundaries and issues which transcend those boundaries. Happily that imbalance in the concerns of political philosophy is now being put right and the philosophical literature on international and transnational issues has grown rapidly in recent years. Students of international relations are also increasingly turning to the normative dimensions of international politics. This volume is a contribution to current debates about the moral significance of nationality and the foundations and extent of transnational rights and obligations. It has its origins in a Colloquium on national rights and international obligations held at the University of Newcastle in January 1995. We are indebted to the contributors to the Colloquium for making it such a stimulating and informative occasion and for making our tasks as editors in preparing this volume so painless and agreeable. We are also indebted to the Department of Politics at Newcastle for providing financial support for the Colloquium, and to the University's Research Committee for its financial assistance. Sue Miller of Westview Press, who has been the book's Commissioning Editor, has given us invaluable help and encouragement, and Jim Grode, also of Westview Press, has been a much appreciated source of technical advice. Finally, we are very grateful to Joan Davison for the patience and good humour with which she produced successive versions of the manuscript and for the care and efficiency with which she has prepared the final text.

Simon Caney
David George
Peter Jones

About the
Editors and Contributors

Helen Batty is a postgraduate student at the University of Newcastle. Her recent work has focused on UK environmental policy and on the idea of environmental justice.

Chris Brown is Professor of Politics at Southampton University. He is the author of *International Relations Theory: New Normative Approaches* (1992) and numerous articles on international political theory. His most recent book is the edited collection *Political Restructuring in Europe: Ethical Perspectives* (1994).

Simon Caney is Lecturer in Politics at the University of Newcastle. He has published articles in politics and philosophy journals on liberalism and communitarianism. His current research interests include normative international political theory and Rawls's political liberalism.

Margaret Canovan is Reader in Politics at Keele University. She is the author of *Hannah Arendt: a Reinterpretation of Her Political Thought* (1992) and *Nationhood and Political Theory* (1996) as well as other books and articles on political theory.

John Charvet is Reader in Political Science at the London School of Economics. He is author of *The Social Problem in the Philosophy of Rousseau* (1974), *A Critique of Freedom and Equality* (1982) and *The Idea of an Ethical Community* (1995). He is currently working on the ethical theory of international society.

David George is Lecturer in Politics at the University of Newcastle. He has published journal articles and book chapters in his three areas of research interest: terrorism and related low-intensity conflict, nationalism and political Islam.

Paul Gilbert is Senior Lecturer in Philosophy at the University of Hull. He is author of *Human Relationships* (1991) and *Terrorism, Security and Nationality* (1994). His current research interests are divided between philosophy of mind and political philosophy, in particular the nature of nationalism.

Tim Gray is Senior Lecturer in Politics at the University of Newcastle. His publications include *Freedom* (1991), *The Feminism of Flora Tristan* (1992) (with M Cross) and *Burke's Dramatic Theory of Politics* (1988) (with P Hindson). He is presently working on the politics of the environment.

Peter Jones is Professor of Political Philosophy at the University of Newcastle. He is the author of *Rights* (1994) and has also written on liberalism, toleration, democracy and social policy. He is currently working on political strategies for dealing with diversities of belief and culture.

Neil MacCormick is Regius Professor of Public Law at the University of Edinburgh. He is the author of many books on legal and political philosophy, including *Legal Reasoning and Legal Theory* (1978) and *Legal Right and Social Democracy* (1982). He is currently working on legal theory and the European Union. He has been a candidate for the Scottish National Party in several recent elections.

Hillel Steiner is Professor of Political Philosophy at the University of Manchester. The author of *An Essay on Rights* (1994), he has contributed articles on liberty, rights and moral reasoning to various philosophy, politics and economics journals and collections, and is a member of the editorial boards of *Ethics* and *Social Philosophy & Policy*.

Yael Tamir is Senior Lecturer in Philosophy at Tel-Aviv University. She is the author of *Liberal Nationalism* (1993) and the editor of *Democratic Education in a Multicultural State* (1995). She has written extensively on theories of nationalism, individual and collective rights, and philosophy of education.

1

Introduction

Simon Caney, David George and Peter Jones

Few will doubt the major importance of the revival of nationalism during the late twentieth century. Together with the eruption of militant political Islam, the collapse of the Soviet bloc, the consolidation of democracy in the West and its spread elsewhere, it is among the most globally significant political phenomena of our time. While this may readily be admitted, the moral meaning of the phenomenon is a much more difficult and obscure matter. This is especially true at present, since it is the ugly, brutal and even barbaric face of nationalism that has been most frequently and conspicuously presented to the world. In raising the question of whether a more reasonable, liberal form of nationalism is possible, a form that avoids the sheer inhumanity of so much contemporary nationalist practice, we immediately begin a philosophical engagement with one of the numerous moral issues that surround nations and nationalism, and with which the contributors to this volume are concerned. Their philosophical business, in short, is with the ethical significance of nationality.[1] However, before its moral meaning can be properly assessed, the concept of nationality itself needs to be fully analysed, and this is a focus of attention in several chapters. The resulting assessments of the moral implications and significance of nationality fall into three main groups: the first group is concerned with the moral legitimacy of the claims of nationality; the second, with the issue of whether moral obligations are invariably transnational, or if there are special moral obligations to compatriots; and the third, with the problems of reconciling global norms of behaviour with the fact of cultural (including value) diversity, both within nation-states and transnationally.

The Claims of Nationality

International law endows all individuals with a plethora of positive entitlements, their human rights. It also accords universal legal rights to various kinds of human groups, including groups labelled as "peoples". The common first article of the two *International Covenants on Human Rights*, adopted by the UN General Assembly in 1966, declares: "All peoples have the right of self determination. By virtue of that right they freely determine their political status and freely pursue their economic, social and cultural development"; though neither here, nor in any other international legal document, is the bearer and beneficiary of this right, the "people", defined. The ambiguity this creates is, perhaps, resolved by current state and UN practice which restricts the right to colonies; to trust, non-self-governing and mandated territories; and to citizens subject to racist regimes—that is, to groups that are generally accepted as political units and whose basis of association therefore includes a territorial element with fixed boundaries. Current practice is not criterionless, then, but the criterion is one that largely confines the self-determination of peoples to colonies or quasi-colonies (which rarely are nations), and consequently excludes minority nationalities within the state, such as the Bretons, the Basques, the Catalans, the Scots and the Welsh, as they are not colonies or quasi-colonies.[2] Since that is its apparent effect, it is unsuitable for present purposes, for these are precisely the kinds of group that are normally thought of as bearers of a moral right, the right of national self-determination.

If individuals are the bearers of many and varied moral rights just because they are human beings, all national groups are normally thought to have a single, collective moral right, that of self-determination. A self-determined nation is one that is politically autonomous; that is, it is a group that has its own political institutions, through which the members collectively decide and implement legislation and policies concerning the group. National self-determination therefore denotes the condition of a self-governing nation. Its antithesis is alien rule. This rule is imposed upon the nation from outside by the government of a state against which the right of national self-determination is claimed. Alien rule thus entails the absence of national political institutions and implies that the policies that prevail in the nation are not its own.

To a certain extent, the right of national self-determination is modelled on the right of a human being to be a self-determined person. Individual self-determination, in its Kantian formulation, is the condition of someone who is not subject to the will of another human being or to any other external cause, but only to his or her own will and then only in so far as it is determined by the rational moral law. This condition of the will is one of moral autonomy and personal freedom. A free person is one whose actions are not the outcome of personal desires, passions or interests, but are the exclusive result of that person's own reason and are thus performed for their own sake, or as ends-in-themselves. Analogously, a nation is self-determined when its collective actions are determined by the national will and are not subject to any other (alien) will or wills. Nationalists frequently describe the achievement of this autonomy as national liberation, though it differs from the Kantian conception of freedom in one crucial respect. In the nationalist version, it is not a necessary condition of freedom that the will of the nation is determined exclusively by rational imperatives of the moral law. On the contrary, the policies followed by the liberated nation may well be determined by the national interest or by national passions. For the same reason, it would not be plausible to describe the independent nation as a morally autonomous group. There is also a third important difference between the concepts of individual self-determination and national self-determination. The manner in which the self-determining person acts is unproblematic, but the self-determining nation acts through its own political institutions, and the form they take is a matter of dispute.

Two basic views can be distinguished. On the first, a nation is self-governing only if it acts through the political institutions of its own state. The right of national self-determination is thus a right to independent statehood (which in turn presupposes that the nation has a right to secede from the state of which it is currently a part). In the chapters that follow, Neil MacCormick and David George interpret the right of national self-determination in this way. On the second view, taken by John Charvet, there is no necessary right of national secession, since the vehicle of national self-government can be either the institutions of independent statehood or political institutions that fall short of independent statehood. In the latter case, the nation's claim to be self-governing will be met through a set of institutions with limited political powers and operating within the existing state. There are several varieties of these political institutions, ranging from states in a confederation or a federation through to regional or local councils exercising powers that have been devolved from the central government. Whichever variety is selected, it will result in a limited form of national self-determination. As the powers of the sub-state institutions are less than those of an independent nation-state, the nation will still be subject to more-or-less extensive external interference by the government of the state within which it remains. Nevertheless, this limited degree of political autonomy will count as national self-determination, provided the political institutions are freely chosen by the nation and not imposed upon it by the government of its state.

On this second interpretation, then, the right of national self-determination is either a right to independent statehood or a right to self-government through institutions providing a lesser degree of political autonomy within the existing state. If it is the latter, this is either because nation-statehood is impractical (for example, because the nation is not territorially concentrated); or because it is morally undesirable (for example, because the nation-state will wrong the citizen body of the state if it secedes, by depriving it of what is economically or militarily necessary for its continued viability or survival); or because, as Charvet argues, rational contractors would not agree to principles of co-operation that did not thus protect (national) minority rights. All three contributors agree, however, in rejecting a variant of the first view of national self-determination that is frequently held by nationalists. This is that the right of national self-determination not only includes a right to a fully sovereign state, but also entails that the actions of this nation-state must result from a wholly autonomous, or externally unconstrained, national will. On this particularist view of national self-determination, only self-imposed limitations on the legislation and policies of the autonomous nation-state are legitimate.

There are two important reasons for rejecting such a claim to national self-determination. In the first place, the absolute degree of political autonomy that is sought here is impossible to achieve. Not even the most powerful economic country on earth is able to determine the exchange rate of its own currency—the US dollar, for example—and neither can any national culture, however strongly rooted, be wholly insulated from the impact of global culture by a nation-state. In the second place, there cannot be a moral right to perpetrate injustice on other groups and individuals which this absolutist formulation of political autonomy allows. There cannot, for example, be a moral right to wrong another nation by denying or withholding from it its right to be self-determined; nor can there be a moral right to sacrifice at will the lives and property of men, women and children of other nationalities just in order to achieve national objectives, whatever these may be. If national self-determination is a moral right, then not only must it be applicable to every nation, but it must also be a right to a lesser degree of political autonomy than is demanded on this particularist, and evidently illiberal, version of the claim. In summary, it must be either a right to the institutions of statehood with less than absolute autonomy in matters of policy and legislation, or a right to sub-state political institutions which facilitate national self-government. In both cases, the right is to choose the institutional vehicle of national self-government. If nation-statehood is that vehicle, two further rights are implied. The right to a nation-state implies, first, a right to select the institutional form of self-government within the nation-state. Thus, the nation that opts for a one-party regime is exercising its right of self-determination, though perversely, as much as the nation that chooses a liberal-democratic form of government. It implies, second, a right of secession from the state of which it is a part, to enable the nation either to join, or to form, a nation-state. Finally, it should be noted that the right of national self-determination, and the further rights that it implies, is always against a state, and not against any other kind of human group, nor against particular individuals.

Moral arguments about human rights attempt to ground them on some relevant feature or features of human individuals such as their claims to be owners of themselves, or to be ends-in-themselves, or to be right bearers under natural law, and so forth. In other words, the relevant facts used in attempts to ground human rights are not natural (or empirical) facts, but moral features of human beings. Arguments over national self-determination similarly attempt to justify it as a moral entitlement by referring to some morally significant feature or features of nations. These attempts can be divided into two broad groups, namely, the individualist and communal approaches. The former locate the moral value of nations in their consequences for the welfare of their individual members. The latter ground the right of national self-determination on the moral fact, or potential moral fact, that nations are inherently ethical communities.

In arguing the case for a liberal form of nationalism, liberal political theorists deploy one or the other version of the individualistic approach to ground national self-determination as a moral right. They may, like David Miller in *On Nationality*,[3] argue that members of nations have obligations to meet the basic needs and interests of each other that they do not have to non-nationals, and that a nation-state can ensure that these reciprocal duties are fulfilled by co-nationals by enforcing them on them as fellow citizens. Or they may, like Yael Tamir in *Liberal Nationalism*,[4] argue that the right of national self-determination is grounded on the value of the distinctive life and character of the nation, as an encompassing cultural group, to the self-identity and well-being of its individual members, which is to say, on its instrumental moral value.

Neil MacCormick presents a variant of this second line of argument. He contends that nations as cultural groups form an important element in constituting the personal identity of their individual members as "contextual individuals". On a Kantian ideal of respect for persons (understood in this way), their nation ought also to be respected, most importantly by ensuring its continuation through an independent, though not a sovereign, state.

Charvet, by contrast, maintains that it is senseless to ask whether nations have a moral right to statehood, as there is no way of distinguishing nations from non-nations among pre-politically organized groups and because, from a contractarian perspective, moral rights accrue only to members of politically organized bodies, that is, to states. Thus, while the cultural commonalities to which nationalists commonly appeal are relevant to the organization of just states, no group exhibiting these commonalities is wronged if self-government is denied; its claim to this status is to a natural right to do the best for itself, not a moral right of self-determination. Charvet admits that unfair discrimination against minority cultures could still occur within the state, the social and political arrangements of which satisfy the general principles of justice. But this outcome is avoided by rational contractors recognizing that they may turn out to be members of a minority culture and so, for self-interested reasons, contractually agreeing to principles of co-operation that preclude this possibility, rather than by granting the minority a moral right to express its culture.

Finally, David George takes a broadly communal approach to grounding the right of national self-determination, but argues that nations are not independent ethical communities on any conception of nationality. He maintains that, in so far as they are ethical communities at all, nations are institutionally organized within states and therefore are incapable of independently generating a moral right to national self-determination.

The ethical significance of nationality is not exhausted in the debate over the right of national self-determination, however, for much contemporary normative political theory tacitly presupposes the phenomenon of nationality, according to Margaret Canovan, and her chapter discloses its extent. She suggests that the beliefs and sentiments of nationality provide a political unity that underpins the principles and ideals that liberal and democratic theorists wish to see implemented. This unifying function is performed unconsciously and without acknowledgement, and it also enables political theorists to appear more thoroughly universalist than they really are. Nationhood meets their need so successfully because it allows members of a state to think and to feel as if they belonged to a natural community.

Should normative political theory therefore come clean and either assert its nationalist foundations loudly and fully or jettison them altogether? Canovan suggests it should do neither, but should recognize the benefits of a balanced combination of particularist and universalist commitments, even though that mix of commitments may not easily be rendered coherent.

Canovan's suggestion is that nationality is essentially a mediating phenomenon which unites the dichotomies of state and community; individual and community; ethnicity or birth and individual identification or choice; past and present; and so on. Yael Tamir explores the mediating function of nationality further by focusing on the role of national myths in this process. In a largely post-religious social world, she claims, national myths, which are typically historical, or rather pseudo-historical, in content, have come to supplant the myths of religion, and it is their socially functional efficacy that commands her attention. She is no less concerned with the moral, epistemological and other problems arising from the fact that efficacious national myths are commonly those that spread illusions, misrepresentations and falsehood. As well as developing Canovan's concept of the mediating role of nations and their myths, and exploring the implications of her own most recent definition of nationality in this connection,[5] the remainder of Tamir's chapter serves a mediating role in this volume, for she vigorously defends her conception of nationality in *Liberal Nationalism* against criticisms made in the chapters of Charvet and George.

National and Transnational Obligations

The ethical significance of nationality, it has already been argued, is not simply a matter of the contested right of national self-determination, but is also the issue of what morally significant function or functions nationality may perform. It further involves the no less controversial question of the ethical significance of national boundaries in terms of duties to compatriots and to others. Do we have obligations that are special to the members of our own nation or more extensive than those that we owe outsiders? Or are our moral obligations owed equally to both?

Two distinctions will be helpful in answering these questions. It is important, first, to distinguish between obligations of justice (a subset of moral obligations, which claim that someone is entitled to some goods) and other types of obligation. The distinction is important because one might accept some sort of obligations to all human beings, but deny others. A libertarian might, for instance, maintain that justice does not require wealthy countries to give assistance to members of impoverished countries, but might also argue, consistently, that members of wealthy countries none the less have a moral obligation to do so.[6] Alternatively, on a theory of global justice, a redistribution from wealthy to poorer countries may be required, and yet it may be claimed, without inconsistency, that every compatriot also has a (non-justice-based) moral obligation to prioritize the well-being of other compatriots. A third possible position is taken by Brian Barry in *Liberty and Justice*. He contends that wealthy countries have both obligations of justice and *humanitarian* obligations to impoverished people in other countries. The distinction he draws between the two types of obligation is not one of enforceable obligations of justice and unenforceable humanitarian obligations, for Barry is willing to accept that the latter kind should also be enforced; rather, the difference is that humanitarian obligations derive from a certain goal, whereas obligations of justice are rights-based. Barry further points out that this classification is not exhaustive since an individual might also have obligations of charity or benevolence.[7]

As well as clarifying what *types* of obligation are appropriate, it is also important to distinguish between theories that affirm a principle of impartiality and those that require (or allow) partiality. What is at stake here is the *scope* of our obligations. To whom do we owe obligations? Impartialist theories require that moral and political principles are not biased towards any individuals and that, in consequence, we have obligations to all human beings regardless of nationality, ethnicity or citizenship. Recent examples of this cosmopolitan approach include Peter Singer's *consequentialist* argument for global redistribution on the basis of individuals having a duty to prevent bad states of affairs, and members of wealthy countries therefore having an obligation to alleviate suffering in impoverished countries.[8] Charles Beitz, by contrast, defends a *contractarian* argument for global redistribution in *Political Theory and International Relations*.[9] Taking as his premiss Rawls's idea that justice should apply within systems of economic co-operation, Beitz argues that principles of justice should apply transnationally rather than within states, because of international economic interdependence. Onora O'Neill provides a third example of the cosmopolitan approach with her *Kantian* theory of international distributive justice in *Faces of Hunger*.[10] Everyone has a duty to assist needy human beings, she claims, regardless of the nation of which they are members, or the state of which they are citizens.

In contrast to impartialist moral and political theories, preferential treatment of some people is enjoined (or allowed) by partialist theories. Michael Sandel's *Liberalism and the Limits of Justice*,[11] Yael Tamir's *Liberal Nationalism* and David Miller's *On Nationality* all take a more communitarian approach than the cosmopolitans with their argument that, as members of a particular community, individuals have special obligations to its other members. A purely cosmopolitan approach, they contend, fails to recognize the special obligations we have as members of groups like families or nations or states. It is, of course, possible to embrace both partialist and impartialist principles and to adopt the position of acknowledging some obligations to all human beings and other, special, obligations to certain people (friends, members of one's family, compatriots).

Both partialist and impartialist accounts of our obligations are considered by the contributors. Paul Gilbert first assumes the existence of special obligations to compatriots and goes on to explore four conceptions of nationality in order to establish which, if any, is capable of accounting for them. Two civic conceptions analyse nationality in political terms, so that national obligations are intelligible in terms of political ones; two culturalist conceptions characterize nationality as a cultural phenomenon, thereby representing national obligations as a species of cultural ones; but none prove capable of accounting for special obligations to compatriots. Gilbert concludes by delineating an alternative, societal, conception of nations as self-constituted, interdependent communities, which, he claims, not only accounts for our national obligations, but also explains their relation to our political obligations.

In his discussion of national obligations, Simon Caney adopts the reverse procedure to that taken by Gilbert. He begins by defining nationality and proceeds to address the normative issue of whether membership of this kind of group does imply special obligations of partiality. Caney distinguishes between two types of defence of special obligations: the "value-independent" and the "value-dependent" approaches. Value-independent defences state that, simply in virtue of belonging to a group, one has special obligations to the other members, independently of the moral value of that group. Value-dependent defences maintain that one can have a special obligation to members of a group to which one belongs only if that group is morally valuable. Altogether, five of the former and three of the latter types of justification of national obligations are examined, but Caney finds none of these communitarian defences to be persuasive.

Turning from national to international (or transnational) obligations, Hillel Steiner and Helen Batty and Tim Gray consider the question of what international obligations, if any, we have. Steiner rejects the partialist approach to justice endorsed in nationalism, which distinguishes between people on the basis of their communal membership, in favour of a cosmopolitan theory of international justice which is universalizable in its approach and treats every human being simply as a human: each individual is a right-holder, each holds the same rights, and no rights may ever be overridden. Drawing on his *Essay on Rights*,[12] Steiner argues each human being has an equal right to equal freedom and claims that this entitles everyone to ownership of their bodies and to an equal share of global natural resources. Both moral claims have implications for normative political theory. The ownership right justifies a right of immigration and emigration; the right to resources justifies secession and, more importantly for Steiner, requires global principles of justice. His theory of justice, like those of Beitz and O'Neill, is cosmopolitan, then; but, unlike them, it primarily appeals neither to our duties nor to a hypothetical contract, but to our rights.

Tim Gray and Helen Batty raise a double question over transnational obligations: is there such an obligation to protect the environment, and if there is, is it compatible with the right of all nation-states to be self-governing? They begin by evaluating arguments in defence of state sovereignty, but find none of them overwhelmingly convincing. They then consider whether the international obligation to protect the environment is best captured by rights discourse (discussing, among others, Beitz's treatment of this issue), but raise numerous objections to this thesis. They conclude that, while we all do have a transnational obligation to protect the environment, there is no human right to an adequate environment.

Global Norms and Local Values

As we move from the nation-state to the world as the arena of our moral life, we increasingly encounter difficult questions posed by the fact of diversity. Given that the world is composed of societies with different values and cultures, how can we identify a set of norms that will tell us what our international rights and duties are? Is it possible to find a set of principles that are already recognized by all societies in spite of their apparent differences? If it is not, should we set about constructing global norms, or should we resign the world to an anarchy of moral relativism? Questions about how we should provide for human conduct in the face of value diversity are not, of course, unique to international life. Within societies, individuals dispute with individuals and groups vie with groups over how we should live. In addition, now more than ever before, societies are themselves multicultural. But the phenomenon of value diversity is most imposing when we look beyond any single society to the world as a whole, and our aspiration to develop and implement universal norms is, perhaps, most inhibited when we confront whole communities whose beliefs, values and ways of life are different from, and incompatible with, our own.

Chris Brown identifies and examines a number of ways in which philosophers have responded to the problems posed by cultural pluralism. One strategy, to be found in the work of Terry Nardin, attempts to evade a clash of global and local values by conceiving international society as a "practical" rather than a "purposive" association. A practical association regulates relations between its members without imposing any goal or conception of the good upon them. So conceived, international society avoids confronting the diverse values of its constituent peoples. Another approach, represented by Kant, Hegel, Marx and their contemporary disciples, spurns that evasion and remains uninhibited by cultural pluralism in propounding universal norms. In the eyes of some, this amounts to cultural imperialism, but universalists themselves understand their norms to be right independently of any culture. A third approach shuns universalism, resigns itself to cultural relativism and engages in a postmodern celebration of difference. Finally, writers such as Michael Walzer and Martha Nussbaum seek to reconcile particularism and universalism by finding space for local values within a universalist framework.

Brown identifies strengths and weaknesses in each of these approaches but concludes that, given the recent and continuing character of the debate, it is still too early to pronounce a verdict upon it. However, he does suggest that it is an approach of the sort proposed by Walzer and Nussbaum that is most likely to yield a satisfactory response to cultural pluralism. There is, indeed, much that is plausible and appealing in a strategy that combines universalism and particularism. Consider how we think about the conduct of individuals. Most theories that prescribe universal norms give individuals some space within which to shape their lives, even though theorists differ over the proper size and content of that space. Analogously, when we develop universal norms for the conduct of international life, we can still allocate to states or nations or peoples a moral space within which they are left to their own discretion. To that extent, the issue is not whether we should be universalist or particularist, but what sort of combination of those two positions we should endorse.

That is how John Rawls conceives the task of developing a theory of justice for the international community.[13] He constructs a law of peoples that is universal in that it provides for international society as a whole. Yet it also leaves ample room for particularism in that it allows individual societies to have very different internal arrangements. Thus, as well as embracing liberal democratic societies, his international law accommodates and gives equal standing to societies based upon conceptions of justice very different from that which Rawls himself sets out in *A Theory of Justice* and, more recently, in *Political Liberalism*. For example, his law of peoples accepts on equal terms nonliberal societies that are committed to specific religious faiths and that are hierarchically organized, provided that they are "well-ordered". Rawls tries to achieve this combination of universalism and particularism by constructing a law of peoples that is entirely "political", in that it derives from fundamental political ideas already shared by the international community, rather than from any specific philosophical, religious or moral doctrine or from any particular intranational conception of justice.

Rawls accepts, however, that there must be some limit to the types of society that the international community can tolerate. Tyrannies and dictatorships, for example, should not be tolerated. Only well-ordered societies should be accepted as "members in good standing" of international society. Well-ordered societies are, *inter alia*, societies that are guided by "common good conceptions of justice" and that respect human rights. Rawls's law of peoples does, therefore, intrude into the domestic arrangements of societies, although he continues to insist that his law, including his account of human rights, remains entirely "political" in that it draws upon political principles shared by the international community rather than upon a comprehensive doctrine or principles unique to liberalism.

In the final chapter of this volume, Peter Jones examines Rawls's attempt to develop a "political" conception of human rights. He questions whether the consensual materials Rawls uses to construct that conception are adequate for the task and whether Rawls's political conception of human rights can avoid colliding with comprehensive doctrines that offer alternative accounts of human rights, or with cultures that are incongruent with human rights thinking yet genuinely embraced and widely shared.

Notes

1. This useful phrase was coined by D. Miller, "The Ethical Significance of Nationality", *Ethics*, Vol. 98 (1988), pp. 647–662.

2. M. H Halperin, D. J Scheffer and P. L Small, *Self-Determination in the New World Order* (Washington, DC: Carnegie Endowment for International Peace, 1992), provides a recent, accessible exposition of the issue of self-determination of peoples in international law. The broader legal issue of peoples' rights is explored in, J. Crawford, ed., *The Rights of Peoples* (Oxford: Clarendon Press, 1988).

3. D. Miller, *On Nationality* (Oxford: Clarendon Press, 1995).

4. Y. Tamir, *Liberal Nationalism* (Princeton: Princeton University Press, 1993).

5. Y. Tamir, "The Enigma of Nationalism", *World Politics*, Vol. 47 (April 1995), p. 425.

6. P. Singer attributes a position like this to R. Nozick: see P. Singer, "Reconsidering the Famine Relief Argument", in P.G. Brown and H. Shue, eds, *Food Policy: The Responsibility of the United States in the Life and Death Choices* (London: Collier Macmillan, 1977), p. 41.

7. B. Barry, "Humanity and Justice in Global Perspective", in *Liberty and Justice: Essays in Political Theory* , Vol. 2 (Oxford: Clarendon, 1991), pp.182–210.

8. P. Singer, "Famine, Affluence, and Morality", *Philosophy and Public Affairs*, Vol. 1, No. 3 (1972).

9. C. Beitz, *Political Theory and International Relations* (Princeton: Princeton University Press, 1979).

10. O. O'Neill, *Faces of Hunger* (London: Allen and Unwin, 1986).

11. M. Sandel, *Liberalism and the Limits of Justice* (Cambridge: Cambridge University Press, 1982).

12. H. Steiner, *Essay on Rights* (Oxford: Blackwell, 1994).

13. J. Rawls, "The Law of Peoples", in S. Shute and S. Hurley, eds, *On Human Rights: The Oxford Amnesty Lecture 1993* (New York: Basic Books, 1993), pp. 41–82.

2

National Identity and
National Self-Determination

David George

Nationalism, the late Elie Kedourie argued, is a relatively modern doctrine, and the no less modern political practice with which it is associated. Briefly stated, the doctrine maintains that "humanity is naturally divided into nations, that nations are known by certain characteristics which can be ascertained, and that the only legitimate type of government is national self-government".[1] For present purposes, this short statement of nationalist doctrine may be glossed as follows. Nationalism has two core doctrines. First, there is the doctrine that all nations are morally entitled to be self-determined or self-governed. A self-determined nation is one subject to a national government and national laws, both of which presuppose that the nation is organized as a territorial, sovereign state; in a strict sense, the self-determined nation is one that is organized as a nation-state. Second, there is the doctrine that only national governments and nation-states are morally legitimate.

This chapter will not be concerned with the second core doctrine, except to note that among the reasons why non-national states and governments are frequently regarded as morally illegitimate is that they inevitably wrong some particular nation or nations by denying them their (alleged) moral right to national self-government. The putative right of national self-determination is violated in the case of a given nation when some part, or all, of its membership and territory is included within that of a non-national state and is prevented from secession. However, the concern of the present chapter is only with the first of the two core doctrines. Its purpose is to elucidate those characteristics of nations that give them, or are supposed to give them, moral rights of national self-determination, understood as entitlements to join, or to become, independent nation-states. In short, its concern is with the concept of nationality or the identity of nations.

Before starting this conceptual analysis, it seems that nations that are capable of generating this right of national self-determination must satisfy five general conditions (or criteria). They must, in the first place, be determinate because, among other reasons, the right to statehood they are supposed to generate is itself determinate, as is statehood too. In the second place, the nation must either be a voluntarist or an involuntarist association: it cannot be both. In other words, the existence of the nation either depends solely upon the will or consciousness of its members (a voluntarist association) or else exists independently of their will or consciousness by virtue of shared features among the group's members, such as the possession of a common language (an involuntarist group). In the first case, the nation is constituted subjectively: in the second, it exists as a matter of objective fact. In whichever of these two, mutually exclusive, ways they are constituted, nations must be separable from states since the right they are supposed to generate is a right to form or to join a state.

This third general condition that a right-bearing nation must satisfy is sometimes formulated as "the nation is a pre-political group". It means that the moral right to statehood must result from some indigenous feature or features of the nation, that is, from features that are not derived from, or dependent upon, its past or present membership of a state. Fourth, since the right to statehood is a moral entitlement—the fact that it may also be a legal right in international law is irrelevant for present purposes—the nation must possess some morally valuable quality or qualities which alone can generate this entitlement. If nationality consists merely of one or more empirical facts, there is then no moral right of national self-determination. Lastly, there is the general criterion that the right of self-determination is universal. All determinate, voluntary or involuntary, separable and morally valuable nations must possess a right to national self-determination if any do, provided, of course, that the exercise of this right does not wrong some other nation (or nations), notably by interfering with its own right of national self-determination. Consequently, the destiny Mill envisaged for what he termed "inferior and more backward" nations , namely, their complete and permanent absorption in "civilised and cultivated" nations, must be excluded.[2]

Whether the fulfilment of these five necessary general conditions is sufficient for a nation to generate a moral right to statehood it is not necessary to consider, for no conception of nation or nationality, it will be argued, meets them all. In the present context, it is also inessential to determine their exact logical relationship, including their logical order of priority (if any), and so this issue will be left as an open question.

Involuntarist Conceptions of Nationality

Nations are normally conceived of as involuntarist bodies, that is, as groups that exist independently of the will or consciousness of their members. Their objective, independent existence is said to be constituted by several, observable, empirical features. The objective characteristics of nationality that are standardly appealed to include a common language, a common culture, a common race, a common religion, a common past and a common territory. Since none of these features is necessarily derived from membership of a state, the condition of separability is, *prima facie*, met. All of them can be exclusively indigenous features of nations, and indeed this is how they are represented. However, it has been almost as often noted that none of the groups normally recognized as nations possesses the entire list of these features. Yael Tamir summarizes this widespread view well when she writes:

> all attempts to single out a particular set of objective features—be it a common history, collective destiny, language, religion, territory, climate, race, ethnicity—as necessary and sufficient for the definition of a nation have ended in failure. Although all these features have been mentioned as characteristic of some nations, no nation will have all of them."[3]

Possessing all the objective characteristics of nationhood is thus too stringent a criterion when it results in no potential national groups qualifying as nations. Equally, however, to possess only one such feature is too loose a criterion of nationality: it results in indeterminacy. Suppose language is taken to be the constitutive tie and indication of nationality. All speakers of Serbo-Croat would then be members of a single Serbo-Croat nation within the territory inhabited by the southern Slavs. But since Serbo-Croat is a Slavonic tongue, on the same linguistic criterion they could just as easily be part of the membership of a wider, pan-Slav, nation. If, however, religion is taken as the best index of nationhood then native speakers of Serbo-Croat constitute (at least) three nations, with mutually exclusive memberships.

Nations will thus be determined by whichever tie and indicator of nationality is selected and will therefore have overlapping memberships and hence either overlapping or identical territories—their national homelands. Could this indeterminacy be avoided if more than one, but less than all, of the objective characteristics of nations that are appealed to count as the necessary and sufficient criteria of nationhood? Unfortunately, this proposed compromise solution does not work either. If it is assumed that all members of the putative nation possess certain features in common, but not all possible traits of nationality, then the indeterminacy of national identity will survive for as long as there is at least one other feature of which this is not the case. Only one such feature is required for there to be nations with overlapping memberships.

The involuntarist conceptions of nationality that have been considered so far make the set of defining constitutive characteristics of nations the common (and exclusive) attribute of all its members. Yet, in reality, these objective national characteristics are frequently not shared by members of the nation. Language and culture, it has been argued, for example, are not, or are not normally, the common property of the members of a nation. A portion of this argument merits quotation in the present context:

> many nations include, on any account of linguistic community, quite distinct language groups within their borders. More significantly, the idea of a common language relies on a quite narrow conception of what it is to belong to a linguistic community. While there may be a large overlap in the vocabulary and grammar of "the language of a nation", the linguistic communities within the nation are quite distinct. The language spoken in the inner cities is not the language spoken in the suburbs. The language spoken by one religious or "ethnic" group might be quite different from that of another. The languages of one region may differ markedly from another. These differences are not merely differences. Divergences in language map onto other social and cultural antagonisms. The inhabitants of a nation do not inhabit a common culture. They exist within distinct cultures dependent on their class, region and ethnic history. The appeal to a national culture or tradition is uniformly an appeal to the culture and tradition of one component group of a nation and the call for its hegemony over others.[4]

To avoid this objection that supposedly common national characteristics are both attributable to only part of the nation's membership and internally differentiated, the involuntarist concept of nationality can be reformulated as a cluster conception.[5] On this version of the involuntarist concept, the members of a nation do not necessarily share all the characteristics that count as a sufficient number to define the nation; indeed, logically, there need not be a single objective national characteristic which all members have in common. Members of the nation acquire their membership simply because they exhibit a family resemblance to its other members; that is, they share some of the defining national characteristics with some of its other members. Yet family resemblances are not sharply demarcated and some members will have similar relations to individuals outside the nation, in which case the national boundaries—the members of the nation and the territory they inhabit—could always have been delineated in some other way or ways.

Redrawing national boundaries of nations as family resemblance groups alters their identity, however. The new demarcation may be regarded either as the same nation with an enlarged or reduced membership and, correspondingly, with changed territorial boundaries, or, if the alterations are more extensive, as a different, though similar, nation, which resembles the first one on account of its overlapping membership and hence partly shared national territory. In the former case, the nation can achieve the requisite fixity of its boundaries for the precisely determinate borders of statehood only from an external source, and that source, it seems, must be a territorial state's highly determinate borders. If so, this violates the separability condition, for nationality no longer consists exclusively in the indigenous features of the nation, but depends for its character partly upon membership of a state. Alternatively, in the latter case, as both nations must have a right of self-determination, neither could become a state, or join a state, owing to their shared membership and territory (i.e., their overlapping boundaries). A further possibility is that one nation exercises its right of self-determination to become a state, either by violating another nation's right of national self-determination (which would seem to undermine the moral quality of its own right), or because the other nation lacks that right, in which case the universality condition is violated. Nations cannot be determinately individuated as family resemblance groups then (i.e., as cluster concepts), either because the nation's borders fluctuate as resemblances are deemed to be more or less inclusive, or because distinguishable nations have overlapping borders, that is, a partly shared membership and territory.

Tamir's definition of a nation as a cluster concept is of a group with a sufficient number of shared, objective characteristics—such as language, history or territory—and, in addition, the possession of a common consciousness by all the nation's members, which she claims is the only necessary, albeit an insufficient, condition of nationality.[6] National consciousness, it might be thought, as a supplementary, subjective criterion of national identity, is capable of overcoming the problems of the objective indeterminacy of nations and the lack of commonality in their objective features, which have already been noted as significant features of the involuntarist conception of nationhood, in whatever way that conception is formulated.

National consciousness, as a criterion of nationality, can itself be formulated in one of two ways: as either a passive or an active awareness. On the first formulation, it consists in a shared awareness on the part of members of a nation of those shared, objective characteristics by virtue of which they constitute a nation; the national consciousness is a passive reflection of the independently existing nation, the mere mental record of a fact. This first formulation of the subjective criterion is therefore not constitutive of nationality, and for this reason it is difficult to see why it should even be thought of as a necessary condition for the group to be defined as a nation. Moreover, when formulated in this way, national consciousness neither eradicates, nor even mitigates, the indeterminacy of a nation, since it does not affect it in any way whatever. Indeed, given the previous argument that nations, on the standard objective criteria of nationhood, have indeterminate memberships, it follows that the passive national consciousness of those members must be correspondingly indeterminate.

Since this interpretation of the cluster version of the involuntarist conception of nationality, with its supplementary criterion of national consciousness, remains devoid of precise limits, it cannot generate a right to national self-determination. Any morally valuable qualities it may possess are also indeterminate. Nor can it achieve a complete separation of the indeterminate nation from the state, for it is always possible that at least some features of such a nation will be derived from its membership of a state because of that very indeterminacy. Nevertheless, this conception of nations does appear to meet the second general condition, namely, that it is a consistently involuntarist conception of nationality. This is due to the fact that national consciousness has been formulated as an intrinsically inactive awareness; it is a wholly inert reflection of empirically observable, objective, national characteristics, and it is these that alone are constitutive of nationality.

In the philosophical literature on national identity, on the other hand, a standard move combines the objective features of nationality with an appeal to an active or constitutive national consciousness. David Miller, for example, argues that five elements in combination distinguish nationality from other sources of collective identity. Three of these features are on the standard list of objective characteristics of nationality—a common past; a common territory; common and differentiating traits like language, culture and race—which suggests that his conception of nationhood is an involuntarist one. To these empirical features of nations, however, Miller adds the apparently voluntarist notion of an active national identity (a community that acts together as a single body) and an unmistakably voluntarist conception of nationhood, namely, a constitutive national consciousness. He writes:

> national communities are constituted by belief: a nationality exists when its members believe that it does. It is not a question of a group of people sharing some common attribute such as race or language. These features do not of themselves make nations, and only become important insofar as a particular nationality takes as one of its defining features that its members speak French or have black skins.[7]

Yael Tamir's cluster concept of nations, on an alternative interpretation, similarly combines an involuntarist with a voluntarist concept of nationality. That is, the cluster concept of nationality is a composite of a number of shared and distinctive objective features in conjunction with a subjective awareness on the part of the members of the nation of those distinctive characteristics which, on this other interpretation, form an active, or constitutive, national consciousness. Were it merely an inert reflection of national characteristics, and hence non-constitutive, it would be difficult to see how national consciousness could be a necessary condition of national identity, as Tamir claims.[8]

In both cases, the outcome of this conjunction of the objective features of nationality with subjective national consciousness is a radical incoherence. The voluntarist and involuntarist conceptions of nationhood cannot be composited because they are mutually exclusive. Either the beliefs of members constitute a nation with a valid claim to statehood, in which case the shared, objective characteristics of nationality will be unnecessary or non-constitutive features, or, alternatively, those very same empirical features do constitute the nation with a right to self-government, in which case any appeal to a national consciousness is necessarily superfluous.[9] It has previously been argued that national consciousness of the inert variety leads to a consistently involuntarist conception of nationality; correspondingly, the active variety of this consciousness relied upon by Miller, and (apparently) by Tamir, results in an inconsistently involuntarist conception of the nation. Other liberal political theorists, like Neil MacCormick, Joseph Raz and Avishai Margalit, may also have adopted a similarly inconsistent conception of nationality and hence embraced the radical incoherence involved.[10]

Neither the consistent nor the inconsistent versions of the involuntarist conception seem to purge nations of indeterminacy, however. As has already been noted, it is analytically true that a purely passive national consciousness has no affect on that indeterminacy. If, instead, national consciousness takes an active or constitutive form, as in the examples of inconsistently involuntarist conceptions of nationality in Miller and Tamir, it also does nothing to modify the defining features of nationality, such as speaking French or having a black skin, in order thereby to remove the indeterminacy of the nation's boundaries (i.e., of its membership and territory).

From these general considerations about indeterminacy, and from particular considerations about the extent to which it can lead to a violation of the separability condition and must rule out national self-determination as a universal right, about the mutual exclusivity of the voluntarist and involuntarist conceptions, and because nations must satisfy all five general conditions if they are to be right-generating groups, it follows that, on any version of the involuntarist conception of nationality, nations must inevitably fail to generate the required moral right of national self-determination. This does not mean that an examination of the alleged ethical value of nations (i.e., as ethical communities), on the involuntarist conception of nationality, is a pointless exercise, however. Given that the logical relationship between the five general conditions that must be satisfied by any valid conception of a moral right-bearing nation was earlier left as an open question, it is a logically permissible move to consider the general criterion that nations must be ethical communities capable of generating a moral right of national self-determination before examining those four other general conditions which must also be satisfied by the involuntarist conception of nationhood. Two lines of argument about the ethical status of nations as involuntarist groups will therefore now be examined: on the first, nations are conceptualized as cultural groups; on the second line, they are viewed as historical communities.

The Moral Significance of Nations: Involuntarist Versions

Empirical facts about a nation, such as that its members speak French or have black skins, are irrelevant to the issue of the ability of nations to generate a right of national self-determination; what is required are moral facts about these and other objective national characteristics. Liberal political theorists commonly claim to find those moral facts in the conception of nations as cultural groups which they favour. Arguably, this is an arbitrary choice among objective national characteristics, unless, that is, national culture is conceptually stretched to include all the other objective features, or else because it is the only empirically observable characteristic of nations that is consistent with liberalism, and that is dubious.

Leaving aside this objection, the liberal political theorist's argument is that it is the moral value of the national culture to individual members that generates the moral right of national self-determination. Neil MacCormick and Yael Tamir both ground a moral right of national self-determination on the individual rights of the members of a nation. MacCormick argues that the distinctive life and character of a cultural nation forms an important element in the personal identity and self-realization of its individual members. Personal identity is, to some extent at least, constituted by membership of the national community, which is also a medium of the members' self-realization; they are "contextual individuals". On the Kantian ideal of respect for persons, their nation ought also to be respected, notably by ensuring its continued existence through independent statehood.[11] On Tamir's version, national self-determination is not a collective right, but the cumulative rights of autonomous, individual members of a nation to make constitutive choices and thus "to express their national identity, to protect, preserve, and cultivate the existence of their nation as a distinct entity", through the political institutions which they establish. Tamir adds that these politically organized bodies need not be nation-states.[12]

Avishai Margalit and Joseph Raz offer a third version of this argument. Nations are cultural groups which have an important ethical value to their individual members; but it is their interests, not their rights, that are the beneficiaries of its moral worth.[13] In each of the three cases, therefore, nations, as cultural groups, are claimed to be of importance to the lives and well-being of their members, and it is this that gives them their morally valuable character. What does not follow, however, is that nations, as ethical communities, are of greater moral value than any other similarly embedding groups, like families, kinship groups or religious communities. In particular, to acknowledge the moral fact that nations as culture groups are important to the lives and well-being of their members is no more a ground for a right to opt for statehood than it is to acknowledge the same moral fact in the case of families, of tribes or of religious communities. At the very least, it would need to be shown that nations are of pre-eminent importance to the lives and well-being of their members in comparison with all other kinds of group to which they also belong—such as a religious community; the family, clan or tribe; the state; the market—and that only by being organized in independent or sovereign nation-states can their pre-eminent moral value be maintained. Moreover, whether or not any of these different groups merit that sort of treatment cannot be determined collectively and *a priori*; their actual moral character is an open question which can be settled only by investigating the facts in each individual case. Thus, for example, if it is admitted that a normal family deserves our respect, a family in which (say) children or the elderly were abused and exploited would not deserve that respect on account of its lack of moral worth. Similarly, a religious community that practised "brainwashing" on its members, or was one the rituals of which included human sacrifice, would not merit our respect because of its morally reprehensible character, no matter how "embedded" were its members.

These examples show that, in certain circumstances, a Kantian respect for persons may require their protection from the group of which they are members and, therefore, a withholding of respect for it.[14] This conclusion is equally applicable to nations. Since a nation can be harmful to the lives and well-being of its members, and, what is no less morally important, though very much more likely, since it may harm the lives and well-being of those people who are not its members, a universal moral right of national self-determination cannot be grounded on an *a priori* claim about the moral value of every national culture; nations, as cultural groups, are not necessarily ethically valuable communities and therefore do not invariably generate a right of national self-determination.

Nor should Mill's "purely moral and social consideration", that not all national cultures are equally valuable to the lives and well-being of their members, be overlooked in this connection. Some national cultures are relatively impoverished, he claims—for example, the Breton and Basque cultures in relation to that of France, or the Welsh, Highland Scots and Irish national cultures in relation to that of Britain. Mill further claims that it is to the advantage of nations with impoverished cultures to be absorbed by those with a relatively richer national culture. He writes:

> Experience proves that it is possible for one nationality to merge and be absorbed in another: and when it was originally an inferior and more backward portion of the human race the absorption is greatly to its advantage. Nobody can suppose that it is not more beneficial to a Breton, or a Basque of French Navarre, to be brought into the current of the ideas and feelings of a highly civilised and cultivated people—to be a member of the French nationality, admitted on equal terms to all the privileges of French citizenship, sharing the advantages of French protection and the dignity and prestige of French power—than to sulk on his own rocks, the half-savage relic of past times, revolving in his own little mental orbit, without participation or interest in the general movement of the world.[15]

   Relatively impoverished national cultures restrict the possibilities for
personal growth (or self-realization) by the nation's members, just as surely as
a relatively impoverished class culture does. Participation in the richer culture
of a different nation or social class offers wider scope for personal self-realization, yet this benefit is withheld from individuals by either a rigid system of
social stratification or by a nation-state, the purpose of which is to protect and
foster the impoverished national culture. On Mill's argument, then, withholding national self-determination in the case of some nations of ethical value
would be of greater value to the lives and well-being of its members than
granting that right, provided there is some other national culture of greater
ethical value in which they will be included. Some losses, as well as gains, to
members of the included nation are probable, however, as the processes of
inclusion are likely to require more or less stressful adjustments in the personal
identity of members. There is no reason in principle though why these should
be any greater than the stresses involved in a transition from one social class to
another in an upwardly mobile society. When these losses are balanced against
the greater opportunities for personal growth within the new nation, it is likely
that the lives and well-being of the members will be enhanced overall.

   An alternative involuntarist conception of nationality remains to be considered in terms of the moral right of national self-determination. Nations, it has
been claimed by David Miller, are historical communities which are simultaneously communities of obligation. That is, national identity "embodies historical
continuity" of a community that "stretches back and forward across the generations", whose members "practise mutual aid among themselves". The governing element in this conception, however, remains that of belief or a constitutive,
national consciousness. Miller's claim is that "national communities are constituted by belief: a nationality exists when its members believe that it does".[16] If
beliefs hold the nation together, in what sense then are nations historic
communities? The nature of Miller's answer is perhaps best understood in
terms of the late Michael Oakeshott's distinction between a practical and an
historical past.

   A practical past is one related to a practical present and future in the sense
that it is one created in order to meet practical concerns; that is, it is
constructed with a view to satisfying present and future wants. It consists of a
vast miscellany of recorded actions and statements which are, as Oakeshott
observed,

   recognised as an almost inexhaustible source of analogies and resemblances
   in terms of which to express our understandings of ourselves or to interpret to
   others our purposes and actions. It extends the range, the vocabulary and the
   idiom of our self-understanding (or at least our self-image) by providing a
   gallery of familiar persons and situations with whom we may identify ourselves or with which we may identify our current circumstances. It offers a

collection of allegedly well-known exploits which in approving, reprobating or excusing we may disclose our current allegiances. It reveals customs and practices which we may view with horror, with admiration or with indulgence and thus protest our own virtue. It provides relics which in venerating, respecting, disparaging or ridiculing we declare our own dispositions. In short, this is a "living" past which may be said to "teach by example", or more generally to afford us a current vocabulary of self-understanding and self-expression.[17]

When all these bits and pieces are assembled in narrative form, they are made to yield important conclusions to those whose past it is, about themselves and about their present circumstances. Among other important conclusions, this narrative provides them with a practical guide to present and future conduct.

That David Miller understands nations as historic communities in this sense is revealed in his comments about some of the beliefs which he maintains are constitutive of nationality. He argues, among other things, that they provide reassurance that the national community is solidly and continuously based over the generations; that "they perform a moralizing role, by holding up before us the virtues of our ancestors and encouraging us to live up to them"; that they increase the members' sense of solidarity with, and obligation to, their co-nationals. This is indeed what Oakeshott terms a living past teaching by example. Parts of this practical past will also tell members of the nation about themselves, about their national character and about how to interpret their current circumstances which, more often than not, appear to be those of a predicament. (Frequently, their predicament is represented as victimisation by another correlative group.) Miller's discussion of the Dunkirk myth is an excellent example of this aspect of the practical past of the nation, the totality of which comprises his understanding of nations as historical communities. Not all the beliefs that Miller argues are constitutive of nationality are myths, but he admits that "national identities typically contain a considerable element of myth". However, whether a constitutive belief is mythical or not is irrelevant to its place within this understanding of nationality: all that is required is that the belief performs the function or the functions required of it within a practical understanding of past, present and future in terms of the category of nationality.

This account of how historical communities have understood themselves in the past and present is a convincing one (though why a liberal political theorist should feel it incumbent upon himself to defend a large amount of known mythological beliefs is, perhaps, somewhat surprising). Though an outline only, it is an historically accurate, general account of their self-interpretation. It is consistent, for example, with Linda Colley's elucidation of the mythical beliefs about themselves that Britons held during the period she labels as, "Forging the Nation, 1707–1837".[18] (The British nation, on Colley's account, was first forged by the Act of Union of 1707 enacted by the Parliament at Westminster, a fact that violates the separability criterion of nationality established at the outset of this chapter.) The principal objection to it is merely that these largely mythological accounts of themselves are not what constitutes the historical character of historical communities. Rather, these beliefs constitute them as legendary communities tied to a practical past, a practical present and a practical future. They are communities, in other words, that are specified in terms of a practical, not a historical, past, and in such a way that their practical usefulness to the current generation will be maximized. A pragmatic test of effectiveness—not the criterion of truth—is the relevant rule by which to assess them.

Though David Miller is not dealing with nations as genuine historical communities, this does not impinge on his argument for national self-determination. A central part of that argument grounds a moral case for the political self-determination of nations. Miller broadly endorses the case made by Margalit and Raz for national self-determination in terms of protecting a national culture which is ethically valuable to the members of the nation. He further argues that nations are ethical communities, in that members have special obligations to meet the basic needs and interests of one another that they do not have to other human beings, and that a national state can ensure these special obligations are performed by enforcing them.[19] This second line of argument (the first has already been considered) is open to several objections, of which two are pertinent here. First, if it is allowed that co-nationals incur special obligations to one another through their membership of the national community, it does not follow that the nation is an ethical community. Special obligations need not be moral ones. They will be if, and only if, the nation is itself an ethical, or morally valuable, community and that moral fact must be established on independent grounds. It cannot be assumed *a priori*. Second, while special obligations may sometimes be moral, it is difficult to see how they can be ascribed exclusively to nations, as distinct from to nation-states, or to any other politically organized community; to put it another way, it is not obvious how the alleged mutual obligations of nationality are distinguishable (other than nominally) from the mutual, civic obligations of citizenship. Nations and states are not historically separable groups in practice, and Miller's own description of special obligations to co-nationals as stemming from a public culture that has been shaped by past political debate presupposes this. So, for example, the moral obligation to sacrifice personal life and property in defence of compatriots in time of war is an obligation to fellow members of the *patria*. Yet, historically, the *patria* has never been merely a national community: it has always been a politically organized community which is sometimes a nation-state and sometimes, as in the case of the Athenian *polis* and the British Empire, is not.

Another example given by David Miller of special obligations to co-nationals is the obligation to pay taxes.[20] This duty can be fulfilled only if they are members of a (recipient) nation-state, which immediately raises the issue of the separability of nation and state. Miller argues that individuals ought to pay taxes to support common projects and fulfil each other's needs, as members of the nation; as citizens of the state, they have the same obligation to pay taxes, only now it is to sustain institutions from which they expect to benefit. It does seem an excessively narrow, instrumentalist, conception of citizenship which makes the duty to pay taxes depend on sustaining beneficial institutions, but does not include determining the beneficial purposes for which these institutions supposedly exist. However, supposing that taxes are for the purposes of pursuing common projects and for fulfilling the needs of members of the community, there is no reason why that community must be a national one: it can be any national, or transnational, socio-economic association that is politically organized as a state. Special obligations, in short, are civic: they are owed to fellow members of civil society who are necessarily fellow citizens and who may also be, contingently, co-nationals. On these considerations about special obligations, there are no good moral reasons why the borders of the state should be made to coincide with the boundaries of nationality. Whether this is also true in the case of nations as historical communities must now be considered.

A historical community is one the identity of which lies in a historical, not a practical, past. This means that its correlative present is not the practical present of transactions, reassurances, moral and other lessons, the satisfaction of wants and so on, which the practical past serves in various ways. It is, Oakeshott argues, a chosen present made up of survivals from the past which constitute the primary evidence from which the historical past of events is constructed, or rather, inferred.[21] What happened in the historical past is inferred from this surviving evidence and is understood as an outcome of what preceded it; that is, it is mediated by other, antecedent, historical events. The historical past then consists exclusively of these historical events and their contingent relations to each other, which is to say it is made up exclusively of differences. Unlike the practical past, which does contain unchanging identities, in the historical past nothing is immune from change.

Every historical identity exists in and through change; it is an identity that is located in the continuity in the different historical events. Historical identities are made up exclusively of historical events, and nothing but such events connects together other historical events. The contingent connection between them, as antecedent and consequent, is that of continuity or contiguity. Daphne's metamorphosis into a laurel tree, bit by bit, is, in Ovid's account of the change, very nearly a model of historical identity. Nothing of Daphne survived: the laurel tree was different from her (apparently) in every respect, and yet the change from a woman to a tree was continuous. Matter, form and final cause of the tree were all completely different from the same three causes in Daphne. One factor, however, prevented the metamorphosis from being a perfect exemplification of historical identity: the efficient cause of the change was the same throughout, namely, Daphne's father, the river-god. In genuinely historical identities the differences are not organized around something that is unchanging, but in terms of each another. What, then, does this rough-and-ready version of Oakeshott's account of the historical past imply for nations when understood as historical communities?

First, the relationships between the members of historical communities through time will obviously be exclusively contingent. This means that any historical community of whatever kind will have no necessary features such as a common language, a common culture or a common territory, whether these are thought of as constitutive or not. The same is true of any beliefs its members may have about themselves. Not only are they not a necessary feature of the community, far less constitutive of it, but also, where they are present they are in a permanent state of flux. Similarly, if a historical community happens to have common purposes at any particular time, though they may be long-lasting, they can never be immutable.

Thus, second, there is no *necessary* distinction between what are normally termed "national communities" and any other kind of historical community. The distinction between them is the contingent one of how they are institutionally organized. For example, the Islamic *umma* or the historical community of Muslims was originally organized as a polity under the rule of Mohammed and subject to divinely revealed law, the *Sharia*. This historical community of religious faith is currently organized exclusively in terms of that law and the apparatus of courts that go with it and no longer as a single polity. This example points to an essential feature of historical communities: namely, that none are devoid of institutionalization, however minimal those institutions may be.

Third, examples of historical communities like the Athenians, the British and the *umma* either have been, or still are, active communities, though they never act through self-appointed proxies who, in some mysterious fashion, are supposed to embody a general or national will, as nations are sometimes supposed to do (for example, by David Miller). Historical communities can act collectively, but only through an apparatus of institutions. Consequently, if a nation is a historical community it will be a corporate body which is institutionally organized for action through political and other institutions. Historical nations are, or, like the Medes, were, political communities, although, like Scotland at present, they need not be organized as nation-states. The contingent fact of being organized in terms of political institutions, as opposed to, say, being institutionalized as a social group, is what fundamentally differentiates nations from other kinds of historical community. Patriotic heroes who sacrifice themselves to their communities do so to institutionally organized, political communities—like kinsmen in the organized Arabian tribes; martyrs in *jihad* to the *Sharia*-organized, Muslim community; soldiers to the sovereign state—not to a social or economic group.

Political organization will not be the only tie that binds together the members of a historical "national" community, however. Other bonds, such as shared, basic moral values and norms of conduct, a shared conception of the good life, mutual obligations, cultural affinities and a host of other individually inessential, because contingent, ties may unite the members of a historical community. These ties, in diverse ways, pervade the attitudes and animate the actions of the members of the "national" community and thereby serve to integrate them. That same function is also performed by the different laws, customs and other institutions of the "national" community—which also embody these shared moral values, norms, affinities and so forth—notably when regulating the conduct of its members. Every basic norm or value will be institutionalized somewhere within the state. Exactly where (and how) is explored at philosophical length by Hegel in his *The Philosophy of Right*, and for this reason not even the barest summary of the argument will be attempted here.

The conclusion to which this sketch of an argument leads about the nature of nations as historical communities is fairly obvious. First, a community whose members have shared moral values and norms of conduct that infuse their attitudes and determine their conduct to each other, and which, additionally, are objectified in laws, customs and other institutions, is an ethical order or community. Second, and crucially, the political institutions of this historical, ethical community are one of its integral aspects like all its other institutions, such as social classes and private property. The notion of an acephalous, national, ethical community, one that pre-exists the political institutions that subsequently are superimposed upon it, is just a historical *fata morgana*. Nation and state are intertwined historical communities. On this strictly, or consistently, involuntarist conception, national communities are determinate bodies in terms of their membership and territory; they may enjoy a shared ethical life (Hegel's *Sittlichkeit*), but their ethical character is historically embodied, *inter alia*, in a whole range of institutions that includes their political organization. In short, although they may be (contingently) ethical communities, they are incapable of independently generating a moral right to statehood, because they violate the separability criterion. There cannot be an independent moral right to statehood derived from the nation, when its features are derived from, or dependent upon, its past or present membership of a state.

National Self-Determination as a Moral Right: The Voluntarist Version

On the alternative voluntarist conception, will or consciousness is constitutive of nationality. That is, a nation is a group constituted by the individuals who believe themselves to be a nation, or, alternatively, who have willed themselves to become one. Benedict Anderson's well-known concept of the nation as "an imagined political community—and imagined as both inherently limited and sovereign", and Seton-Watson's claim that "a nation exists when a significant number of people in a community consider themselves to form a nation, or behave as if they formed one", are examples of the belief-constituted, voluntarist conception of nations.[22] (For Anderson and Seton-Watson, the belief of a collection of individuals that they form a nation is based on a further belief that they share various characteristics such as culture.) Schiller's drama, *William Tell* (Act II, scene 2), provides an example of the other volitional, version of the voluntarist conception of nationality in a scene that depicts the historic oath sworn in 1291 at the Ruetli by representatives of the inhabitants of the Forest Cantons of Schwyz, Uri and Unterwalden—"We will to be a nation of brothers, one and indivisible"—by which the Swiss nation was (re)constituted. *Prima facie*, then, when nations are conceptualized as voluntarist groups, the subjective criterion of will or consciousness is a necessary and sufficient condition for any group to be defined as a nation.

Yael Tamir denies that an occasional group of individuals, lacking any shared characteristics, can "turn into a nation . . . merely by the power of its will".[23] Her denial may be tested out through a consideration of the events depicted in Schiller's drama, *William Tell*. Historically, it is probable, though not certain, that the men of Schwyz, Uri and Unterwalden who met on the banks of the Ruetli river in 1291 formed a political union, the "Everlasting League", which eventually became the Swiss Confederal Republic that exists today. In Schiller's dramatic account of their meeting, no new union was formed, but "an ancient league" was re-formed through an *al fresco* social contract consisting in the men of the three cantons assembling beside the Ruetli as a corporate body with the intention to re-form it in mind. It was to this body—a state, or perhaps a proto-state—that the Ruetli oath was sworn.

The significance of the oath in the drama was two-fold: first, it was an oath of allegiance to the resurrected League, which was sworn only after allegiance to the Holy Roman Emperor had been renounced, though not abjured; second, the oath was an act of will which expressed the re-constitution of the Swiss as a nation. A complicating factor was that earlier in the scene the principal character, Werner Stauffacher, had affirmed that the Swiss were a nation by virtue of their common descent. (That the men of Schwyz, Uri and Unterwalden presumably spoke the same low dialect of German, shared a common Germanic culture, were all baptized Roman Catholics and lived in the identifiable geographical area surrounding the Vierwald Statter lake were facts not viewed by Schiller as pertinent, dramatically, to their nationhood.) Stauffacher had asserted that the Swiss community of common descent was divided geographically and by its three-fold "tribal" divisions, its three cantonal governments and three sets of cantonal laws, divisions which he indicated had led to the loss of their ancient rights and liberties and the lapse into disuse (and disunion?) of their "ancient league". This predicament was to be overcome by three separate acts of will by the same individuals, the men of the three cantons, on the same occasion. By their first act, a social contract, the league was re-formed; by their second, allegiance to the Emperor was renounced; by their third act, the oath of allegiance, the Swiss nation was re-constituted as a association united by a common purpose of recovering lost rights and liberties and by a common allegiance to the re-formed league, through which that purpose was to be pursued. The old, divided, common descent community was not thereby restored and reunited, however: rather the Swiss nation, from this point onward, existed on an entirely new basis, on one that totally superseded the old. To put it another way, in the drama an involuntarist conception of nationality was replaced by a consistently voluntarist conception.

On a single occasion, then, and through a concurrence of their multiple wills, the men of the three cantons created a Swiss nation-state. The new nation-state was unmistakably a determinate body comprising the members of the cantons whose representatives were parties to the compact of 1291 and the fixed territory of the three cantons. How far the newly constituted, one and indivisible, Swiss nation of brothers was separable from the re-constituted and no less fraternal league is a moot point, however; for the same set of male individuals—women and children were excluded—constituted a state to which they swore allegiance, and by virtue of which they constituted themselves as a nation. By their acts of will, the Swiss nation was thus assimilated to the Swiss state, or proto-state, from the very beginning.[24] In that case, it would be nonsensical to attribute a right of statehood to nations, for, on this version of the voluntarist conception, they are already citizens of the state of their choice. In other words, the volitional version of voluntarist nationality does not meet the third criterion, namely, that the nation must be separable from the state in order to generate a right to statehood. This right, it was argued, must result from indigenous features of the separate nation, that is, from features that have not been derived from, or depend on, the nation's past or present membership of a state. It remains to be seen if the alternative version of this criterion—national consciousness—avoids this failure to generate a right to national self-determination through violating the separability condition.

According to this version, individuals form a nation if they think they form a nation and behave accordingly. As this point is commonly argued, they entertain the belief that they form a nation when they believe that they share certain characteristics such as a common language and culture, a common past and so on, or share certain family resemblances, and which they further believe to be "national" characteristics or resemblances. Now it is not logically necessary that these individuals share a single common characteristic, or even that any family resemblance exists among them; and if either happens to be present, this empirical fact will not affect the voluntarist character of the nation. For, on this version of the subjective criterion of nationality, a nation exists when, and only when, it is believed to exist, regardless of whether other beliefs upon which this constitutive belief is based have any basis in empirical fact. Only where the involuntarist criterion of nations is at issue does the truth or falsity of beliefs about common features, shared resemblances and the "national" quality of both become a pertinent consideration. Only there is the national consciousness either a purely passive awareness of the objective facts of nationality or else an equally passive, false consciousness of them. Either way it is non-constitutive. But an active, constitutive national consciousness, one that is logically independent of the truth or falsity of the beliefs upon which it is based, is a puzzling consciousness.

It might be supposed that the nation thus founded is an illusion, or perhaps a delusion, a figment of the imagination as opposed to Anderson's "imagined political community", or, in the words of Ernest Gellner, an invention. "Nationalism", he writes, "is not the awakening of nations to self-consciousness; it invents nations where they do not exist".[25] But if national consciousness does not spuriously fabricate nations, and if it is also not tied to the truth or falsity of beliefs about objective, empirical facts of nationality, then it can be constitutive of nationality only as a shared awareness of a common purpose or a shared allegiance on the part of the future members of the nation; that is, it must be tied to the will to nationhood on the part of a multiplicity of individuals. In this case, the national consciousness as a consciousness of wills is open to the same objection as before: namely, that it is not easy to see how a nation is generated with a right of statehood since what is constituted is a nation-state, where the nation and state appear inseparable. Though the first (determinacy) and second (exclusively voluntarist) general criteria have been fulfilled in this voluntarist conception, the third criterion (separability) has not. For this reason it cannot qualify as a concept of nationality capable of generating a right of statehood. Thus it could be the case that members of a nation-state founded by the decision or consciousness of its members do enjoy a morally valuable way of life, and this valuable way of life may well be a realistic prospect before the nation-state is established; but neither moral fact, if they are moral facts, is strictly relevant, for it is impossible to determine whether or not such an ethically valuable way of life can be attributed exclusively to the nation.

There are good grounds for supposing that nations conceived in this way need not be ethical communities, however. On the voluntarist conception of nationality, the moral right to national self-determination is founded on the moral right of individuals to associate freely with others of their choice, and this in turn is derived from their moral right to live self-determined lives. In other words, it is a moral fact about individual members of the nation and their wills, and not a moral fact about the national community (which, as yet, does not exist), that generates the moral right of national self-determination. Thus, although the individual acts of will or consciousness by which this national community is constituted are morally valuable, it does not follow that the resultant nation will itself be a morally valuable community. If a nation happens to be an ethical community, this is a purely contingent moral fact on the voluntarist conception of nationality, and this fact consequently cannot ground a universal moral right of national self-determination.

Conclusion

None of the conceptions of nationhood that have been examined in this chapter has proved capable of this; none has been able to show that nationality is a good reason for political independence or statehood. This may cause some discomfiture, intellectual or otherwise. Paul Gilbert once put it this way:

> the idea that a nation has a right to statehood comes down to this: a nation just *is* that (or, at least, the primary case of that) which has a right to statehood. We do not, on this hypothesis, have an understanding of the concept of a nation independent of that of the state, such that on the basis of our understanding we can grasp the propriety of this right. Rather the ability to support a claim to statehood is partly *constitutive* of our notion of a nation.[26]

My reply to this is to reiterate a point once made by Elie Kedourie when he said that not the least of the triumphs of nationalist doctrine was that its propositions have become accepted as self-evident in the contemporary world.[27] To suppose that nations just *are* entitled to be self-determined, and that this entitlement is partly constitutive of the concept of nationhood, is simply to embrace the core of nationalism which is a doctrine of political legitimacy.

Notes

1. E. Kedourie, *Nationalism,* 4th edn. (Oxford: Blackwell, 1993), p. 1.
2. J. S. Mill, *Utilitarianism, Liberty, Representative Government* (London: Dent, 1910), pp. 363–365.
3. Y. Tamir, *Liberal Nationalism* (Princeton NJ: Princeton University Press, 1993), p. 65.
4. J. O'Neill, "Should Communitarians be Nationalists?" *Journal of Applied Philosophy*, Vol. 11, No. 2 (1994), pp. 140–141.
5. In chapter 6, Yael Tamir rightly takes me to task over her discussion of nationality and cluster concepts in *Liberal Nationalism* (pp. 65–66) in an earlier version of this chapter presented to the Newcastle Colloquium. A group counts as a nation, on her account, if it exhibits some ("a sufficient number"), but not all, of the objective characteristics of nationality and all its members share these. Such groups exhibit a family resemblance to one another. This version of the involuntarist concept of nationality, I argued then and now, is clearly indeterminate in its application, and is therefore incapable of grounding a right of national self-determination. Subsequently, I examined the cluster version of the involuntarist conception of nationality (which I incorrectly attributed to her), where the concern is not with family resemblances

between nations, but with those existing within them, that is, among the members, to see if it avoided the indeterminacy of her conception. It did not. Whatever the objective characteristics of a nation, not all members of the nation share them all, on the cluster conception. Each member will share some of these characteristics, but there will be non-members who also share some of these features. The point is argued more fully than in the earlier version of this chapter. I cannot detect confusion arising in either. The cluster conception of nationality is, of course, universally applicable and is not restricted to some particular nations and their boundaries.

6. Tamir, *Nationalism*, pp. 65–66.

7. D. Miller, "In Defence of Nationality", in P. Gilbert and P. Gregory, eds, *Nations, Cultures and Markets* (Aldershot: Avebury, 1994), pp. 19–21.

8. Tamir, *Nationalism*, p. 65.

9. P. Gilbert, "Criteria of Nationality and the Ethics of Self-Determination", *History of European Ideas*, Vol. 16, Nos. 4–6 (1993), p. 517. My debt to Paul Gilbert's argument about voluntarist and involuntarist criteria of nationality in this article is extensive. I am also indebted to him for his very helpful written comments on an earlier draft of this chapter presented to the Newcastle Colloquium on National Rights and International Obligations, 4–5 January 1995.

10. For example, A. Margalit and J. Raz, "National Self-Determination", *The Journal of Philosophy*, Vol. 77, No. 9 (1990), adopt an involuntarist conception of nations as encompassing, common culture groups (pp. 443–444) but add a form of national consciousness in the mutual recognition of membership: "Typically, one belongs to such groups if, among other conditions, one is recognised by other members as belonging to it." (p. 445). Similarly, N. MacCormick in chapter 3 below, postulates an involuntarist conception of nations as "cultural (but not necessarily ethnic) communities", adding that these communities are composed of "persons conscious of their attachment to a culture as a historically evolved social reality, particularly attached to a particular place, and of significance to those who live there, because they belong to it quite as much as it to them" (p. 42; also p.46). See also N. MacCormick, "Is Nationalism Philosophically Credible?" in W. Twining, ed., *Issues of Self-Determination* (Aberdeen: Aberdeen University Press, 1991), p. 16.

11. N. MacCormick, pp. 40–42 below "Is Nationalism Philosophically Credible?" pp. 8–19; "Nation and Nationalism", in N. MacCormick, *Legal Right and Social Democracy* (Oxford: Clarendon Press, 1982), pp. 247–264.

12. Tamir, *Nationalism*, pp. 69–74.

13. Margalit and Raz, "National Self-Determination", pp. 439–461.

14. I argue this point more fully in "The Ethics of National Self-Determination", in Gilbert and Gregory, eds., *Nations, Cultures and Markets*, pp. 76–78.

15. Mill, *Representative Government*, p. 363.

16. D. Miller, "In Defence of Nationality", in P. Gilbert and P. Gregory, eds, *Nations, Cultures and Markets* (Aldershot: Avebury, 1994), pp. 19–21. David Miller has recently reformulated this concept of nationality: "national communities are constituted by belief: nations exist when their members recognize one another as compatriots, and believe that they share characteristics of the relevant kind". D. Miller, *On Nationality* (Oxford: Clarendon Press, 1995), pp. 22–24.

17. M. Oakeshott, *On History and Other Essays* (Oxford: Blackwell, 1983), pp. 18–19.

18. L. Colley, *Britons. Forging the Nation, 1707–1837* (London: Random House, 1992).

19. Miller, *On Nationality*, pp. 65-66.

20. Ibid., p. 57.

21. Oakeshott, *On History*, pp. 30–33, also chapters 2 and 3.

22. B. Anderson, *Imagined Communities. Reflections on the Origin and Spread of Nationalism*, rev. edn. (London: Verso, 1991), p. 6; H. Seton-Watson, *Nations and States. An Enquiry into the Origins of Nations and the Politics of Nationalism* (London: Methuen, 1977), p. 5.

23. Tamir, *Liberal Nationalism*, p. 66.

24. Maybe the Swiss nation has continued to exist inseparably from the Swiss state thereafter through a mute daily plebiscite, *"Wir wollen sein ein einige Volk von Brüdern"*. Voluntarist nations do not continue to exist after their initial foundation unless the constitutive act of will continues.

25. E. Gellner, *Thought and Change* (London: Weidenfeld & Nicolson, 1964), p. 169. Elsewhere he suggests one important reason why national self-determination cannot be a universal right of nationhood: namely, that the number of potential nations considerably exceeds the number of possible viable states: E. Gellner, *Nations and Nationalism* (Oxford: Blackwell, 1983), p. 2.

26. Gilbert, "Criteria of Nationality", p. 516.

27. Kedourie, *Nationalism*, p. 1.

3

What Place for Nationalism in the Modern World?

Neil MacCormick

Is nationalism a threat to peace or a noble ideal? A danger to the integrity of individuals or an element in their individuality? An enemy of human rights or a vital component of humanity?

At present, a peace-threatening, individual-suppressing, anti-humanistic face of nationalism is particularly prominently in view through the media. Mr Zhirinovsky in Russia, Mr Karadzic in Bosnia, Mr Milosevic in Serbia; the reviving right in the eastern Länder of Germany; Mr Le Pen; Italian neo-Fascists and other rightist manifestations—all give their kiss of death to the name and concept of nationalism, and make it stink in liberal nostrils.

Contrary opinions assert nationalism and related ideals of autonomy and subsidiarity in the name of human rights. Self-determination is a basic human right for this approach. Rights of minorities, rather than being threatened, are in principle defended, even asserted, under this conception.

Can such a liberal nationalism really offer a coherent political vision? Is it compatible with a universalistic vision of the common humanity of human beings? Is respect for persons possible where the political significance and value of national identity and cultural community are also proposed as foundational political principles?

The European Union has brought about a new form of legal and political order in Western Europe. This creates a politics "beyond the sovereign state". Old conceptions of state sovereignty and of the absolutism of the nation-state are consigned to history. This does not abolish nations as politico-cultural communities. It may create space for the flourishing of nationalism tamed—a fully liberal and humanistic nationalism.

The survival of more atavistic nationalisms in less favoured parts of the world does not negate this possibility. They show, on the contrary, how urgent it is to make progress with extending the model (whether or not enlarging the Union) so as to give space for reasonable national and cultural aspirations without unleashing fascism and inhumanity in their wake.

The other possibility, of trying simply to re-absorb minorities in grander unities upheld in the last resort by force, is not a liberal but an imperialist solution. The revival of imperialism, however tempting, should not be confused with rights-based liberalism.

Liberalism: Universality and Individualism

These summary remarks assume that there can be such a thing as liberal nationalism. This is an assumption I share with the penetrating Israeli scholar, Yael Tamir, whose book *Liberal Nationalism* appeared recently.[1] In a spirit similar to hers, I shall argue that there is an important place in the contemporary world for a liberal nationalism, and that the liberal version of nationalism is one for which it is vital to argue most vigorously just now. Otherwise, we leave the field wide open for intolerant, illiberal, racist or even fascist forms of nationalism. This case has to be upheld against arguments which say that liberal ideals are wholly incompatible with nationalism in any form, so that so-called liberal nationalism is a mixture of contradiction in terms and dangerous illusion.

Liberalism itself is a much-contested concept. The version of it that I favour shades over into social democracy, rather than embracing a purely market-economical view of the good society.[2] My social-democratic liberalism is both universalistic and individualistic. It is universalistic because it holds that whatever rights or duties attach to any particular human being in given circumstances must be considered as universalizable. The same rights and duties must attach to any human being in like circumstances. It also upholds a presumption in favour of more inclusive over less inclusive characterizations of relevant human circumstances. Universality is a necessary feature of moral justification. Hence morally justifiable political principles have to be universalizable, and principles that have a narrowly discriminatory application to narrowly specified characteristics or external circumstances of individuals are to be considered suspect despite being logically universal in form. The less inclusive the categories they stipulate, the stronger the justification they require.

For example, "all white male adult citizens may vote in parliamentary elections" is narrower than "all male adult citizens may vote in parliamentary elections"; it in turn is narrower than "all adult citizens may vote in parliamentary elections", and it than "all citizens may vote in parliamentary elections", and it than "all human beings resident in the state may vote in parliamentary elections", and it than "all human beings may vote in parliamentary elections". Assuming that we are referring to a particular state's Parliament, we may be inclined to think a voting qualification based on citizenship is justified; if not, we may favour at least a residence qualification, since a Parliament's chief task is to legislate for, and to supervise, the government of the territory of the given state and those who live there and are committed to its long-term well-being. Many might go further and argue that some degree of political maturity is relevant to voting, and hence that a restriction of voting rights to adults (judged by a relatively arbitrary age qualification) is justified. But all attempts to provide satisfactory justifications for voting qualifications on the basis of gender or skin colour have been totally discredited. So one can justify some narrowing of principle from "all human beings may vote" down to a more restricted formula; but some further narrowings fail to find relevant justification.

The individualistic element in the proposed version of liberalism has two internal principles. The first makes an assumption *about* value: namely, that nothing can be deemed a fundamental human good unless it is capable of being enjoyed as an enhancement of life by a human being as a distinct individual. The second makes an assumption *of* value: namely, that a social situation in which human individuals have scope for self-development and self-realization through autonomous decisions and choices taken either individually or in free collaboration with others is of value both to the self-realizing individuals and to others. Of these principles, the former rejects claims on behalf of superhuman or collectively human entities to be repositories of ultimate human values —there cannot, for example, be "national values" enjoyed by nations as such but incapable of being enjoyed or experienced as values by human individuals as individuals. The second asserts a particular claim on behalf of individuals: there is special political value in securing a social situation where self-aware individuality and self-fulfilment are possible for individuals.

Neither of these individualistic principles adds up to, or gives any support or backing to, such absurd, or anyway wrong, theoretical positions about the character and existence of human beings as social atomism or ontological or methodological individualism. It is clearly not possible to understand humans as intrinsically extra-social atoms who come together voluntarily or otherwise to form human societies or communities. Nor can human individuals be conceived as existing with the very nature they have independently from, or in abstraction from, social relationships and connections. Nor can social organizations, activities or phenomena be described or conceived in terms of simple aggregations of individual human actions. Without the participation of individuals, it would be logically impossible for there to be families, football matches and symphony concerts, but there is no individual activity or aggregation of individual activities that amounts to constituting a family, playing a football match or playing a symphony. Moreover, the individuals who take part in these activities have acquired an individuality, and a sense of their own being and character, through participation in a multiplicity of also irreducibly social relationships and activities. We have all known since Aristotle said it that humans are irreducibly social animals; Yael Tamir adds, in a happy turn of phrase, that human individuals are necessarily "contextual individuals",[3] a thesis about which more will be said later.

This being so, the value of individual self-realization, though it depends on extensive political and economic liberty for individuals, also depends on a substantial degree of support for individuals so that each may have the social and economic backing that makes possible coming to maturity as a potentially self-realizing individual. It also gives reason to oppose acceptance of legally conferred economic liberties so extensive that differences of wealth between different persons can become so gross as to make impossible any serious adherence to equality of self-respect among different persons. Equality of this sort is essential to such persons' participation as equals in the same political community. The upshot is that, when one adds together universalistic and individualistic principles in the senses here proposed, one establishes relatively clear criteria for preference of certain political programmes, situations and systems.

One ought always to prefer social situations in which there is more rather than less autonomy for individuals, and situations in which more individuals are able to pursue self-realization over those in which fewer can. One ought to rule out forms of self-realization involving the exercise of autonomy by some individuals in ways that exploit others through denial of, or severe constraint upon, their chances for achieving real autonomy as individuals. (Slavery is an extreme example, but others can be envisaged, including the condition of women in many types of society.)

The commonly recognized human rights of the present epoch—those for example contained in the European Convention for the Protection of Human Rights and Fundamental Freedoms, or in the UN Covenants on Civil and Political Rights and on Economic and Social Rights—correspondingly express basic requirements for human autonomy. This is because of the way they are linked with a set of reasonable assumptions about the human condition and about human goods in contemporary human circumstances. The need for some recognition of economic and social rights is tied up with the bar on improperly exploitative exercises of autonomy, and with the need accordingly to supplement substantially, though not to supplant, the market as the mechanism for distribution of social products. Due observance of human rights by government, with some form of judicial scrutiny, is a reasonable contemporary requirement for anything that aspires to be a liberal state. Constitutional entrenchment of human rights is highly desirable, and where it is missing, the kind of external guarantee of human rights achieved in countries such as the United Kingdom through the European Convention is a requirement for any serious pretension to liberalism in the state.

In summary, the present version of liberalism is universalistic and individualistic, gives a large place to the working of markets but also requires state intervention of a redistributive kind, and requires states to be subjected to a guarantee of human rights. This is not very original, and nowadays not even particularly controversial. Relative unoriginality is, however, a virtue in this present context. For the task of the moment is not to reconcile nationalism with any highly eccentric conception of liberalism: rather, it is to establish that there are kinds of nationalism that are fully compatible with a reasonable, acceptable, and quite commonly accepted, liberalism. The tenets I have set out exhibit, I think, just such a commonplace quality. The time has therefore come to move towards an investigation of such a nationalism. Movement in that direction is best achieved through reflection on possible objections to the kind of liberalism I have been sketching here.

Objections to Abstract Individualism

The ideas of universality and of individualism that I have supported here some-times attract criticism for ignoring the true substance, the flesh-and-blood actuality, the idiosyncratic and personal character, of real live human beings. Immanuel Kant is usually picked out for specially unfavourable mention in such a setting, and not without reason. For the idea of universality, or indeed universalizability, found its classical expression in Kant's "categorical impera-tive", whose simplest form requires the moral agent to act only upon such maxims of action as can at the same time be willed as universal laws applying to every moral agent. Notoriously, this categorical imperative of Kant's addresses humans as purely rational moral agents, as "noumenal" or "intelligible" selves, not as the sensual-cum-rational creatures that humans actually are. Notoriously, it fails to make contact with the merely phenomenal world of desires, friendships, pleasures or pains. It poses moral demands of an abstract kind, apart from earthy reality. Between abstract universal principles and concrete decisions affecting real people, there is often considered to be an unbridgeable gap.

Liberal individualism comes often under similar attack. The "individual" envisaged by liberal individualism can be so conceptualized as to lack the true individuality that makes real people real to us—and to themselves. Likewise, the abstract equality of all rational agents or legal persons before moral or economic principles or before the law ignores or obscures the huge inequalities that divide and differentiate different members of class- and gender-divided societies, to say nothing of differences of skin colour or ethnicity. The promise of equal and identical human rights for all is hollow mockery in real societies whose institutions, including those articulated around legal rights, constitu-tional rights and human rights, have evolved and been designed under the guidance of the dominant groups of the societies whose institutions they are.

The proper response to these by no means unreasonable lines of criticism is to revise the position in such a way as to ensure that real flesh-and-blood individuals are built into it in the first place. Kant may have held that rational agency is extraneous to the phenomenal world of desire, feeling and fellow-feeling. But we need not. The rationality we ought to contemplate is the rationality of at-the-same-time flesh-and-blood humans, each belonging in a particular familial, social and historical context. The principles we set up are principles that take account of human sense and sentiment. The acceptability or unacceptability of a universal principle depends on our view of its impact on flesh-and-blood humans.

It is indeed necessarily true that general principles have an abstract quality, and address individuals in terms of some of their qualities—as persons wishing to vote in an election, or parents, or promisers, or scholars, or citizens of a state, or members of a nation, for example—in abstraction from the totality of their personal qualities. This, however, is not an abstraction that ignores concrete human realities. It is simply a logical feature of having principles that are the same principles for everybody, or for every participant in some actual or ideal dialogue or discourse. It does not require us to ignore the fact that people have a multiplicity of other characteristics seen from a multiplicity of possible points of view and schemes of classification.

What happens if we examine our principles in the light of the fact that humans have a multiplicity of features potentially relevant for moral deliberation either at large or (even more) in relation to particular situations engaging particular individuals? The answer seems clear: it has to be the case that there can be a plurality or even a multiplicity of acceptable and relevant principles bearing on any particular situation of moral significance. So it must be acknowledged that any final judgement in any concrete case will involve taking into account a plurality of potentially applicable principles. To reach a satisfactory final judgement calls for a capacity to enter sympathetically into the position of all parties involved, and to weigh the subjective importance for them of the interests and values at stake.

On this view, it is always possible that the final judgement about what is right for one person at her junction-point of relevant and applicable principles differs from the equally sound judgement about another person at his junction point—for differences of individual character and situation may entail different relative weights in the given context even of the same abstract principles. To give a trivially easy, and indeed rather abstract, example, if two people have promised to attend an important meeting, but a third party is dangerously ill, and if one of the two is a close and valued relative of the ill person while the other is merely a colleague and friendly acquaintance, then the former ought to visit the hospital at the cost of missing the meeting, while the latter ought to attend the meeting rather than visit the hospital. Somebody who is a native speaker of a minority language might have to weigh different factors about whether to rear her children as speakers of her language than one who speaks a widely used language like English.

We should reject any approach that says or suggests (as, for example, both Kant and his contemporary follower John Rawls at least seem to suggest) that ideas about individuals as moral agents have to be formed in abstraction from their flesh-and-blood actuality.[4] Every individual, to take up again Yael Tamir's vivid phrase, is a "contextual individual". Each of us occupies a physically distinct human body from every other, each with a unique (identical twins aside) genetic inheritance, and each with a unique (identical twins included) social situation, in the form of a set of relationships to other individuals, and to communities and cultures, and to social organizations, associations and institutions. To become a full human individual involves things like acquiring a name, learning to speak a language and becoming acculturated into some culture, or into some sub-culture in some idiosyncratic mix with some wider and more inclusive culture or cultures. Schooling and further education, work and the workplace, marriage and family, friendship, engagement in sport or voluntary activity or politics—all such engagements and relationships with other persons make us the persons we come to be, and account for the continual evolution of character and individuality in our lives as human persons.

As Francis Hutcheson, and even more his intellectual successors David Hume and Adam Smith, observed and argued with great force, humans as moral and practical beings have ties and links of sympathy and fellow-feeling with other individuals, and in a more diffuse way with groups and communities of people. These particular links of sentiment are not just accidental features of phenomenal human beings aside from their rationally intelligible moral character. They are a part of what makes it possible for people to have moral character at all. It is in one's becoming capable of seeing the world as it must seem from someone else's point of view that one can grasp the validity of a universal principle applicable to both of us, and be motivated to act on it. Without the gift to see ourselves as other see us—and to feel their potential engagement in situations in which we are engaged—we would lack the psychic equipment essential to entering into any moral discourse whatsoever with others.

This is all a matter of what it is subjectively like to be a human being. Our feelings and attachments and bonds with, and commitments to, other people participate at least as fully in what makes us human and makes us individual as our faculty for rational calculation, universalization, abstraction. So again we must insist that liberal individualism, although it treats "individuality" as a morally significant abstract category, is properly envisaged as applying that abstraction to the concrete individuality of each human being at his or her unique junction-point of genetic and social influences, together with his or her distinctive self-awareness grounded in a (possible) conscious reflection on these influences and on abstract principles. The abstraction involved in universalistic individualism need not and should not amount to a bland indifference to the concrete individuality of the human individuals it envisages. It would be self-contradictory if it were.

Universality and abstraction express our commitment to impartiality in interpersonal dealings; but the impartiality proper to abstract moral thought sometimes reveals the legitimacy of a kind of partiality in practical conduct. I should be impartial among qualified applicants in allocating council houses as a councillor. But I should not be equally impartial in the face of need when it comes to allocating beds in my own house; family members there have rights to prior consideration even over others whose needs, objectively considered, may be greater. Moreover, even in the case of a public housing authority, impartiality seems to have its limits. Residence in the local authority area and, *a fortiori*, permanent residence in the state in question, if not indeed citizenship of that state as well as residence, are properly taken into account alongside of need. The criterion for access to municipal housing is not pure neediness, nor is the whole homeless population of the world admitted to the housing list.

The right to reside in a country is not impartially allocated either. Amidst all the controversy about immigration and rights of asylum, it is widely taken for granted that governments do and should treat existing citizens and established residents differently from those who seek to change their domicile by moving from one country to another. In discussions of asylum, mere economic motivation—which includes attempting to escape from starvation—is treated as different from political persecution. That someone only wants to escape abject poverty is not an accepted ground for automatically being permitted international migration. Yet if the only principles at stake were ones concerning human need, this could not be so. As Tamir observes, most current liberal theories take for granted the legitimacy of states (and frequently denominate them "nation-states"), and elaborate theories of justice in the political sphere that simply take states as the given units of political discourse and practice, and discuss the special obligations of government to citizens and of citizens to each other. Nationalism is not a widely favoured doctrine, but unargued nationalist or statist ("nation-statist") assumptions in fact lie unexamined behind such theorizing. Either the hidden assumptions should be taken out of their closet and brought up to scratch as an acceptable part of liberal political philosophy, or the whole project should be abandoned.

I am in danger of running ahead of my theme. So far, what I have essentially tried to establish is something like the following: To make sense of the idea of an individual, we need to conceive of each individual as having some social location and context. A sound individualism concerns individuals as contextual individuals. Thus, Alasdair MacIntyre's paradoxical dictum that the individual is as much an abstraction as society is not so odd a saying after all. Individuals, including autonomous self-determining individuals, emerge from social contexts that are essential to their development and formation. Societies are conceptual communities supervening upon the sets of relations between individuals who can come to be what they are only by virtue of the relationships in which they participate, and whose sense of themselves would be radically different if they were to have emerged from some different set of relationships, even if their biochemical and genetic make-up were otherwise unchanged.

One of the corollaries of the categorical imperative considered earlier is the duty of respect for persons. In Kant this no doubt refers to the purely abstract rational agent. Robin Downie and Elizabeth Telfer gave the idea a more satisfactorily substantial quality in their book of several years ago.[5] With them, if with necessary adaptation to the ideas now in play, I want to insist on respect for persons as implying respect for contextual individuals in the sense just explained.

Let us now postulate an idea of nations as cultural (but not necessarily ethnic) communities of persons conscious of their attachment to a culture as a historically evolved social reality, particularly attached to a particular place, and of significance to those who live there, because they belong to it quite as much as it to them. Communities of this sort seem to be among the most effectively dominant contexts in terms of which human beings acquire their sense of identity and belonging. Probably nobody identifies solely with national attributes, all having other focal points of their sense of identity and belonging, be these family, city, parish, workplace, professional community, religious tradition, school, college or whatever. Doubtless some have a sense of identity that omits and some a sense that actively excludes any national identification. Doubtless nations as relevant communities are a comparatively modern cultural form. They may indeed prove less than permanent in the further unfolding of human history. Nevertheless, if for many humans as humans are today individuality includes subjective commitment to some national culture, perceived as such, then respect for humans as contextual individuals must include respect for their sense of nationality among other things. Individual self-realization will require a context of participation in some mode of collective self-determination. This implies a right that is eminently universalizable, whether or not all to whom it applies would wish to exercise the right, or to exercise it in a determinate political way. It seems fully compatible with the two basic principles of liberalism stipulated above.

Nationalism Defined

I turn therefore to some more articulate reflections on nationalism, having established at least a *prima facie* case for some kind of right to respect for national identities as a part of respect for persons, and implicit in that respect for human individuals and for all that goes into their individuality. To the extent that a sense of nationality is intrinsic to the fabric of individuality and vital for many individuals to their sense of belonging and to their self-respect as acknowledged members of some recognized and respected community of people, morally justifiable political principles have to take this into account.

As for a definition of nationalism, Kenneth Minogue, in his already classical *Nationalism* of 1967, gave this characterization of the idea: "Nationalism is a political movement which seeks to attain and defend an objective we may call national integrity."[6]

No great stress has up till now been laid on politics in the sense of programmes for political action, yet it is obviously right to accept Minogue's stress upon this in a definition of nationalism. Nationalism is indeed a political movement or programme, or a family of overlapping movements or programmes. The character of members of the family may, however, differ quite largely, depending on the other elements or principles built into such a movement or programme. Here, it will be recalled, the aim is the construction (if possible) of a liberal nationalism. This will take national integrity seriously, but will advance claims for it only in a way that is compatible with the basic liberal principles already enunciated.

The issue is not only about the sense of identity or belonging that individuals have, nor only about the moral rights we may found upon that. The issue is also about individuals acting collectively to attain and defend identity through distinctively national political institutions. Culture is conceptually essential to the being of a national, as distinct from some other kind of human, community; yet purely cultural or related religious organizations or the like are not usually accepted as sufficient guarantors of a nation's integrity, however significant a role they may play alongside of more strictly political institutions. Even so, the question may arise as to which institutions of state, or which political arrangements, meet the need described.

To take the case of Scotland, the absence of the full panoply of statehood is not incompatible with certain institutions of state. There is a complete system of courts and of civil and criminal justice, there is an administratively devolved executive branch of government under the Secretary of State for Scotland, there is an established national church (and the non-established churches have a Scottish national mode of internal government), and there are all manner of state and public bodies such as the National Library, national museums and galleries, national orchestras and opera companies, national sporting associations active in international sport, national newspapers, broadcasting stations and so on. There is no doubt that such institutions and agencies play a powerful role in sustaining and even in part defining the contemporary sense of Scotland and of "Scottishness". One form of nationalism in Scotland argues that the defence and nurturing of such institutions is the most desirable way of upholding Scotland's position as a contemporary nation embedded in a larger state (and some would say a more comprehensive nation). This is spoken for in the Government's recent White Paper, *Scotland in the Union: A Partnership for Good*.

Others argue that further political and constitutional change is required for the securing of Scottish identity and enabling Scotland as a politico-cultural community to thrive fully in contemporary circumstances. The reason for this is akin to that in favour of democratic institutions. Processes of autonomous self-realization are of fundamental value to humans, as argued earlier. Sometimes this requires no more than negative liberty and private opportunity to get on with one's own life. But a life that is a human one can only be lived in society, and the legal framework within which one's liberty and privacy are shaped is necessarily a common framework for the collectivity in which one lives. How shall the laws that define the framework then be made and upheld? By external fiat, or by some process of participative decision-making? The latter engages individual autonomy in a collective process of law-making. The self-determining individual participates in determining the collective conditions of the common life which forms the essential context of individualistic self-realization. So by liberal premisses, democratic and thus partially autonomous processes of decision-making about common rules are preferable to purely heteronomous processes. It has been said that good government is preferable to self-government; despite the fact that some experiments in self-government have ended in catastrophic failure, this is unacceptable. Good government in a real sense has to be self-government, even though not all self-government is good, and sometimes effective externally imposed rule may be better than home-grown chaos.

But democracy as majority rule always poses the questions: What majority? A majority of whom? The current state of debate in Ireland, and the question whether relevant majorities must always be all-Ireland majorities or must for some purposes be majorities in Northern Ireland only, provide a vivid example of how problematic this can be. Any answer to the question anywhere has to include some perception of common and mutual loyalty such that a momentary minority can reasonably accept that it should go along with a majority choice. In some communities there is the possibility of a reasonable understanding that all political majorities are in principle temporary, and all political minorities likewise. This suggests that there must be some ground of belonging other than the mere existence of a legally constituted constitution that confers power to vote and rules about the establishment and working of a legislative assembly. Thus, viable political societies have an existence conceptually apart from any particular constitution giving them a determinate legal character.

This both explains and justifies the ideas of nation or people that are enshrined in legal attempts to grasp the right of self-determination as a collective right. The International Covenant on Civil and Political Rights and the International Covenant on Economic, Social and Cultural Rights both open with the stipulation that

> All peoples have the right of self-determination. By virtue of that right they freely determine their political status and freely pursue their economic, social and cultural development.

Notwithstanding the assertion of this right in so solemn and authoritative a document, a common response among intellectuals is one of extreme scepticism alike towards nationalism and towards claims for national self-determination outside of such very special contexts as decolonization. This scepticism has commonly challenged the whole idea of the "nation" and has denied the principle of "self-determination" as a moral principle. Kenneth Minogue's book is itself a highly sceptical account. He describes nationalism as a political phenomenon, but in terms of the holding of ideas that in his view are mainly false and mischievous. He considers, and largely deplores, the effects of nationalism. But he does not entertain it as a justifiable political ideal in any form.

Among persons of liberal disposition, exactly those most favourable to universalistic and individualistic ideas, there has been a long-standing suspicion of the notion of national independence or integrity, and of politics that promote the values of a nation as a whole as against those that promote the ability of citizens as individuals and in their freely chosen groupings to choose and pursue what they think valuable, even against actual or supposed national preferences. Liberals on the whole mistrust nationalism. Yet I have tried to show how self-determination as a collective right of appropriate groups may be a necessary element in individual self-realization as a fully self-realizing member of a political community. There are forms of nationalism that are fully compatible with forms of liberalism; and forms of liberalism that do not give place to liberal-nationalist values do not properly allow for the "contextual" character of the contextual individual, that is, for the real human being as distinct from some purely theoretical abstraction.

Perhaps even yet we have not sufficiently pursued one key point. Why in this setting are people apt to insist on such ideas as self-determination for such puzzling entities as "peoples" or "nations"? The doctrine that "peoples" have the right to self-determination was once taken for granted as an element in liberal internationalism, though in classical works such as J. S. Mill's, *Considerations on Representative Government* it is treated as axiomatic that the members of smaller cultural or ethno-cultural groupings ("peoples" perhaps?) such as the Welsh or the Basques or the Scots Highlanders ought to seek their good in some larger and more politically advanced state or supposed "nation-state" like France or the United Kingdom ("England", as Mill and his contemporaries usually called it).[7] Anyway, the doctrine itself has been found problematic because of the difficulties of applying it *in concreto*. Woodrow Wilson's famous attempts to apply the doctrine through the Versailles settlement, and all the problems of sorting out people from people, and minorities within minorities within minorities, have led many to the same position as Hugh Seton-Watson, i.e., that of rejecting the basic idea as not merely impracticable but essentially chimerical, postulating the existence of metaphysical objects such as "nations" or "peoples" where no identifiable such entities really exist.[8]

How should we then deal with this challenge? I return to the theme that all individuals are "contextual individuals". Our sense of identity arises from our experience of belonging within significant communities such as families, schools, workplace communities, religious groups, political associations, sports clubs—and also nations, conceived as cultural communities endowed with political relevance. A nation is constituted by a sense in its members of important (even if internally diverse) cultural community with each other based on a shared past, a "heritage" of common ways and traditions, including at least some of a family of items such as language, literature, legend and mythology, music, educational usages, legal tradition, religious tradition, all of which cumulatively are regarded as bearing on the legitimacy of government, at least in the sense that governmental decisions that denigrate or belittle any of the focal elements in a given cultural tradition are viewed as abusive of power. Nations exist wherever there are substantial numbers of individuals who share in some degree a common consciousness of this kind. This gives them a possibility of mutual loyalty and a common patriotism of the kind that seems essential to any form of long-run viable democracy.

But such national identities do carry political aspirations. The relation between the existence of a nation and the perceived conditions of political legitimacy was noted a moment ago. So respect for nationality does require some acknowledgement of political demands grounded in the needs of national communities for political conditions hospitable to their continuance and free development. Further, the whole idea of the desirability of creating the conditions for autonomous self-determination, both of individuals—contextual individuals—and of the groups and collectivities constitutive of them, leads back to the claim of self-determination as quite properly a claim on behalf of each nation on similar terms to any and every other.

This is fully capable of being stated as a universal principle. It couples up naturally with the earlier noted and equally universal imperative of equal allowance for equal respect among national identities, just like other identities. A part of the odium attaching to nationalism (and richly earned by not a few nationalists in political arenas from Bosnia Herzegovina to Iraqi Kurdistan and elsewhere) lies precisely in its failure to universalize and treat essentially like claims in like manner. But this in itself can no more discredit the legitimate claims of liberal nationalism than the rampant selfishness and non-universalism of some individualistic persons discredit of themselves universalistic liberal doctrines of political individualism.

Nevertheless, a hitherto unexplored implication of the whole argument up to this point concerns the non-exclusiveness and non-absoluteness of national claims. Since the French Revolution, there has been, until a few years ago, an insistence both on the exclusiveness and on the absoluteness of national rights.

Nation-states were sovereign states, and sovereignty had to be absolute. There was a parallel doctrine of unity: for every state, but one nation, whatever violence this might do to the facts of history or the consciousness and self-respect of minorities. Ernest Gellner has pointed out how the politics of large-scale modern political societies has required an assertion of a "flat" common nationality through educational and communications systems—has required, that is to say, an assertion of a "nation" for the state.[9] Historians have tended to treat these theses as paradigmatic for nationalism, and thus to treat nations and nationalism as features exclusively of the post-revolutionary world. I have else-where argued that this is an unduly restrictive model for a descriptive theory of nationalism that could fit credibly with the history of, for example, the British Isles.[10] Rather, the virulent doctrine of the sovereign and absolute nation-state which arose after the revolution, important though it may have been in the rise of modernity, is but one conception of a concept that has a longer past and still, I hope, a future.

Nationalisms Differentiated

So it is indeed proper to distinguish various strands within nationalism. It is a phenomenon with more than one face. There is the imperialistic nationalism of successful nation-states. This is a nationalism of which I have already spoken slightingly. It has often both attacked internal minorities and imposed itself on external victims or rivals, defining enmity so as to justify territorial aggran-dizement and enhanced state power. At the same time, it defines a tendency towards exaltation within the state of a single dominant national tradition and culture, and a disregard for minorities or deviant traditions. It is easy to read this in the reported speeches of Mr Zhirinovsky. Nationalism in this sense always shades over towards fascism and is the enemy of human liberty. Nationalism of this kind and appeals to nationality and identity are often used ideologically (in the adversative sense) to stamp out liberal democratic parties and socializing institutions like free trade unions and social democratic parties, exalting national unity against any mere partisanship or any politics of class rather than country. Nationalism in this mode is seen as the embodiment of exclusivism, intolerance and racial hatred. In this model, nationalists cannot see the universal of humanity in the many versions of human identity, but only the particularity of the favoured or asserted nation exalted over all its internal or external rivals. This is indeed so much the prevalent image of nationalism that it can be difficult even to pose the possibility that nationalism could have a different and acceptable face.

There is a different face, though, and one that starts from a universally statable principle, not from rampant particularism. The principle is that of the right of self-determination of those politico-cultural communities that have evolved as "nations" in the history of Europe and, no doubt partly under European influence, elsewhere. This principle is not only compatible with, but has as its necessary corollary, the duty of mutual respect among those who claim the right. The assertion of national aspirations does not have to be, and rationally ought not to be, a ground for the denial of other aspirations similar in kind. This is a principle that can and should be recognized among the principles of right (or justice) that set the terms of shared democracy in a large-scale meta-community such as that of the European Union.

Further, if one asks about the values represented by the principle of self-determination, these unquestionably include a certain appreciation of cultural individuality and diversity. If I ask why there *should* be a Catalonia after years of a unified Spain, why there should be a Lithuania or an Estonia after two generations of incorporation in the USSR, the answer must presumably include the proposition that the existence of these cultural diversities and the possibility of their political recognition adds to the wealth of human experience and enhances human possibilities. No less important, of course, is the proposition that there are many people who want to be recognized as Catalan, or as Lithuanian, or as Estonian, and to enjoy the same opportunities of individual and collective cultural self-expression in that identity as can easily and uncontroversially be enjoyed by those who identify with the state culture of Castilian or Russian or the like. But for such wishes to be rational, they must be rational for a state of affairs that is itself of some value. That condition is satisfied if we ascribe positive value to variety in the human experience; the existence of a plurality of expressions of human culture adds to the richness of life. This seems to me a value with much positive appeal. It is a value each can appreciate for herself or himself as an individual, even though that which is appreciated has an irreducibly collective rather than purely individualistic character.

But what is then required is some form of universally statable acceptance of diversity in human groupings with mutual respect and like rights to respect. So conceived, nationalism is absolutely incompatible with fascism, racism or majority discrimination against national (or other) minorities. The critique of nationalism in its virulent forms simply would not apply to nationalism defined as implying a right and duty of mutual respect among diverse national traditions, with appropriate political expression of national identities.

The question seems to me to be not whether this argument is rationally acceptable, but whether the state of affairs that it envisages is a serious practical possibility given the real political, sociological and psychological circumstances of human beings now. It might be argued that any political approach that allows of, let alone contemplates, celebrating the collectivity as such—the cultural group, the nation—is bound to lead on into the kind of mass hysteria, the mindless self-exaltation and other-denigration, the exacerbation of suspicions and hatreds, the intercommunal violence, the massacres, the death camps, that history has so often associated with actual movements of national self-determination, and that political science predominantly deems to be inevitable con-comitants of anything meriting the name "nationalism".

The years of disappointment that have followed the year of triumphs and liberations in Eastern and Central Europe in 1989–90 seem almost to prove the point. Certainly newspapers throughout democratic Europe are full of forebod-ings about the outbreak of destructive and intolerant nationalisms that have blown up in many parts of Central and Eastern Europe, and the new fascisms that are creeping up on us in the West. Movements that started with the joy of the liberation of individuals and their societies have continued into more ques-tionable and exclusivist reassertions of the nation and of national authoritarian-ism. Or so it is said. But the truth by no means seems to bear this out every-where. So far, at least, conditions in the Baltic republics, for example, do seem to be a good deal closer to those required by a tolerant and liberal democracy than those in many other parts of the former USSR.

Anyway, to carry on with arguments I have stated in other places, I should like to suggest that the problems associated with nationalism lie more with the state and with statism than with the nation. The doctrine of the self sufficiency of sovereign states, and (as in some nineteenth-century thinkers) the doctrine of their right to dominate to whatever extent they had power to dominate—the doctrine that legitimated imperialism and the nationalistic wars of the nine-teenth and earlier twentieth centuries—has been in large part the source of the odium attaching to nationalism. For the idea that the "nation-state" must have absolute and uncontrollable control of a territory and all (everyone) that is found within it necessarily creates incurable tension between those who are defined as belonging and those who are defined as not belonging, or who so define themselves. The contemporary fate of the Kurds, who lack a state, but who define themselves (and are for some purposes defined) as not Iraqi, makes a dismal contrast with that of the Kuwaitis, who have, on however shaky historical foundations, a state of their own, and thus have had their national independence rigorously vindicated under the full authority of the United Nations.

The principle of national self-determination becomes morally and practi-cally problematic because (or when) it is coupled to the concept or doctrine of the absolutely sovereign state. For in this form it stipulates that whoever consti-tute a nation have the right (unless they freely renounce it) to constitute them-selves into a sovereign state. But the distribution of people and territory makes all the familiar problems almost inevitable once you try to implement this principle. As Gellner says, there are too many possible nations for the capacity of our planet and its geopolitical systems to embrace as many states.[11] In the world as we find it, there can be no practical universalizability of the right to respect for national identity and the duty of mutual respect if one insists on strong self-determination coupled with the doctrines associated with state sovereignty.

On the other hand, given that the world is one in which there are sovereign states which clothe themselves also in the trappings of nationality, the sense of, and the reality of, injustice to national minorities who are denied a full place in this scheme of things is obvious. It is one consequence of the non-universaliz-ability of the maxims governing the international order of sovereign states under the current arrangements approved by dominant majorities (or, just as likely, minorities). Thus, it appears that problems of national minorities are practically by definition injustices, but injustices of that special kind whose rectification cannot but involve the infliction of like injustices on different persons or groups.

The European Opportunity

Hence there arise some grounds for optimism about the new order represented by the European Union. For this is a new form of political order which offers the hope of transcending the sovereign state rather than simply replicating it in some new superstate, some new repository of absolute sovereignty. It creates new possibilities of imagining, and thus of subsequently realizing, political order on the basis of a pluralistic rather than a monolithic conception of the exercise of political power and legal authority. By creating a framework of political and economic order across many states and national cultures, and by guaranteeing free movement of people, goods and services throughout the whole, Europe necessarily weakens somewhat the idea of the exclusive territo-riality of its parts without however derogating from internal jurisdictions and democratic institutional authorities within the parts.

In such a setting, by escaping from the apparent conceptual necessity for some single repository of absolute institutional sovereignty (as distinct from underlying popular sovereignties), we make possible a solution of the problem considered above. If choices can cease to be between rival claims to sovereign statehood over disputed territories and populations, but can become choices about the allocation of levels of political authority within a transnational com-munity embracing many nationalities and cultural traditions or groupings, a choice guided by some version of the principle of subsidiarity, some dilemmas are greatly eased. The recognition of one identity ceases to be necessarily at the price of denying another.

Still, of course, there remain institutional problems. The European Union remains at this time rather too noticeably a collection of states with a sover-eignty still to assert, as Mr Major's government so ineptly attempted during the debates on enlargement in early 1994. Too much still rests with the Council of Ministers, too little with seriously democratic organs. The unrepresented nationalities are most acutely unrepresented so long as the key decisions rest exclusively with ministers representing the member states. The Committee of the Regions remains untested and has a curiously skewed membership such that, for example, five persons elected by nobody in Scotland to this end represent the whole of Scotland as an entity otherwise unrepresented, while Denmark, with its population also of five million, has eight elected representatives of its regions, with also full representation for Denmark at Council, Commission and Court.

But imperfection in essentially good institutions drives us only to further improvement. It is a matter of continuing political debate among us in Scotland, and indeed in the rest of the United Kingdom, which forms of internal constitutional ordering and relationship to the European Union best satisfy both our own local sense of nationality and our bonds of amity and interrelationship with our immediate neighbours in these islands and our wider neighbourhoods in Europe and in the international community. Some, as noted, are happy with Scotland's place in the existing constitutional frame of the United Kingdom inside the European Union; others (probably the largest proportion of us at present) favour federal arrangements for the nations and the English regions within the UK, connecting these to the Committee of the Regions, on a parallel with Bavaria, Corsica, Catalunya or Euskadi; others again, myself included, would prefer the status of EU member statehood, in parallel with other small countries like Finland, Norway, Sweden or Denmark. This debate continues, and meanwhile nobody in Europe considers the Union Treaty of Maastricht to have had the last word. The extension of the Union first to the Nordic countries and Austria, and later perhaps further east into the democratizing and liberalizing states beyond the former iron curtain, is almost *fait accompli*, and may be the best road to undercutting atavistic nationalisms that may otherwise spread like wildfire across the Continent. Europe's present institutional and governmental forms do not, however, seem capable of accommodating much further expansion without radical transformation.

The world and the Europe that are to come will not I think find it possible to abandon every sort of nationalist principle The realistic, but profoundly difficult, aim ought to be that of securing acceptance only of liberal nationalist principles, and of trying to devise institutional frameworks in which whatever nationalisms remain in being or come into being are all liberal in their principles and in their practice.[12]

Notes

1. Y. Tamir, *Liberal Nationalism* (Princeton: Princeton University Press, 1993).

2. See N. MacCormick, "Nation and Nationalism", *Legal Right and Social Democracy* (Oxford: Oxford University Press 1982), pp. 247–264.

3. Tamir, *Liberal Nationalism*, pp. 32–34.

4. J. Rawls, *A Theory of Justice* (Oxford: Oxford University Press, 1972).

5. R. Downie and E. Telfer, *Respect for Persons as a Moral Principle* (London: G. Allen and Unwin, 1968).

6. K. Minogue, *Nationalism* (London: Batsford, 1967), p. 25.

7. J. S. Mill, *Considerations on Representative Government*, in *Utilitarianism Liberty, Representative Government*, ed. H. B. Acton, (London: Dent, 1972), pp 363–364.

8. H. Seton-Watson, *Nationalism and Communism* (New York: Praeger, 1964).

9. E. Gellner, *Nations and Nationalism* (Oxford: Blackwell, 1983).

10. MacCormick, "Nation and Nationalism".

11. Gellner, *Nations and Nationalism*, p. 2.

12. This chapter is a revised version of the Stevenson Lecture in Citizenship which I delivered at the University of Glasgow in January 1994. It is published here by kind permission of Edinburgh University Press and the David Hume Institute, having been published in a slightly different version under the same title in H. MacQueen, ed., *In Search of New Constitutions*, Hume Papers in Public Policy, No. 2 (Edinburgh: Edinburgh University Press, 1994), pp. 79–95.

4

What Is Nationality, and Is There a Moral Right to National Self-Determination?

John Charvet

This chapter defends a civic nationalist use of the term "nation". According to this usage, it makes no sense to ask whether a nation has a moral right to self-determination unless this question is to be understood as one about the right of the people of a state to democratic self-government. I do not think that the standard usage of the term "nation", present in the question of whether nations have the right of self-determination, and containing the belief that a certain type of group constitutes a nation independently of its organization in a state, is meaningful. I do not believe that there is any way of distinguishing pre-state-organized groups that are nations from those that are not. Ideally, the term "nation" should be abandoned altogether, since it encourages conceptual and political confusion, but as this is too much to hope for I retain a residual use for it in the civic nationalist mode.

Despite being so critical of the standard usage of the term, I believe that nationalist-type concerns—namely the relevance of cultural commonalities to the distribution of human beings among states—are both intelligible and reasonable. Their discussion and evaluation are greatly assisted, nevertheless, by abandoning the illusion that some of these commonalities are attributes of distinct entities called nations. It is, I think, hopeless to attempt to determine the proper weight to be given to such considerations independently of a general theory of normative association. At any rate, in this chapter I shall pursue my two questions in the context of such a theory. This theory is a contractarian theory of moral and political association. In the first section of the chapter I provide a brief sketch of the theory. It should be broadly familiar, but it has distinct characteristics of my own invention. In the second section I turn to the question of what a nation is, while in the final section, having abolished nations so to speak, I attempt to assess the importance of cultural commonalities in the organization of just states.

Contractarian Theories of Moral and Political Association

The particular form of contract theory I espouse follows in the first instance what may be called the Rawls–Scanlon theory of just association.[1] What is just is what cannot reasonably be rejected, under certain ideal conditions, as principles for regulating their interactions by persons who desire to co-operate in order to further their interests defined in terms of certain basic goods, which I shall call life, liberty and access to resources.

It should immediately be emphasized that this theory of just association is perfectly compatible with the recognition that persons can develop to the point of becoming ideal contractors only through their initial formation as reason-following, morally co-operating beings in some society. They will have developed the capacity to reflect abstractly about the terms of moral co-operation in society only after having learned to think and act in accordance with the moral beliefs and practices of their society. The contractors stand back from that formative embeddedness in traditional ways in order to subject those ways to a critical appraisal.

A major difficulty in the Rawls–Scanlon approach arises from the uncertainty as to whether, in the end, the contract plays any necessary role in the derivation of the principles. This is because the ideal conditions that structure the contractual situation appear to contain a prior commitment to the equal positive worth of persons, so that the fundamental principle of justice in the scheme—namely, equality—is somehow established or presupposed independently of the agreement. To avoid this complete collapse of the contractarian element, and the consequent necessity of treating the value of persons as inhering in them in a manner that is justifiable only from an ethically realist standpoint, we must be able to derive the equality principle from the agreement. I shall have to say a word or two about how I think this is to be done, since the character of the argument and its conclusion greatly affect everything that is to follow.

In the first place, then, we must adhere strictly to an anti-realist position on moral value.[2] The moral principles, and so the equality principle, are grounded in nothing other than the reasoned agreement of human beings. Second, we must reject the rational choice interpretation of the contract. To do this we need an account of why the contractors have an interest in imposing on themselves the impartiality conditions reflected in the Rawlsian notion of the veil of ignorance. The argument proceeds as follows. Social co-operation on the basis of morally authoritative norms—that is, norms that are accepted as regulative of the co-operators' pursuit of their self-interest—is enormously profitable for human beings in terms of each person's interest in the social primary goods. Such norms make stable social co-operation possible. However, norms that simply reflect the relative bargaining power of the contracting parties cannot have that authority. The self-interested ground licenses a person to renege on the agreement whenever he is in a position to do so. A genuinely authoritative norm is one that persons would have reason to accept whatever position they came to occupy in society. To achieve that result, the contractors can see that they must, in making the agreement, abstract from their particular characteristics and situation in the world and consider only their general nature and interests as persons.

Third, the reasons for the contractors to adopt the impartial standpoint are still only prudential ones, and as such they are an insufficient basis to support the authority of the norms over self-interest. They are necessary but not sufficient reasons. Yet, from an anti-realist perspective on ethics, there cannot be any other reasons for a person to acknowledge moral authority. He must make an existential commitment to live his life from the moral standpoint. However, this is not a completely irrational choice, since he has very good prudential reasons to make it. In making such a commitment, a person undertakes to pursue his good together with the other contracting parties under the authority of the moral norms. Co-operation in accordance with the norms constitutes a common good for the contractors, and the engagement to make oneself into a moral being is at the same time a recognition of a community of interest with the others and an acceptance of the superiority of one's common identity and good over one's personal identity and good.

At this point in the argument I supplement the Rawls–Scanlon type theory with arguments to be found in Hobbes, Rousseau and Kant for the identity of moral and political association. The moral contract is not an unconditional commitment to live a moral life. It is a conditional agreement to interact with others who are so willing on moral terms. But one's necessary prudential reason to be moral is dependent on one's having the assurance that the others will reciprocate. The Hobbes–Rousseau–Kant argument is that in a state of nature, which should, of course, be understood as a non-political condition and not a non-social condition, one cannot have that assurance, and that in its absence one has no obligation to interact with others on moral terms. Hence, the advantages of a mutual commitment to moral interaction can be secured only through the constitution of the moral community as at the same time a political one with a collective coercive authority.[3]

There is an additional argument for the identity of moral and political association present in the classic contractarians, and which I take to be of major significance for the nationality issue. This is what I call the determinacy argument. The fundamental principles of moral interaction to which the contractors commit themselves require that persons have equal rights over the basic goods.

In a state of nature, each person must judge for himself what his entitlement is under the scheme. But since what he is entitled to is only relative to the entitlements of others, there being no absolute rights, a person's just claims are quite indeterminate independently of a judgement about priorities when one person's life, liberty or property interest conflicts with another's. If each must judge for himself, and if there is no reason to suppose that individual judgement on priority claims will coincide, there can be no obligation on anyone to recognize what the other claims for himself. The solution once again is to substitute for the multiplicity of private judgements a collective or public judgement of priority rules.[4] As this issue is of such importance for an evaluation of nationalist-type considerations, I shall return to it again later.

The assurance and determinacy arguments for the moral community taking a political form do not in themselves require the world to be divided up into separate communities. They could in principle be satisfied by a global political community of humankind. For obvious, but contingent, reasons, a world state could not have been the first form of human political association, and is even now in a centralized form not a sensible goal to pursue. So the contractarian theory that I have sketched in effect justifies the division of humankind into separate moral–political communities, which must be the primary focus of a person's moral commitments. There are nevertheless good reasons for these separate communities to form an international political community of communities, as indeed exists to some degree at the present time.

What Is Nationality?

According to my contractarian theory, the legitimacy principle for states is egalitarian and voluntarist. The authority of the state and its laws is grounded in the equal wills of its members to pursue their good together as a common good through moral norms. So if we ask the question, on what principle should the division of humankind into distinct states be based, it might appear that a voluntarist answer is dictated by the underlying normative theory. By "voluntarism" here I mean the view of Harry Beran, who believes that any self-supporting collection of human beings who inhabit the territory of an existing state should be allowed to secede if they wish, provided that they themselves permit any minority within their territory to exercise the same right and provided that certain other not very demanding conditions are met.[5]

However, voluntarism in that form would involve a misunderstanding of the contractarian theory of political legitimacy. The contractor commits himself to co-operation on moral–political terms with anyone who is willing to reciprocate. Thus, a person who finds himself a citizen of a state which satisfies in its arrangements the moral–political conditions that as a rational contractor he would endorse, has at least a *prima facie* obligation to that state and to his fellow citizens. His reasons for moral–political association are in fact met by his existing state, so he can have no good reason having to do with the purpose of states to secede from it. Still, it may be thought that a person has a natural right to associate politically with whomsoever he pleases provided they are so willing and provided that no substantial injustice is done to third parties by the secession. A natural right on the Hobbesian view of the state of nature that I am broadly following is, however, not a moral right. There can be no moral rights in a state of nature because the assurance conditions of moral obligation are not fulfilled. Once they are met by a state, which thereby claims jurisdiction over a person and his possessions, that person's moral interests are realized through the political order, and he can have no moral reason to secede. His actual reason for seceding would then be arbitrary from a moral point of view.

The arrangements of a state may, of course, be morally deficient in some way. Such deficiencies, however, would provide a citizen in the first place with a reason to seek to remove them rather than himself, and could constitute a ground for secession only if the injustices were directed at a territorially based group of which he was a member and only if the majority of the state's citizens supported the injustices. The justification for secession in that case would not be the right of the group as a collective identity—for instance a nation—to determine itself, but the interest of its members as individuals in associating on just terms. So if there is to be something like a right of groups called nations to be politically autonomous, then, to be compatible with the contractarian theory of legitimacy, the right must be located in the political conditions of moral community, the most promising of which from this point of view will be the determinacy condition. However, before investigating that possibility, I must first seek to give an answer to the question, what is a nation?

On my contractarian theory, every legitimate state needs a communal identity strong enough to ensure the loyalty of its citizens in any conflict between the common good of the whole as realized through the norms of justice and the particular good of individuals and groups. On one understanding of what a national identity may be, such a communal identity will necessarily be a national identity. This is the so-called civic idea of nationalism. On this view, the nation is the body of citizens of a state. It will, then, make no sense to talk of a right to national self-determination unless this means either the right of the subjects of a state to be democratically self-governing or the right of the nation-state to its sovereignty *vis- -vis* other states. Since my contractarian theory with its egalitarian basis almost certainly establishes a presumption in favour of democratic self-government, it could be said to be completed in the civic nationalist idea. But this would be merely to repeat that the theory requires a strong sense of communal identity in the citizens of a state. Furthermore, this communal or civic national identity is simply the sentiment of a collection of persons that their fundamental moral–political interests are tied to the success of this state and hence are dependent on their mutual commitment. From this point of view, any collection of persons will do.

Yet such a conclusion is very implausible. It is very unlikely that a sufficient condition for a successful moral–political community is that the members acknowledge their interest in being a member of some state organized on contractarian principles and see that here is such a state of which they happen to be members, unless present in the determinacy argument in the contractarian theory are more demanding conditions that point to the need not simply for common agreement on general contractarian principles, but also for agreement of a more particularist nature. Let us assume for the moment that something along these lines is required, and that a more substantial idea of the nation than is contained in the civic conception of it might provide the additional particularist element necessary for a successful communal identity. Is there a viable substantive idea of the nation?

It seems to be widely agreed among contemporary writers on the subject that it is impossible to define a nation in purely objective terms, that is to say in terms of features of a collection of persons that are independent of the members of the collection believing that they are a nation. The objective features that are standardly appealed to are ancestry, language, religion, culture, history, territory. The trouble with an objective definition is that successful political groups calling themselves, and called by others, nations may share very few of these characteristics. Perhaps it would be sufficient to say that for any group to count as a nation it must possess some common features in the above list. But this is so vague a criterion that it will be impossible to differentiate on its basis those collections of people whose members share objective features and do not think of themselves, and are not generally thought of, as nations from those whose members may have even less in common than the former and yet who are considered to be nations. There are simply too many commonalities of the designated kind that people share at many different levels. Thus, a person may be, at the same time, a Londoner, an East Ender, an Englishman, a Briton, a European, a Christian, a member of Western liberal society, and even a human being! Where are we to find in these various commonalities the objective facts that make some of these collections a nation but not others?

At this point a fairly standard move is to add to the objective factors a subjective element—namely, the belief of persons who share a number of the standard objective characteristics that they are a nation.[6] But what is it that they believe? It would seem that they believe they possess certain objective features in common and by virtue of that fact constitute a nation. This must be a false belief, because we have already seen that it does not follow from the common possession of these features by a collection of persons that they are a nation. The proposal would seem to be that, just in so far as a collection of people falsely believe that possessing certain common features makes them a nation, then they are a nation. Such a proposal is manifestly absurd. We are not inclined to say, for example, that, just in so far as someone falsely believes that in virtue of being self-conscious he has an immortal soul, then he has an immortal soul! So the whole weight of the subjective element must be separated from the objective features and lie in itself. This would be to say that, besides the objective features, what it is to be a nation is simply to believe that you are a nation. But then, the crucial subjective element would be empty of meaning. For if what makes a collection of persons a nation is essentially the belief that they are a nation, and the content of the belief that they are a nation is the belief that they are a nation, the belief is subject to a meaning-destroying infinite regress.

David Miller says that nationality exists when, besides the stock objective features, its members believe that it does, but adds that they believe that they belong together and constitute a community of obligation.[7] The national community should also have an active identity by doing things together as a group. It should take decisions and achieve results. Let us concentrate first on the suggestion that the content of the subjective belief is that of belonging to a community of obligation. There are many kinds of groups the members of which may believe that they belong together and constitute a community of obligation—for instance, families, tribes, churches, universities, trade unions, businesses. A nation is presumably more like a family or a tribe than like the other groups, for there seems to be very often or perhaps always a belief in the common ancestry of the members of the nation. Nevertheless, in all the examples cited, the belief that one is a member of a community of obligation is tied to some real function that the group fulfils in its members' lives. Families fulfil sexual and reproductive functions, tribes are decentralized political associations, while the other groups define their identity by the particular purpose for which they are organized. What is the function of a nation? It would seem to be something like that of a tribe. But the tribe is a political association, and only on the civic nationalist definition is a nation essentially a political entity. The view of the nation that I am now exploring is that of a group that is not necessarily a political entity, but may have a right to form such a unit.

So what is a nation on this view? In virtue of what do the members believe themselves to be under mutual obligation? No doubt it is in virtue of the commonalities shared with other members of the group. However, as I have already claimed, a person shares such commonalities at various levels, and no doubt feels an obligation to give preference to other members of these groups in suitable circumstances. Thus, he may at different times, or indeed at the same time, feel under obligation to attach moral weight to his relations to fellow Londoners, East Enders, Englishmen, Britons, Europeans, Christians, members of Western liberal society and even human beings! One cannot identify the collectivity that constitutes a nation by reference to feelings of obligation alone. Perhaps there is a special type of feeling of obligation that is characteristic of national sentiment. Perhaps it involves a sense of belonging together in a special kind of way. But what could this be? One cannot define the peculiar nature of the national sentiment in terms of the members' belief that they are a nation. For doing so would merely return us to the emptiness of the infinite regress. If the meaning of the "national" element in the sentiment is the belief that they are a nation, then one can always substitute for the object of the belief, the belief that they are a nation, and so on *ad infinitum*.

Perhaps a national identity is a rock-bottom primitive group identity of a human being, the primitiveness of which consists in the fact that it cannot be analysed into further components. A human being is necessarily a national being, for it is as a national being that his humanity as a self-conscious, reason-following and language-speaking being gets given a determinate content in the national culture. On this view, a person's nation is a constitutive part of his essential identity, so that he is essentially who he is only by virtue of being a member of his nation. Perhaps Herder held such a conception of the nation. But it involves attributing to the nation an organic unity as an original individual existence in the world that is frankly ridiculous. One cannot read the histories of the so-called nations without recognizing that national identity is a radically contingent construction. Even if it is true, as Anthony Smith claims, that the successful modern nations have had as their original nuclear core a dominant ethnic group such as the Anglo-Saxons, the Franks and so on, ethnic or tribal identity may be just as contingent and constructed an identity resting on invented ideas of common ancestry as the nation itself that it is supposed to explain.[8] Furthermore, a "Herderian" notion of national identity would be incompatible with the belief in the freedom and separate individuality of persons. For a person would be essentially a part, or a "member", of a specific greater whole—his nation. Even if it is accepted that human beings are essentially social beings in the sense of needing to be brought up in a cultural group in order to realize their human capacities as self-conscious, reason-following beings, they are not as such essentially members of any particular group, but have the potentiality to be members successively, or even at the same time, of a multiplicity of them, and to re-form or reconstitute the collectivities of which they are part into smaller or larger entities.

It will be recalled that David Miller includes as part of his definition of a nation the requirement that it do things together, take decisions and achieve results. This is to give to the collectivity not just a passive commonality of beliefs and practices, but an active unity. But I do not think that such organizational unity can, together with the other requirements, be a sufficient condition to identify some group as a nation since such criteria will not distinguish a "nation" from other organized groups with a common history and a sense of communal identity and obligation, such as churches, trade unions or tribes. It cannot even be a necessary condition. For if, to be a nation, a collectivity must already be organized as a unit, then it must either now enjoy a degree of recognized political autonomy or possess this in illegal form as a rebel movement. It would, then, make no sense to talk of the right of nations to self-determination, where this implies that some group, identifiable as a nation but not already politically organized, has a right to the political expression of its group identity. For, on the supposed definition to claim such a right, either one must now have it, in which case it cannot be a moral right affirmed against the legal status quo, or one must be an organized rebel group seeking political autonomy, and one is said to have the moral right to a legally recognized autonomy just in so far as one is an illegal "natural" organization. The content of the claim to the right in the latter case would seem to be that one's group had succeeded in achieving a degree of illegal organization in opposition to the established political order. How could such illegality of itself establish a moral right?

Nevertheless, it does seem to be the case that the claim to political autonomy is a central element in the idea of a nation. A nation is perhaps a group the members of which think of themselves as being entitled to a degree of political autonomy. On this view what distinguishes groups conceived by their members as nations from groups that do not is simply the fact that the members of the former class believe that as a nationality they have a right to a degree of political independence.

However, the trouble with this formula is that the claim to political autonomy is made on the basis of the group's being able to identify itself as a nation independently of its political claim. It is entitled to make the claim because it can be so identified. But, as we have seen, there is no way of doing this. There are no nations in that sense. In so far as a group is claiming its political independence by virtue of its nationality, this is necessarily a fraudulent claim. Could one save the meaningfulness of the term by saying that a nation is a group claiming a degree of political autonomy—a collectivity aspiring to self-government? Provided that the claim is not based on the prior existence of the nation, we would have a clear and distinct use for the term. But it would have the drawback that one could not, on this usage, talk of groups that already enjoyed political sovereignty, and so would not need to claim it, as nations. It would seem to me better to say, then, that a nation is a self-governing group with a sense of communal identity, and that groups aspiring to be self-governing are groups seeking to acquire national identity or to become nations. They are not, as such, already nations. This commits us, in effect, to the civic idea of nationality.

If we say that a group aspires to the status of a nationality when seeking to acquire political autonomy, then we must require it to have reasons for making the claim, and those reasons cannot appeal to its existing nature as a nation. They must be reasons that are relevant to the formation of politically autonomous units. What they are is not difficult to see. They consist in the claim that this group is an appropriate collection of persons to form a polity by virtue of the significant commonalities that already exist among them, and that distinguish them from other groups including the group of persons with whom they now share a state and a nationality. To appeal to such commonalities is similar to, but not the same as, giving as one's reason the fact that one is already a nation. It appeals to the same sort of objective features to which "nations" appeal in asserting their identity, but drops the pretension that these features as such make them a nation. The objective commonalities are the reasons why the world should be divided into states in one way rather than another. Political divisions should correspond as much as possible to differences in the significant commonalities.

Cultural Communalities and Just States

What is the validity of the political appeal to such commonalities? In order to appreciate its significance we need to return to, and elaborate upon, the determinacy argument. This argument holds that in a state of nature—that is to say, in a non-political, but not non-social condition in which there are no collective procedures for determining the claims of individuals under the equal rights principle, but each uses his private judgement in interpreting the rule—it will be inherently uncertain what anyone's just claims are. This is because what a person's entitlements are in respect even of the rule against physically harming another depends on whether or not a harm is legitimately inflicted in a person's defence of his liberty or property rights, so that we have to settle the latter before we can adjudicate upon the former in any particular case. There is no valid private decision in these cases. What we need is an agreement among the interacting parties as to individual entitlements over resources on the one hand and priority rules governing conflicts of liberty on the other. But there is no reason to suppose that the collective decision of each political association in giving determinacy to the equal rights principle will yield an identical set of rules. There are many possible property arrangements and priority rules which could count as instantiations of the general principle, and which one is best for a particular group must depend on considerations that are accidental from the standpoint of the principle itself, and have to do with the peculiarities of that group's situation and make-up.

When we add to the fundamental equal rights principle a further principle, such as the difference principle or the Pareto principle, which legitimizes departures from a baseline equality and which also cannot determine acceptable outcomes in a unique way, we recognize that there will be additional substantial areas of indeterminacy which require collective agreement governed not by reasoned deductions from universal principles but by appeals to particularistic considerations. By the latter I mean reasons that involve the adaptation of universal principles to the peculiarities of a particular people and its situation. The authority of such reasons for that people cannot then depend on a claim that they are valid for human beings as rational beings, but must rest on self-understandings that are limited to that specific collection of persons. The success of the collective authority in this respect requires an ability to articulate the potential agreements among those people.

Some of the commonalities that nationalists appeal to as the basis for their claim to be a nation and enjoy the rights of nations, or, as I would put it, as the basis of a claim by a group to form its own state and become a nation, are the sorts of considerations that facilitate the achievement among a collection of people of political agreement on particularistic reasoning. The most important commonalities from this point of view are cultural ones. A culture is a way of organizing beliefs and values over some range of human interests shared by a group of persons. This is not to say that a culture cannot contain conflicting views within it, but there must still be something distinctive about the way those conflicts are apprehended in that culture if it is to be marked off from other cultures. It is not to say either that cultures are distinct individual wholes. There is no clear and settled way of counting cultures, and as I use the term it is perfectly meaningful to talk of cultures overlapping, exhibiting a nested character, and of persons participating in many cultures at the same time. A person's beliefs and values may reflect English, European and Western culture simultaneously, and may combine a Catholic religious culture with an intellectual culture formed by Anglo-American analytical philosophy. The "nationalist" claim, then, might be formulated in terms of the importance of cultural affinity for political agreement. A successful polity on the contractarian theory must create its own distinctive political culture, and this will be greatly assisted if its citizens possess a common culture in other areas.

Should we recognize, then, a right of cultures to political autonomy? This would be a revised version of the nationalist claim that nations have a right to self-determination. However, since there is no unique way of counting cultures, this claim looks as insubstantial as the nationalist one. It would clearly be lunatic and incoherent to propose to give political autonomy to everything identifiable as a culture. So at most we would have to say that, where there exists among a collection of people significant cultural affinities bearing importantly on matters of social and political organization, then such a people has a right to political independence. Suppose that we can pick out on this basis some reasonably clear cases of such cultures which are not already organized in their own states: do we want to say that they have a *prima facie* right, at least, to a state of their own?

We must first distinguish between cultures that are compatible with the contractarian principle of just association and those that are not. I shall assume that the best interpretation of contractarian principles of equal rights over life, liberty and resources is a liberal one broadly understood so as to include theorists as diverse as Locke, Rousseau, Hume, Bentham, Burke, Kant, Hegel, Mill and so on. In fact, liberalism as I understand it excludes only a communist interpretation of equal rights, for which there is, I believe, little to be said. So cultures compatible with contractarian justice will be broadly liberal ones. Illiberal cultures have no right to political autonomy, since one cannot have a right to promote unjust practices. From a pragmatic point of view, of course, it may be advisable to accommodate such cultures with a state of their own, or to tolerate them if they have one. But this would be a defeat for contractarian justice. From an ideal point of view, the issue of a right of cultures to political autonomy can arise only in relation to ones that can reasonably count as liberal.

Is there a moral right for broadly liberal cultures to be self-determining politically? The trouble is that the supposed beneficiaries of the right simply do not have the necessary exclusive individual identity. For example, English culture may be broadly distinguished into northern and southern and is itself a sub-set of British culture, which can be subsumed under European and more broadly Western culture, not to speak of humanity itself. A participant in English culture has multiple nested cultural identities; and, from the point of view of the public–political expression of these identities, he has in principle many choices as to the level at which he might seek political independence for a cultural identity. There is no way of establishing that one level has such a right and others do not on the basis solely of cultural identity. One cannot say that British cultural identity alone has that right, for it is perfectly possible ethically speaking for the British polity to be divided into separate states, or to become unequivocally part of a European federal state, or even of a world state.

Could it be, then, that there is a right of any collection of persons who think of themselves as sharing some cultural identity of socio-political relevance to elect for political independence, so that in principle there would be a right of East Enders, Londoners, Cornishmen or whoever to declare themselves politically independent, provided they could form a viable state and could do so without substantial injustice to third parties? This would no doubt be practically equivalent to the pure voluntarist principle, but would it fall to the same objections? Not if one can derive such a right from the determinacy argument. That argument establishes that political community requires agreement not only on general principles but also on particularistic reasons. But this requirement can be met by collections of people who possess at some level strikingly diverse cultural identities, such as the Swiss. So we cannot say that it follows from the determinacy argument that there must be a non-political cultural uniformity as the basis for political community, and then justify on these grounds the right of any cultural group to choose independence. To accept such a claim would be to acknowledge that any degree of cultural diversity constituted a threat to political community—a view that is quite false and that would be madness to endorse.

There cannot in any case be a natural moral right of individuals to associate on the basis of their cultural identity, since, on the "Hobbesian" version of contract theory that I add to my modified Rawlsianism, there are no natural moral rights. As I have already claimed, persons can have moral rights only as members of a political community. So they could not have the supposed moral right to cultural self-determination. If there is no right for any cultural group to secede from an existing state as it chooses, is there a duty on the group not to secede, if it has the power and the will to do so? Do its members have a duty to remain in the existing state even though they can establish themselves in a viable state of their own without injustice? It is difficult to see that there is such a duty. Of course, the other members of their state have no duty to let them go. Since, *ex hypothesi*, members of the seceding minority are not unjustly treated and, let us say, participate to some extent in the formation of the overall political identity, as the Scots in the British identity, and the Québecois in the Canadian, they would appear to have no claim on general contractarian principles to be allowed to go freely. However, they wish to be politically independent and have a state of their own. They believe, perhaps, that they could do better for themselves through the greater accentuation given to their Québecois or Scottish identity that political independence brings, just as many British/English dislike the European Union largely because of the attenuation of the British/English identity that the Union's successful development would involve.

I do not think that there is any way of settling such disputes from a general moral point of view. Since the relevant identities of persons as members of groups are not given naturally but are alterable, and since on the contractarian theory persons are fundamentally free beings with the capacity to take responsibility for who they are, each person must ultimately decide for himself in the light of his history and circumstances where his preferred political identity lies and what he must do to realize it. This is not a moral right of self-determination, but a "Hobbesian" natural right to do whatever one thinks best for oneself, which underlies and grounds the political system of moral rights and duties and can never be surrendered. Because it is not a moral right, and because the minority is not being unjustly treated, the cultural majority has no duty to let the minority go without a fight. It is the natural right of the majority to choose to insist on the preservation of the union. Of course, to compel a reluctant minority to remain in a loveless union may not be a prudent policy, and it may very well be prudentially rational for a multicultural regionally based federal state to allow secession solely on the basis of a qualified majority vote in a referendum. In this way, for federal states at least, voluntarism would be accepted as a constitutional procedure for settling claims to secession, but not as a substantive moral principle. The reason for supporting voluntarism as a procedure would be a pragmatic one.[9] It prevents disputes over secession from degenerating into civil or terrorist wars, when no alternative adjudication of the issue on the basis of substantive criteria is likely to be acceptable to both parties. On the other hand, such a constitutional right to secede may encourage secessionist movements to try their luck. It may be better not to have explicit rules on the question or even to recognize a right of secession at all, and so avoid giving a secessionist movement any moral or constitutional status.

Whether procedural rights to secession are recognized or not, the substantive moral point is that there is no moral right to secede on cultural grounds. Nevertheless, we still need to consider the case of a minority culture that is discriminated against by the majority culture whose members control the state in such a way that, although the general principles of justice are satisfied and majority agreement on particularistic reasons is secured, the minority remain unfairly treated. If they are subject to such an injustice, what are their rights? Once again, on "Hobbesian" grounds we cannot say that they have a moral right to secession or revolution in order to correct the injustice. For such a right still supposes that they could have natural moral rights independently of the political community, or in other words in a state of nature. Instead, we should say that they are relieved of any obligation to the existing state, and have a natural "Hobbesian" right to reconstitute the state on just terms or, given a malign will towards them on the part of the majority, to secede from the state.

How is it possible for the social and political arrangements of a society to satisfy the general principles of justice but still discriminate unfairly against a minority culture? One could mean by this discrimination that the liberal rights of majority and minority members are formally equal but substantively unequal in a way that is not justifiable in terms of whatever is deemed the appropriate rule for justifying inequalities. But I do not mean this. I mean rather that the agreement on particularistic reasoning required under the determinacy argument may reflect solely or disproportionately the ways of thinking and valuing of the majority culture. No, or little, attempt may be made at the level of the national state to accommodate the sensibility of the minority, with the consequence that the state may reasonably appear to the latter as an alien entity belonging to the majority with which members of the minority cannot identify. Under such circumstances, they either have to assimilate themselves to the majority identity, or have to assert themselves politically as a group and demand the public–political expression of their cultural identity.

Would the recognition of the reasonableness of such a minority complaint not after all commit us to the belief in a moral right to the political expression of a culture? Yes, but only if the right is formulated in the contractarian terms I have sketched in the opening section, and not as a natural moral right. In other words, the rational contractors would acknowledge the force of the determinacy argument and would therefore recognize that they may turn out to be members of a minority culture. Consequently, they would not agree to principles of co-operation which required the euthanasia of minority cultures within otherwise liberal regimes. They would insist either on specific minority rights as part of the agreement, or at least on the general right of a minority to be recognized as an integral part of the national identity and its political culture. The specific minority rights are most easily organized if the minority has its own home territory. It can then be given a substantial degree of regional autonomy, which may include the adoption of its language for all public business and education in the area and which allows the members to arrive at their own agreement on particularistic reasons in respect of the range of affairs reserved for regional determination.

Nevertheless, regionally based minority rights will not be a satisfactory response to the problem if at the level of the national political identity and culture the minority remains excluded, perhaps on the grounds that enough has already been done for it by giving its members regional autonomy. Regional autonomy will then only sharpen the minority's sense of alienation from the majority-dominated nation-state in which it does not feel represented. For the identity and interests of the nation-state must take precedence over the identity and interests of lesser groups within the state in any conflict, and therefore the failure to incorporate the minority's self-identity in the larger whole by relying on regional rights alone is bound not to solve the minority problem. Incorporation at the national level must accompany regional autonomy, whether this takes place through a system of formal power-sharing, as in the so-called consociational model of multi-cultural co-operation, or through informal understandings and accommodations which enable members of the minority to feel that they can be for example Québecois as well as Canadian, Welsh as well as British. Where the minority culture has no territorial base, then it becomes difficult to combine rights for the minority with the individualistic basis of the general liberal culture. It may be necessary to allocate some rights on the basis of cultural affiliation—the right for instance to state-financed schools which may well not be obtainable through the normal operation of the liberal-democratic system.

Would this matter from the point of view of liberal justice? I do not think that the very idea of group rights contradicts the liberal individualist conception of just co-operation. For that conception in my version includes the assurance and determinacy arguments, and both these contingently support the claims of specific collections of people to set themselves up in their own state, and hence to distinguish themselves politically and morally from other people. The assurance argument justifies the separate group by reference solely to the universal liberal individualist values, while the determinacy argument explains the need for persons to form culturally specific collective practices. On both counts the theory holds that persons can effectively have rights only as members of a group. So it cannot be contrary to the principles or spirit of contractarian justice that cultural groups should be designated as the bearers of rights. Nevertheless, it may again be necessary for the state to pursue informal accommodation at the national level with non-territorially based minority cultures to supplement their legal rights in order to ensure that their members can give overriding loyalty to the civic national identity.

Notes

1. The Scanlon part of this dual identity is to be found in T. Scanlon, "Contractualism and Utilitarianism", in A. Sen and B. Williams, eds., *Utilitarianism and Beyond* (Cambridge: Cambridge University Press, 1982); and also in his "The Aims and Authority of Moral Theory", *Oxford Journal of Legal Studies*, Vol. 12, No. 1 (1992).

2. I mean by anti-realism in ethics the view that moral values do not exist independently of human desires and attitudes. This involves a certain subjectivism, but does not preclude the possibility of there being good reasons for everyone to accept contractarian principles of association.

3. Everyone knows that Hobbes has such an argument. For Rousseau see *The Social Contract* (London: Penguin Books, 1968.), book 2, ch. 6, pp. 80–81. For Kant see *The Metaphysical Elements of Justice* (Indianapolis: Bobbs-Merrill, 1965), p. 76.

4. The clearest statement of this argument is Kant's in the same passage cited above. For Hobbes see *Leviathan* (Oxford: Basil Blackwell, 1955), pp. 110, 112.

5. H. Beran, *The Consent Theory of Political Obligation* (London: Croom Helm, 1987), pp. 37–42.

6. See e.g. Y. Tamir, *Liberal Nationalism* (Princeton: Princeton University Press, 1993), p. 66.

7. D. Miller, "The Nation-State: A Modest Defence", in C. Brown, ed., *Political Restructuring in Europe: Ethical Perspectives* (London: Routledge, 1994).

8. A. Smith, *The Ethnic Origins of Nations* (Oxford: Blackwell, 1986), p. 24.

9. I follow Buchanan here: A. Buchanan, *Secession* (Boulder, Colo.: Westview Press, 1991).

5

The Skeleton in the Cupboard: Nationhood, Patriotism and Limited Loyalties

Margaret Canovan

Every patriot hates foreigners: they are only men, and nothing to him.

When first he opens his eyes a child should see his country, and to the day of his death he should see nothing else.

—Jean-Jacques Rousseau[1]

Reflections on the tension between patriotic loyalties and wider moral obligations have a long history in Western political thought. In particular, the republican tradition that ended in Rousseau had at its centre a harsh and disturbing dissonance between the mutual commitment of the select body of free citizens and their chauvinistic comportment outside it. Writing during the first flush of enlightened cosmopolitanism, Rousseau was less militaristic than many of his republican predecessors, but he made a point of drawing attention to that dissonance between inside and outside, defiantly affirming the limited loyalties that were the price of political community and of the freedom and justice it made possible. His doubts about the possibility of being both a good citizen and a good man contrast sharply with the generous universalism that we associate with modern liberal democratic political thought. In this chapter I shall explore the thesis that, if modern political theorists have been spared the strain of facing up to similar dilemmas, it is thanks to the advent of nationhood, which has made political community appear natural and effortless.

The chapter has four sections. The first contrasts Rousseau's pessimistic approach to republican political values with the more sanguine expectations of contemporary political philosophers, and accounts for part of the difference by pointing to the presence of nationhood as a tacit assumption in the thinking of the latter. The second section illustrates this claim by looking at some of the ways in which political thinkers rely on more or less hidden presuppositions about nationhood, while the third considers what it is about nations that makes them so easy to take for granted. In the final section I discuss the advantages of being able to smuggle in a notion of political community that is not usually raised to the level of explicit discussion, but point out that, if political theorists are to avoid damagingly naive responses to some of the most pressing of current political issues, it is as well for them to be occasionally reminded of their presuppositions. I shall begin, however, with a paradox in the reputation of that lover of paradoxes, Jean-Jacques Rousseau.

The Paradox of Rousseau's Relevance

Rousseau's notion of the General Will continues to fascinate us largely because it crystallizes many of the themes that occupy contemporary political philosophy. It is (in the first place) explicitly concerned with democratic themes of the sovereignty of the people and direct participation by citizens. Theorists of social justice find it relevant because, while Rousseau was not concerned with economic redistribution, it expresses the idea of a common interest in fairness transcending selfish and thoughtless desires. Meanwhile, those liberals who are preoccupied with the rule of law can find in the General Will an almost Hayekian stress on the importance of _general_ laws that apply to all, in contrast to the special privileges of the _ancien regime_.[2]

What is interesting about this continuing relevance is that it flies in the face of all Rousseau's expectations. For he made it clear that a state based upon the general will was a utopia, certainly not attainable in France, and possible (if at all) only in a small city-state with exceptional levels of unity, patriotism and public spirit: conditions, he stressed, which do not come naturally. A "people" capable of a general will would have to be welded into unity by a charismatic law-giver, and continuing political community would need to be nurtured by means that strike us as totalitarian. The price of democracy, justice and (positive) freedom within the state was oppressive togetherness at home and chauvinism abroad. Without them the republic would not endure.[3]

No doubt the clarity with which Rousseau articulated this had a good deal to do with his temperamental pessimism and his fondness for paradoxes. In doing so, however, he was echoing a traditional republican pessimism which was based on the discouraging record of historical republics.[4] Experience had given rise to the truism that a monarchical polity was much more likely to be strong and stable than a republic, precisely because it demanded less by way of unity and public spirit from the population As Hobbes saw, if Leviathan is there to provide unity by bearing the person of every man,[5] it does not matter that the subjects are separate and mutually hostile. By the same token, however, there is no collective "people" to whom Leviathan can be answerable. If the people were themselves to be sovereign, then (as Rousseau saw) they would need a corporate identity, which would need to be formed and nurtured.[6]

How is it, then, that Rousseau's successors can be so much less pessimistic? For the contemporary political philosophers who appeal to ideas akin to the general will (in their writings on democracy, social justice and the rule of law) do so in quite a different tone. It is true that they regard their principles as regulative ideals rather than blueprints to be completely implemented, but they do believe that their ideas have a purchase on political actuality that is very far from Rousseau's utopian pessimism, and yet there are few parallels in their writings with his anxious concern for the maintenance of political community. Even "communitarians" rarely address such problems.[7] No doubt there are all sorts of reasons for this change of tone, but we can see part of the answer if we consider how Rousseau's theory was read by the French revolutionaries only a generation after his death. Where he had written about imaginary city-republics, most of them read *The Social Contract* as a book about *nations*. It was the French nation that was the "people", with a sovereign general will, a common good and the right to a uniform law for all members of the nation.[8]

In the short term, these assumptions about France turned out to be premature, and the experiment led to civil war and repression. In the longer run, however, political communities in the shape of nations have in certain parts of the world (not all) proved to have a sufficiently vigorous collective existence to make some of Rousseau's utopian aspirations seem almost attainable. Large populations, far beyond the scale of city-states, have come to feel that they are members of a people, that the state is *their* state, that they share a common good and have public duties, that all their people have a right to equality before the law.

I do not wish to exaggerate this phenomenon, for all such cases have plenty of flaws and ragged edges. France (for example) may today be a model of unity, harmony and public spirit compared with contemporary Rwanda or with France in 1789, but a general will may still be hard to find. Empirical examples of national political community are always messy, imperfect, quite largely sustained by muddling through; but the place where the nation is really firmly rooted, so much part of the landscape that it hardly ever becomes visible, is in contemporary political theory, which (with few exceptions) tacitly presupposes the existence of political communities that are evidently nation-states. These can be tacitly presupposed because (in sharp contrast to Rousseau's patriotic republics, which were explicitly artificial constructions) nations present themselves as *natural* phenomena and are often experienced as such. Relieved of the need to construct and maintain a political community and of the limited loyalties it demands, political theorists have been able to let the presupposition of nationhood retreat below the surface of consciousness, freeing themselves to talk in universal terms without facing Rousseau's dilemmas.

The Nation in Political Theory

Although the presence of nationhood in contemporary political thinking is not often explicitly acknowledged, little excavation is needed to find it, sometimes very near the surface, in other cases rather more deeply buried. It is quite prominent, for example, in the thought of both John Rawls and his critics, as Yael Tamir has pointed out.[9] Having begun by working out his theory of justice in terms that appeared to have a global reach, Rawls turns out to have been talking about discrete nations (and the United States in particular) all along. Although he has now spelt this out, stipulating that his model of "political liberalism" is located in a "closed society" which one enters by birth and leaves by death, he seems still to take nationhood too much for granted to recognize the dissonance between this acceptance of inherited citizenship and his hostility to other kinds of inherited privileges.[10] And yet it is not at all obvious why it should be fair for co-nationals to have special claims upon one another whereas (for example) fellow members of a superior caste do not. As Michael Walzer points out, *membership* of a group within which goods are going to be shared is itself "the primary good that we distribute to one another".[11] Surprisingly little of the voluminous criticism of Rawls's theory has paid any attention to this question of boundaries, suggesting that Rawls's critics as well as Rawls himself have been helping themselves to the idea that humanity is conveniently divided into nations.[12]

The same is true of other areas of political thought, such as democratic theory. Political philosophers are of course much too sophisticated to echo politicians and journalists, who talk about "the people"—"the people of Northern Ireland", for instance—in a way that makes clear both the collectivist nature of the concept and also the problems of applying it to the real world. Academic theorists of democracy usually disclaim any such resort to dubious collectivities. Nevertheless, nations have a way of creeping in and concealing themselves among our tacit presuppositions; many theorists who believe themselves to be thinking in terms only of individuals and smaller groups are actually taking for granted the existence of national political communities. The strongest evidence for this is the curious paucity of discussion within democratic theory of the boundaries within which democratic procedures are to take place. With few exceptions, both confirmed individualists and advocates of local participation take for granted that the boundaries are given, and are those of the nation-state.

It may be objected that taking for granted the state boundaries that happen to have been delivered by history does not amount to any kind of affirmation that those boundaries enclose a nation. If one is to talk about democracy at any level that is not global, one must have *some* boundaries: why not accept them simply as a contingent fact with little bearing on the central issues of democratic theory? But the answer is that democrats cannot treat boundaries so lightly, because unless they enclose a "people"—a political community held together by bonds of loyalty—democratic activity may well challenge the borders themselves. If democracy is (in some sense or other) about giving those at the grass roots access to power, then preferences about allegiance are just as likely to be expressed as preferences about taxation. "Bring the 'people' into political life and they will arrive, marching in tribal ranks and orders, carrying with them their own languages, historic memories, customs, beliefs, and commitments."[13] If we are to have some say in public affairs, then the most fundamental issue for decision is *which* public arena we are to participate in, and of what polity we are to be members.

Charles Taylor, who has long been engaged in the practical and theoretical aspects of this problem in Canada, observes that "a democratic society requires a certain kind of unity, because its people supposedly form a unit of collective decision . . . They have to be able to trust one another and have a sense of commitment to one another, or the whole process of common decision will be poisoned by division and mutual suspicion."[14] To make matters worse, there is (as Frederick Whelan has pointed out) no way in which the boundaries within which democracy is to apply can themselves be settled democratically.[15] Democracy is therefore a recipe for continual tearing up of borders, unless it can be underpinned by the assumption that contingent boundaries enclose a political community with some sort of collective existence, typically a "people" or nation. The extreme rarity of discussion of such questions within democratic theory betrays the tacit assumption made by most theorists that the world is divided not just into states but into nations.

Neo-classical liberals may feel that in finding nations under the surface of contemporary political theory I am merely repeating criticisms made by Hayek long since, when he drew attention to the communitarian assumptions about an entity called "society" that were regularly smuggled into discussions of "social" justice and democracy.[16] But even liberals of this anti-communitarian kind cannot congratulate themselves on being free from assumptions about nationhood. It is such assumptions, surely, that lie behind the curious absence of discussion (so very different from Rousseau) of the political conditions that are necessary if the liberal ideal of individual rights protected by the rule of law is to be possible.

It may be objected that theorists of rights are concerned with normative questions about the justice of claims and obligations, and that it is no business of theirs to think about the empirical conditions in which justice is most likely to prevail. But this will not do. Rights imply some kind of legal order and expectation of enforcement. In the absence of such conditions (in the middle of a civil war, for example) we would find ourselves in the situation described by

Hobbes, in which we have obligations *in foro interno*, but probably not in practice.[17] In so far as it can survive without the sustenance of religious belief, the notion of human rights relies for its plausibility on the practical possibility of something approximating to an impartial rule of law, and that implies a particular kind of political community.

This is a point that is often missed. Because the classical liberal view of the minimal state is often regarded as a deplorably undemanding view of politics, it is generally assumed to be easy to attain. Any fool (it is assumed) can establish a night-watchman state: the hard bit is to create participatory democracy or social justice. But the liberal ideal is in fact very demanding indeed. Consider just a few of the conditions it requires:

- laws that are impartial and fairly administered, and do not (for example) favour one religious, ethnic or status group over another;
- a government that is strong enough to maintain internal order and external defence, but is not arbitrarily coercive;
- a public culture that restrains the rulers and officials from using their positions to further their private interests.

No doubt the conditions listed describe an ideal that is never met in full. But the important point to recognize is that it is rare, both in contemporary and in historic polities, for them to be met at all. Rousseau was right: the majority of governments suffered by the human race are, and have always been, arbitrary and coercive. Most of them have been corrupt, using government and law to serve the private interests of the rulers and their associates. Not only has the administration of justice usually been unequal, but the laws themselves have normally favoured some aristocratic, religious or ethnic group at the expense of others. A condition of equal subjection has been rare enough, let alone one of equal citizenship.

Liberal polities do not exist by nature, and are made possible only by a series of rather difficult balancing acts. The state must be strong and effective without being excessively coercive: it must, therefore, be able to mobilize support from at least some sections of the population. However, if it is also to administer equal justice to its citizens, it cannot support itself (as so many governments have done) by helping one group to keep another in subjection. It must in general be trusted by all sections of its subjects. But if, sustained by a culture of bureaucratic professionalism, it tries (like the Habsburg Empire in some phases of its later existence[18]) to rule impartially over all groups, it is likely to find that it has the support of none. It is scarcely surprising that liberal polities are rare. What is it, then, that has made approximations to them possible in certain places at certain times, without the intensive socialization into citizenship that Rousseau thought necessary? The answer, surely (so much taken for granted that it is hardly even discussed), is a specific, national kind of political loyalty that has (in some imperfect degree) made the state *our* state.[19]

I began by observing that, when Rousseau put forward ideals of democracy, a common good and the rule of law, he supported those ideals with anxious concern about how the political community that was their necessary context might be constructed and preserved. Rousseau worried about this communal context *even though* his theory was consciously presented as a utopia. By contrast, although modern political philosophers usually do not think of themselves as utopians, this problem of political community has dropped out of sight in their theories.[20] They are, I suggest, taking for granted that political communities in the shape of nations are simply *there*, so well-rooted and stable that they can sustain democracy, social justice and the rule of law, and would not be shaken by moves in the direction of participation, redistribution of wealth or the granting of rights to minorities.[21]

The trouble with this widespread assumption is that it is politically naive. Nations are not given by nature, and are not even particularly common. Furthermore, the process through which they typically come into existence is even more dissonant with modern Western political values than the activities of Rousseau's Lawgiver, while the measures necessary to preserve those that already do exist are also unpalatable. Let us first consider, however, what it is about nations that makes them so easy to overlook.

Nations and Naturalness

We have given to our frame of polity the image of a relation in blood.
—Edmund Burke[22]

If modern political philosophers have been able to assume the plausibility of political community without having to resort to Rousseau's anxious efforts to imagine how such a community might be constructed, the reason is that theorists writing in Britain, France, the United States and some other places are accustomed to nations that (however flawed in practice) provide intimations of polities in which "we" would rule ourselves, share our resources or respect one another's rights. Experience of these "imagined communities" (in Benedict Anderson's invaluable phrase)[23] leads some theorists to try to imagine the European Union or even the whole of humanity as a kind of super-nation. But what is a nation, and why does it so easily disappear below the surface of consciousness?

Hugh Seton-Watson observed that "many attempts have been made to define nations, and none have been successful".[24] Bearing in mind this warning, I shall not make the attempt, preferring to suggest that the search for a definition rather than a more phenomenological characterization is one of the reasons for the air of exasperated frustration that hangs over the enormous literature on the subject. The truth is that nationhood (which is much less common than is often assumed) is a phenomenon of great political significance that is too complex to lend itself to brief definition. This point is easily missed because it is of the essence of nationhood to seem natural, to the point, in the most well-established cases, of becoming unobtrusive.

Those who have tried to define nations have often done so by adopting one side or another of a series of dichotomies. Is a nation essentially a *political* entity, typically a state, as suggested by terms like "nationality", "national team", "United Nations" and so on? Or is it essentially a *community*, held together by language and culture (as the Romantic nationalists believed)? Is it constituted by birth or by choice? It is a politicized version of ethnicity, or a matter of individual identification? Are nations natural or artificial? Are they immemorial (as nationalists usually believe) or recent products of modernization (as debunking sociologists and historians often maintain)?

Adequate discussion of these complexities is out of the question here. My suggestion is, however, that these apparently fruitless debates themselves point to an answer, which is that the nation is a *mediating* phenomenon, the strength of which is that it holds together the various pairs of alternatives just listed. A nation is a polity that feels like a community, or, conversely a cultural or ethnic community politically mobilized; it cannot exist without subjective identification, and therefore is to some extent dependent on free individual choice, but that choice is nevertheless experienced as a destiny transcending individuality; it turns political institutions into a kind of extended family inheritance, although the kinship ties in question are highly metaphorical; it is a contingent historical product that feels like part of the order of nature; it links individual and community, past and present; it gives to cold, impersonal structures an aura of warm, intimate togetherness. In other words, nationhood is hard to define not because it is confused and nonsensical, but because it is extremely subtle, and, moreover, because (as perceptive commentators from Renan to David Miller have observed) an element of myth is essential to it.[25]

A phenomenon as complex as this is extraordinarily hard to analyse. It happens, however, that an account of the specifically English/British version was given two hundred years ago by that master of articulacy, Edmund Burke. Nationhood developed early in England,[26] and was by the time Burke wrote in the process of expanding into a wider British nationhood,[27] helped on the way by Burke himself as he strove to explain to the French revolutionaries and to his own fellow-countrymen what it was that was so distinctive and effective about the English/British style of politics. His account is worth quoting at length:

> . . . it has been the uniform policy of our constitution to claim and assert our liberties, as an *entailed inheritance* derived to us from our forefathers, and to be transmitted to our posterity. . . By a constitutional policy, working after the pattern of nature, we receive, we hold, we transmit our government and

our privileges, in the same manner in which we enjoy and transmit our proprty and our lives . . . Our political system is placed in a just correspondence and symmetry with the order of the world, and with the mode of existence decreed to a permanent body composed of transitory parts; wherein, by the disposition of a stupendous wisdom, moulding together the great mysterious incorporation of the human race, the whole, at one time, is never old, or middle-aged, or young, . . . Thus, by preserving the method of nature in the conduct of the state, in what we improve we are never wholly new; in what we retain we are never wholly obsolete. By adhering in this manner and on those principles to our forefathers, we are guided not by the superstition of antiquarians, but by the spirit of philosophic analogy. In this choice of inheritance we have given to our frame of polity the image of a relation in blood; binding up the constitution of our country with our dearest domestic ties; adopting our fundamental laws into the bosom of our family affections; keeping inseparable, and cherishing with the warmth of all their combined and mutually reflected charities, our state, our hearths, our sepulchres, and our altars.[28]

Burke brings out into the open the intricate web of custom, contrivance and fiction that allowed the polity to be experienced *as if* it were a community of kin (and an aristocratic family into the bargain). Notice that he does not claim that the nation is actually a natural entity with common blood and a *Volksgeist*. His account is much more sophisticated and less credulous than the nationalist ideology of many Romantics who thought they were his disciples, no doubt because (as an Irishman with Catholic connections negotiating the hazards of English politics) he had very good reasons for being aware of the mythical nature of the beast.[29] While clothing the institutions of the state in the awesome vesture of family, nature and sanctity, he also makes clear that there is contrivance here and that the appearance of kinship itself contains elements of choice. He speaks confidently of "our forefathers", but not only is he himself, as an outsider,[30] part of that "we" by adoption: he is also aware that no political collectivity is natural, and that any that is to survive must be able to transcend the fleeting existence of individual mortal men.[31] The veil of imagined kinship and pretended naturalness thrown over the constitution becomes for him a rational policy designed to solve the fundamental problem of any body politic, "a permanent body composed of transitory parts". The most remarkable feature of this passage is that, by means of the incantatory magic of his rhetoric, Burke is able to acknowledge the crucial role played by myth in constituting nationhood without at the same time exposing the pretence.

Like other politicians, Burke had his own axe to grind. Nevertheless, he does succeed in conveying the complexity that makes the nation such a formidable political force. This is consistently underestimated because it is of the essence of nationhood to *seem* simple and straightforward. A polity that seems like the family inheritance of an entire population is a very unlikely artefact, but where nationhood exists, it looks "natural". As a result we fail to notice what a remarkable political phenomenon it is, giving rise to an enduring "we" far more relaxed and unforced than Rousseau's *moi commun*,[32] which can form the basis of a strong and stable body politic and give the state unity, legitimacy and permanence. In particular, the existence of a nation makes it possible for the state that governs, coerces and taxes us to do so in the name of the same collective "people" who have to put up with these ministrations.[33] No wonder, then, that aspirations that seemed utopian to Rousseau (who thought in pre-national terms)[34] came to look feasible to his successors.

The Benefits and Costs of Letting Sleeping Nations Lie

If contemporary political theorists are indeed building tacit assumptions about nationhood into theories that purport to be cosmopolitan in their principles, it may seem to follow that this embarrassingly ambiguous situation ought to be resolved in one way or another. Either (as many political philosophers would say) we should eliminate national assumptions, or else (with David Miller) we should bring them out of the closet and defend them openly. In contrast to both these rival calls for clear and distinct ideas, I shall argue that, in this as in many areas of political thinking, a certain degree of vagueness is to be welcomed. Just as nationhood as a phenomenon depends on some level of mystification, so it may also be that some benefits flow from the current incoherent combination of universalist discourse and particularistic assumptions.

There is, it is true, one recipe on hand for avoiding any such confrontation: this involves the substitution of "patriotism" for nationhood as the bond of political community, on the assumption that patriotism is easier to reconcile with universal principles than is nationalism. But this assumption is dubious. Rousseau was an authentic spokesman for the classical republican tradition of patriotism in his defiant vindication of loyalties that were exclusive and chauvinistic (not to mention sexist and militarist). Patriotism of that classic kind is much more explicitly hostile to universal values than are the national loyalties of well-established nations.[35] As for the "constitutional patriotism" that attracts some German and American theorists (according to which loyalty is supposed to be given to institutions embodying universal principles, rather than to a nation), the snag here is that (as Charles Taylor points out) the principles and constitution in question have to be *ours* rather than just anybody's if they are to function as the bond of political community.[36] It is no coincidence that apparently "universalist" loyalties of this kind are in fact highly specific. German "constitutional patriotism" is very obviously a response to the unique post-war situation of a German nation that was not only politically divided but heir to a loyalty that dared not speak its name. In America, as in the French republican tradition, patriotism is indeed linked to a set of universal principles, but instead of freeing patriotism from its narrow bounds, the net effect is instead to take universalism captive, surrounding "our" principles with the glamour of a universal "teaching mission" or *"mission civilisatrice"*, and thereby adding self-righteousness and crusading spirit to chauvinism.[37]

"Crusading patriotism" is one way of reducing cognitive dissonance when faced with the clash between universal principles and the demands of limited loyalties. Another is to adopt a stance of "realism", arguing that, since political philosophers who advocate universal principles are secretly enjoying the benefits of nationhood (in their lives as well as in their theories), the only honest position to take is an explicitly nationalist one that acknowledges and is willing to pay the price of political community. According to Roger Scruton (who provides a powerful defence of this position), it is time that liberals acknowledged "the real price of community: which is sanctity, intolerance, exclusion, and a sense that life's meaning depends upon obedience, and also on vigilance against the enemy".[38]

Scruton's position here sounds very like Rousseau's—something that might in itself make us wary of adopting it too hastily, for Rousseau delighted in the drama that came from pushing dilemmas to extremes. I am inclined to argue instead that to press for too much clarity in this area would be to spurn the real political advantages that can arise from the national solution to the problem of political integration, advantages that are greatest in the cases where nationhood is least explicit. Perhaps the greatest blessing of (mature) nationhood is precisely that it can retreat below the surface of consciousness and allow space for the development of idealistic universalism, very much in the way that successful and sustained military defence can allow space for the development of a civilized distaste for war.

There is something to be said, then, for allowing the nations that sleep beneath the surface of so much contemporary political theory to continue their slumbers. Nevertheless, the justification for occasionally drawing back the covers is that this innocent slumber also has disadvantages, particularly in fostering a complacent lack of realism among those who benefit from it. It is easy for political theorists used to talking entirely in universal terms to forget altogether that underlying their ability to do so is the idea (and usually the experience) of a political community that does have borders, that does need to be able to command the loyalty of its population, and that cannot (for example) treat immigration as a human right to which anyone in the world is entitled.[39]

Perhaps the most damaging disadvantage of keeping the hidden premiss of nationhood well buried is that what is concealed from view is not only the nations that do exist, but also the political hazards where nations are not present or are in the process of emerging. For nations are empirically quite rare, perhaps no more common than the city-republics Rousseau wrote about, though controlling larger territories. Their scarcity is much less obvious because of the myths that constitute nationhood and the mystification with which nations are surrounded. No one ever supposed that city-republics existed by nature, nor did the monarchies of Rousseau's time pretend to be republics. But states around the world today do make implausible claims to nationhood, and the purported naturalness of nations helps them to do this. Although no one now would defend the classic nationalist claim that humanity is primordially divided into nations, there is a widespread tendency for political theorists to assume that, as a result of the process of modernization, every state now contains a nation in the sense of a political community with enough collective identity for notions of democracy, social justice and the rule of law to have some purchase. Unfortunately (as the current instability of borders and proliferation of ethnic civil wars is making increasingly obvious), this is not the case.

Recent attempts at "nation-building" have on the whole been unsuccessful, in many cases merely provoking sub-nationalisms that mobilize people along ethnic lines. Where nations perhaps *can* be seen emerging, this is often at the cost of war, chauvinism and "ethnic cleansing", recalling the bloody histories through which the nations that are now firmly established became so. The fundamental dilemma has been stated with devastating frankness by John Hall:

> In a horrible sense, Third World countries have not had enough war, or, perhaps enough war of the right type. They are quasi-societies, not nation-states. Their states desperately need to be strengthened so that they can provide that basic order which we have come to take for granted.[40]

In other words, if we were to adopt the defence of nationhood as an explicit general principle, we would find ourselves committed to supporting something very different from the humane, flexible, mature nationalism defended by David Miller, which is simply not an option for most of mankind.

Conclusion

I have argued in this chapter that a retrospective glance at the tradition of republican political thought (and especially at Rousseau) can make us more vividly aware of the difficulty of reconciling our obligations to mankind in general with the claims upon us of free (but rare and fragile) political communities. The dilemma has (I suggested) been blurred for us to the extent that we have been able to take for granted national political communities that are experienced as being "natural", and therefore less exceptional and more resilient than the cherished artefacts of the republican tradition. While thinking in terms of universal principles, political theorists have been able to assume the existence of relatively stable and unified political communities and have thereby escaped the responsibility of having to weigh those principles against the demands of political solidarity.

I have, however, refused to draw what may appear to be the obvious conclusion from my argument, namely that we should drop this comfortable fudge in favour of Rousseauian or Scrutonian clarity about the costs of political community.[41] Instead, my recommendation is in a sense for fudge at a higher level, fudge *aufgehoben*. For the main theme of this chapter is that the topic of nationhood calls for a difficult balance to be struck between demythologizing clarity on the one hand, and on the other the myth of naturalness that cloaks and softens the hard outlines of the body politic. We need enough clarity about our own political community and its history to avoid being over-optimistic in our application of universal principles at home, and to approach political upheavals in other countries without unreasonable expectations for peace, democracy, justice and freedom. On the other hand, we need to be sufficiently vague to avoid seeking consistency in a strident Machiavellianism that can easily veer in the direction of fascism. There is a delicate balance to be struck between maintaining contact with the solid ground of reality and avoiding stirring up too much mud. No arena is more appropriate for the practice of the Burkean virtues of prudence and circumspection than the topic of the nation.

Notes

1. J.J. Rousseau, *Emile*, trans. B. Foxley (London: J.M. Dent, 1911), p. 7; "Considerations sur le Gouvernement de Pologne", in *Political Writings*, Vol. 2 (Oxford: Blackwell, 1962), ed. C.E. Vaughan, p. 437 (my translation).

2. J.J. Rousseau, *The Social Contract and Discourses*, trans. G.D.H. Cole (London: J.M. Dent, 1913), pp. 24–26, 240.

3. Rousseau, *Social Contract and Discourses*, pp. 32, 78–79, 87, 110, 243–251; *Emile*, pp. 7–8; *Political Writings II*, pp. 437–441. Cf. P.A. Rahe, *Republics Ancient and Modern: Classical Republicanism and the American Revolution* (Chapel Hill: University of North Carolina Press, 1992).

4. "As hungry men dream of food and frozen men of warmth, so the men of the Italian republics dreamed of concord." D. Waley, *The Italian City-Republics*, 2nd edn. (London: Longman, 1978), p. 126.

5. T. Hobbes, *Leviathan*, ed. M. Oakeshott (Oxford: Blackwell, 1960), pp. 107, 112, 114.

6. Rousseau, *Social Contract*, p. 32. Cf. P. Riley, "Rousseau's General Will: Freedom of a Particular Kind", *Political Studies*, Vol. 39, No. 1 (1991), pp. 55–74.

7. Contemporary "communitarians" rarely address such problems, but see A. Oldfield, *Citizenship and Community: Civic Republicanism and the Modern World* (London: Routledge, 1990), *passim*.

8. See the 1789 "Declaration of the Rights of Man and the Citizen", especially article 3, *Revolution from 1789 to 1906: Documents*, ed. R. Postgate (New York: Harper and Row, 1962), p. 30. On the complexities of revolutionary internationalism, see I. Hont, "The Permanent Crisis of a Divided Mankind: 'Contemporary Crisis of the

Nation State' in Historical Perspective", *Political Studies*, Vol. 42 (Special Issue 1994: "Contemporary Crisis of the Nation State", ed. J. Dunn), pp. 116–231.

9. Y. Tamir, *Liberal Nationalism* (Princeton: Princeton University Press, 1993), pp. 119–121. The view of nationhood expressed in this chapter is elaborated in M. Canovan, *Nationhood and Political Theory* (Cheltenham: Edward Elgar, 1996), in which some passages of the present text also appear.

10. J. Rawls, *Political Liberalism* (New York: Columbia University Press, 1993), pp. 11–12, 271. Cf. J. Rawls, "Justice as Fairness: Political not Metaphysical", in S. Avineri and A. de Shalit, eds, *Communitarianism and Individualism* (Oxford: Oxford University Press, 1992), p. 202.

11. M. Walzer, *Spheres of Justice: A Defence of Pluralism and Equality* (New York: Basic Books, 1983), p. 31.

12. For example, there is no reference to this topic in S. Mulhall and A. Swift, *Liberals and Communitarians* (Oxford: Blackwell, 1992), nor in C. Kukathas and P. Pettit, *Rawls: A Theory of Justice and its Critics* (Oxford: Polity, 1990), nor in N. Daniels, *Reading Rawls* (Oxford: Blackwell, 1975), though see B. Barry, *Theories of Justice* (London: Harvester Wheatsheaf, 1989), pp. 189, 236–241.

13. M. Walzer, "Notes on the New Tribalism", in C. Brown, ed., *Political Restructuring in Europe: Ethical Perspectives* (London: Routledge, 1994), p. 188.

14. C. Taylor, *Reconciling the Solitudes: Essays on Canadian Federalism and Nationalism*, ed. G. Laforest (Montreal and Kingston: McGill-Queen's University Press, 1993), p. 197.

15. F. C. Whelan, "Democratic Theory and the Boundary Problem", in *Liberal Democracy*, ed. J.R. Pennock and J.W. Chapman, *Nomos*, Vol. 25 (New York: New York University Press, 1983).

16. F.A. Hayek, *Law, Legislation and Liberty* (London: Routledge, 1973), Vol. 1, p. 28; Vol. 2, pp. 62–100.

17. Hobbes, *Leviathan*, p. 103.

18. O. Jaszi, *The Dissolution of the Habsburg Monarchy* (Chicago: University of Chicago Press, 1929), pp. 3, 31, 82, 449.

19. This point has recently been acknowledged by Hillel Steiner: "There can be little doubt that, as a matter of empirical fact, the historical advance of classical liberal or libertarian principles was accompanied and on balance aided by the development of the strong nation-state"; H. Steiner, "Libertarianism and the Transnational Migration of People", in B. Barry and R.E. Goodin, eds, *Free Movement: Ethical Issues in the Transnational Migration of People and of Money* (New York: Harvester-Wheatsheaf, 1992), p. 93. On the relationship between national identity and liberal civil society, see A.B. Seligman, *The Idea of Civil Society* (New York: Free Press, 1992), pp. 147–182.

20. Despite the widespread preoccupation with a different "communitarian" agenda, essentially concerned with matters of personal identity.

21. Arguing for minority rights, Will Kymlicka criticizes approaches that "subordinate considerations of fairness to considerations of *realpolitik*", so that "minority rights are still viewed essentially in terms of protecting domestic or international peace": W. Kymlicka, *Liberalism, Community, and Culture* (Oxford: Oxford

University Press, 1989), p. 215. The question how rights are likely to fare in the *absence* of strong institutions that can maintain peace is not asked.

22. E. Burke, *Reflections on the Revolution in France*, ed. C.C. O'Brien (Harmondsworth: Penguin, 1968), p. 120.

23. B. Anderson, *Imagined Communities: Reflections on the Origin and Spread of Nationalism* (London: Verso, 1983).

24. H. Seton-Watson, *Nations and States* (London: Methuen, 1977), p. 3.

25. E. Renan, "What is a Nation?" in *Modern Political Doctrines*, ed. A. Zimmern (London: Oxford University Press, 1939), p. 190; D. Miller, "In Defence of Nationality", *Journal of Applied Philosophy*, Vol. 10, No. 11 (1993), p. 9.

26. Liah Greenfeld argues controversially that nationhood was actually *invented* in England in the sixteenth century: L. Greenfeld, *Nationalism: Five Roads to Modernity*, (Cambridge, Mass: Harvard University Press, 1992), pp. 14, 27–87. Whether or not Greenfeld's argument can be accepted in its entirety, there are strong grounds for accepting that English nationhood was well-established by the sixteenth century; see e.g. the impressive evidence assembled in R. Helgerson, *Forms of Nationhood: The Elizabethan Writing of England* (Chicago: University of Chicago Press, 1992).

27. L. Colley, *Britons: Forging the Nation 1707–1837* (New Haven: Yale University Press, 1992).

28. Burke, *Reflections*, pp. 119–120.

29. Cf. A. MacIntyre, "Poetry as Political Philosophy: Notes on Burke and Yeats", in *On Modern Poetry: Essays presented to Donald Davie*, ed. V. Bell and L. Lerner (Nashville: Vanderbilt University Press, 1988), pp. 147–152.

30. C.C. O'Brien, *The Great Melody: A Thematic Biography of Edmund Burke* (London: Sinclair-Stevenson, 1992), pp. 13, 90–91.

31. Burke, *Reflections*, pp. 193–195; "An Appeal from the New to the Old Whigs", in *Works of the Right Honourable Edmund Burke* (London: Holdsworth and Hall, 1834), Vol. 2, pp. 524–525.

32. Rousseau, *Political Writings*, Vol. 2, p. 33.

33. Jonathan Rée has attacked nationhood for precisely this reason: "it conspires to make us give our consent to state power by disguising it as an expression of our own feelings": "Internationality", *Radical Philosophy*, Vol. 60 (Spring 1992), p. 10.

34. Rousseau, *Social Contract*, pp. 75–76. In his "Considerations on the Government of Poland" Rousseau did of course concern himself with politics on the scale of a nation rather than of his preferred city-state. But the tone of his advice about imprinting Polishness on the minds of young citizens by means of alarmingly totalitarian public education shows that he is far short of the later notion of a nation as a more or less spontaneous form of community.

35. For more extended reflections on this theme, see my essay, "Breathes There the Man, with Soul so Dead . . . ? Reflections on Patriotic Poetry and Liberal Principles", forthcoming in *Political Theory and Literature*, ed. A Baumeister and J. Horton (London: Routledge, 1996).

36. C. Taylor, "Cross-Purposes: The Liberal Communitarian Debate", in N.L. Rosenblum, ed., *Liberalism and the Moral Life* (Cambridge, Mass: Harvard University

Press, 1989), pp. 166–170. Cf. J. Habermas, "Citizenship and National Identity", *Praxis International*, Vol. 12, No. 1 (1992), p. 7. For a demonstration of the acute sensitivity about the German national heritage that has led Habermas and others to try to substitute *Verfassungspatriotismus* for national loyalty, see the documents from the *Historikerstreit* collected in *Forever in the Shadow of Hitler?* trans. J. Knowlton and T. Cates (Atlantic Highlands, NJ: Humanities Press, 1993).

37. This tactic goes back a long way. Here is Thomas Tickell's early eighteenth-century universalist British Patriotism:

> Her Guiltless glory just Britannia draws
> From pure religion and impartial laws
> . . . .
> Her labours are to plead the' Almighty's cause
> Her pride to teach the' untamed Barbarian laws.
> Who conquers, wins by brutal strength the prize,
> But 'tis a godlike work to civilize.

"On the Prospect of Peace", *Poems of Thomas Tickell*, p. 132, *The British Poets* Vol. 27 (College House, C. Whittingham, 1822). Later in the same century the French Revolutionaries became notorious for a form of universalist patriotism that led them to see conquest of their neighbours as "liberation": see C.C. O'Brien, "Nationalism and the French Revolution", in *The Permanent Revolution: The French Revolution and its Legacy 1789–1989*, ed. G. Best (London: Fontana, 1988), pp. 38-43. For a recent and less bellicose assertion of the "teaching mission" of the United States, see J.H. Schaar, "The Case for Patriotism", in Schaar, *Legitimacy in the Modern State* (New Brunswick, NJ: Transaction Books, 1981), pp. 285–311. Like other universalist patriots, Schaar insists that his kind of "covenanted patriotism" is quite different from "nationalism, patriotism's bloody brother".

38. R. Scruton, "In Defence of the Nation", in Scruton, *The Philosopher on Dover Beach* (Manchester: Carcanet, 1990), p. 310.

39. For some bracing remarks on this subject, see B. Barry, "The Quest for Consistency: A Sceptical View", in B. Barry and R.E. Goodin, eds, *Free Movement: Ethical Issues in the Transnational Migration of People and of Money* (New York: Harvester-Wheatsheaf, 1992).

40. J.A. Hall, "Nationalisms: Classified and Explained", in *Daedalus*, Vol. 122, No. 3 (Summer 1993), p. 21.

41. For similar reasons, I am dubious of the likely benefits of the public debate on British national identity called for by David Miller in *On Nationality* (Oxford: Clarendon Press, 1995). For some earlier reflections on letting sleeping collective identities lie, see Canovan, "On Being Economical with the Truth: Some Liberal Reflections", *Political Studies*, Vol. 38 (1990), pp. 5–19.

6

Reconstructing the Landscape
of Imagination

Yael Tamir

HENNA: . . . *This is how it looked until, say 1810—smooth, undulating, serpentine—open water, clumps of trees, classical boat-house—*

BERNARD: *Lovely. The real England.*

HENNA: *You can stop being silly now, Bernard. English landscape was invented by gardeners imitating foreign painters who were evoking classical authors. The whole thing was brought home in the luggage from the grand tour.*

—Tom Stoppard[1]

The recent proliferation of writings on nationalism has unfortunately left the definition of the term *nation* as obscure as it has ever been. Hence we must admit that a statement made by Seton-Watson in 1977 still accurately describes the stage at which the current discussants find themselves. Many attempts have been made to define *nation*, Seton-Watson argued, "and none have been successful".[2] And yet we cannot surrender our attempts to find a more adequate definition of the term *nation,* as without one we would be unable to understand the nature of nationalism and the essence of national rights and obligations. The following discussion will analyse some of the criticisms offered by other contributors to this volume of my definition of *nation*[3] and will examine the implications of that definition for our understanding of the functional role played by nations in general and by national myth in particular. This role, I would argue, is of such importance that national beliefs and myths should be defended and preserved even if they foster a particular kind of false belief.

What Is a Nation?

The crux of my definition of the term *nation* is a refutation of the identification of nation and state. Phrased in this way, it may seem to be a commonplace; but it is not. The term *nation* is often used in English as synonymous with the terms *state* or *country*, meaning a society united under one government. Thus, the term *national* is employed for designating "anything run or controlled by the state, such as the national debt or national health insurance".[4] This sense of the term is more than just a feature of common speech, as such official expressions as "the Laws of Nations" or "the League of Nations" show.

One might then be led to the conclusion that *state* and *nation* are identical concepts, or at least two aspects of the same concept. And yet when one refers to definitions of the concept *state* the picture one gets is very different: the concept *nation*, if mentioned at all, is referred to in relation to the nation-state, as one among a variety of possible forms of state. The contrast between the definitions of the two concepts might result from the fact that, while not all states are nations, all nations are, or must be, institutionally organized as states. Consequently, despite the fact that the term *state* can be defined independently of the term *nation*, the term *nation* cannot be defined independently of the term *state*. This, however, is not the case: whereas the factual claim that all nations are states is plainly false, the validity of the statement that nations must have states depends on the way the term *must* is used. The statement might be read as an expression of instrumental necessity; we should then ask what kind of purposes nations have that only states can fulfil. Or the statement could be read as a normative statement, indicating that nations ought to have states; we would then have to ask what kinds of attributes turn nations into entities that are entitled to have states. I do not intend to embark on either of these lines of inquiry, but it is evident that they are meaningful only if states and nations are separate entities.

If nations are not states, what kind of entities are they? A nation, I have argued,[5] is a community whose members share feelings of *fraternity*, substantial *distinctiveness* and *exclusivity*, as well as a belief that they have *common ancestors* and that their community exhibits a *continuous genealogy*. Let me clarify these terms. The first aspect of nationhood is that individuals see themselves as affiliated with, and committed to, other members. But fraternity, unlike friendship, love or political camaraderie, is not based on intimate relations, on personal likings or on a community of particular values. It is grounded in a view of the nation as a community of common descent and fate. Members of such a community see themselves sharing a common destiny and view their individual success and well-being as closely dependent on the prosperity of the group as a whole. They think of their self-esteem and their accomplishments as related to the achievements of other group members, and take pride in the group's distinctive contributions. Consequently, they develop feelings of care and duty towards one another. These feelings are exclusive and apply to members only, as no nation "imagines itself continuous with mankind".[6]

Yet feelings of fraternity may also be shared by women, homosexuals, vegetarians, Freemasons, members of a university, the kibbutz movement or members of a local community, none of which is commonly considered to be a nation. On closer scrutiny, however, it is clear that these groups lack one or more of the other four elements included in the definition. Women and homosexuals are not nations because their persistent historical presence is not, nor can it be, a continuity of kinship, whereas national continuity embodies a strong sense of genealogy. Vegetarians and the kibbutz movement are not nations because both of these groups uphold an ideology they consider appropriate to the whole of humanity; their exclusivity is therefore contingent, whereas national exclusivity is intrinsic to the nation, as the particular features of a group do not apply, nor are they supposed to apply, to non-members. Nationalists do not believe that their culture, language, or tradition is relevant to the whole of humanity; in fact, they view the restricted scope of these elements as a reason for pride rather than concern. Freemasons and universities are not nations because their exclusivity is elitist and a function of individual attainments, whereas national exclusivity and fraternity are populistic and based on membership rather than achievement. Neither do these groups see themselves as sharing common ancestors.

A state may also fall within the boundaries of my definition of nation. Yet, although this definition may provide an adequate description of some states, it remains incomplete as, intentionally, it makes no reference to the institutional sphere, nor to concepts such as sovereignty and territory, which lie at the heart of any definition of the state. Moreover, states that do seem to fit my definition are invariably nation-states, and it is the national rather than the state elements in this compound that accord with the definition.

The definition given above emphasizes the importance of the subjective element in the definition of the term *nation*. Nations, then, are social entities that are not the product of the mere fact that a group shares a particular set of objective factors, such as language, geography, race or religion; they are a creation of human will and imagination. According to Seton-Watson, a nation exists when "a significant number of people in a community consider themselves to form a nation, or behave as if they formed one".[7] Hence it could be argued that, if a group of human beings share a national consciousness, then it is a nation. The reasons leading individuals to share national consciousness, feelings of fraternity and exclusivity, and a belief in a common ancestry are inherent not in the definition of the term *nation*, but in the explanation of how nations emerge. When the reasons that account for the rise of a nation are mistaken for its characteristic features, the result is an inadequate and confused definition.

How, then, do nations emerge? When does national consciousness arise within a certain group? Why do people share feelings of belonging with certain individuals and not with others? In cases of friendship or love, the relevant others may be chosen on the basis of a broad set of personal characteristics, but in cases of national fraternity, the process of demarcation is far more complicated. The boundaries of national consciousness are not defined by personal attributes, and personal likings are not a criterion of membership. How, then, do individuals define the boundaries of the nation to which they belong? How do they construct its image?

This is the hardest question of all. A nation, argues Smith (mixing again the definition of the term *nation* with the reasons for its emergence), is a "named human population sharing an historic territory, common myths and historical memories, a mass public culture, a common economy and common legal rights and duties for all members".[8] Although sharing these features may enhance communal feelings and encourage the belief that those who share them are, in some way, distinct from those who do not, these attributes, *per se*, cannot define a nation. Individuals often share a historical territory as well as past memories but do not see themselves as members of the same nation, as is usually true for nations competing for the same piece of land. The Israeli–Palestinian conflict clearly shows that a shared territory and common historical memories can be divisive rather than unifying. In many other cases, living together in the same territory and under the same government, or even sharing economic and legal systems, fails to blend different communities into one nation, as is attested by the political reality in Canada, Belgium, the former Yugoslavia and the former Czechoslovakia. For every case in which one of these features did lead to the emergence of a nation, we could point to another where the same features were present but no nation emerged. Clearly, then, our understanding of the term *nation* cannot be contingent on the mere existence of these features.

As no set of objective features—common history, collective destiny, language, culture, religion, territory, climate, race, ethnicity—could be defined as necessary and sufficient for a nation to emerge, it is often suggested that, a "sufficient number" of these characteristics is necessary. In cases in which *no* shared features exist, national consciousness is unlikely to surface. This is why David George's dichotomy between subjective and objective aspects of nationhood is misleading. There is, then, no point in trying to contrast two seemingly incompatible options:

> Either beliefs of members constitute a nation with a valid claim to statehood, in which case the shared, objective characteristics of nationality will be unnecessary or non-constitutive features, or, alternatively, those very same empirical features do constitute the nation with a right to self-government, in which case any appeal to a national consciousness is necessarily superfluous.[9]

The emergence of national consciousness is not impervious to the existence of certain shared objective features that are necessary to support its formation.

Note that according to this definition the concept *nation* is not in itself a cluster concept: the notion of a cluster applies only to the reasons leading to the formation of national consciousness. Hence the objections George raises against it are misplaced. In fact, they would misplaced even if one were to argue that the term *nation* is best understood as a cluster concept. If the term *nation* is defined as a cluster concept, George argues, members of a nation

> do not necessarily share all the characteristics which count as a sufficient number to define the nation, indeed, logically, there need not be a single objective national characteristic which all members have in common. Members of the nation acquire their membership simply because they exhibit a family resemblance to its other members, that is, they share some of the defining national characteristics with some of its other members. Yet family resemblances are not sharply demarcated and some members will have similar relations to individuals outside the nation. In which case the national boundaries—the members of the nation and the territory they inhabit—could always have been delineated in some other way or ways. [10]

There are two problems with this argument. First, the notion of a cluster concept suggests only that the groups that fall under the term *nation* share a family resemblance, and yet it could still be the case that *all* of the members of each particular nation would share the same characteristic features. George thus confuses claims concerning the definition of the term *nation* with claims concerning the indeterminate nature of the boundaries of particular nations. Second, the ambiguous nature of the set of criteria that defines membership supports the importance of the subjective element for the definition of *nation*, which he sets out to challenge. This will be clear if we look at the following example. Members of the Palestinian nation share a religion, language, culture and territory. Not all of them share all four characteristics: some are Christian, others live in the diaspora and as a result do not share the language, the culture or the territory. Obviously it could be the case that a Christian Palestinian who lives in Jerusalem shares no characteristics with a Muslim member of the Palestinian diaspora but shares a territory, and maybe a language, with a neighbouring Jew. Why are the first two members of the same nation while the latter two are members of different nations?

The answer to this question refers us back to the inevitable importance of national consciousness. A nation, like lovers or friends, is the kind of group whose existence cannot be inferred from the mere existence of certain shared objective features but must refer to the members' shared consciousness and feelings of communion.[11] Other groups—for example, those composed of individuals who share a gender, income, place of birth or citizenship—could be defined irrespective of their members' consciousness or feelings. Hence, an external observer would not be able to divide the world accurately into nations, nor could the observer explain, without referring to the agents' feelings, why Ethiopian, Russian and Israeli Jews belong to the same nation, whereas Palestinian, Jordanian and Egyptian Muslims belong to different ones; but given the appropriate records, the observer could divide the population of the world by age-groups or by citizenship.[12]

But what is it that members of a nation believe they share? John Charvet answers: "it would seem that they believe that they posses certain objective features in common and by virtue of that fact they constitute a nation". This, he argues,

> *must* be a false belief, because we have already seen that it does not follow from the common possession of these features by a collection of persons that they are a nation. The proposal would seem to be that, just insofar as a collection of people falsely believe that possessing certain common features makes them a nation, then they are a nation. Such a proposal is manifestly absurd.[13]

But Charvet ignores the fact that, as far as human relations are concerned, the existence of certain objective attributes could generate subjective feelings and perceptions, and these could generate certain patterns of behaviour and relationships. The process is much more complex; the fact that individuals share certain attributes, or believe they do, may influence their mutual relations; they may care more for each other, develop mutual responsibilities, and support each other in pursuing what they see as their common ends. They may then develop a whole network of mutual dependencies, expectations and obligations that are derived not from the mere fact that they share some objective features, but from their awareness of this fact and the importance they attribute to it. Hence, despite the fact that one cannot claim that a certain nation exists just because its members share certain objective features (or have the illusion that they share some), it is still plausible to claim that the fact that they share these features played a constitutive role in the formation of the nation.

This description is very similar to the one Charvet provides for the emergence of specific contractarian communities. All of these communities share a commitment to a common set of values, and, on the basis of this set of values, they later develop distinctive political cultures and foster civic friendship among their members. And yet it would not be misleading to answer the question "what holds this group together?" by making reference to the fact that its member share a certain set of values. This answer will be accurate even if other groups share the very same values.

A nation, then, is a community whose members share certain feelings and commitments that are grounded in the belief that they share certain features. The most important among these features are common ancestors, continuous genealogy and an exclusive culture. This is the essence of nationhood. Even nations whose main moulding power is ideological adopt a genealogical and exclusivist language and symbols. This is well expressed by Burke: "it has been the uniform policy of our constitution to claim and assert our liberties, as an *entailed inheritance* derived to us from our forefathers, and to be transmitted to our posterity."[14]

The definitions of *nation* offered here and elsewhere leave Margaret Canovan unsatisfied. The term *nation* defies definition, she argues, and this is not accidental, as nationhood is a mediating phenomenon whose strength lies in its ability to hold together various contradictory points of view. A nation, Canovan argues,

> cannot exist without subjective identification, and therefore is to some extent dependent on free individual choice, but that choice is nevertheless experienced as a destiny transcending individuality; it turns political institutions into a kind of extended family inheritance, although the kinship ties in question are highly metaphorical; it is a contingent historical product that feels like part of the order of nature; it links individual and community, past and present; it gives to cold, impersonal structures an aura of warm, intimate togetherness.[15]

Canovan points to an aspect of nationhood that has been given far less attention than it deserves. Her claim that nations serve a mediating role is extremely important, but to capture its full significance we must distinguish between our understanding of the term *nation* and the functional role played by nations. In what follows I will argue that the definition of *nation* provided so far can best explain the mediating role played by nations.

The Historical Nature of National Myths

How can nations play the mediating role Canovan attributes to them? Canovan points in the right direction when she draws attention to the notion of myth. Why is the mythological aspect of nationalism so important? In answering this question we must refer to the social function of myth. The function of mythological and ritual instruction, Campbell argues, "is to transform the person who lives for animal ends into one who lives for cultural and spiritual ends".[16] But myth has also a social function. Myth "expresses, enhances, and codifies belief; it safeguards and enforces morality; it vouches for the efficiency of ritual and contains practical rules for the guidance of man. Myth thus is a vital ingredient of human civilisation; it is not an idle tale, but a hard-worked active force."[17]

Keeping the individual and social functions of myth in mind, we may now return to our discussion of nationalism and consider what makes national myths suited to serve these functions. As Canovan indicates, the power of nationalism is grounded in the ability of national myths to allow individuals to enjoy two inconsistent worlds: that of personal autonomy and that of historical determinism. They allow individuals to carve themselves a place in the chain of being, to adopt for themselves a glorious past, a caring community and a hopeful future.

Other mythologies may have been able to play a similar role, and yet national myths are distinctive in the sense that they can fulfil these functions by telling a story that fits well the needs and the forms of thinking of modern rational individuals. For primitive hunting people,

> the sabertooth tiger, the mammoth, and the lesser presence of the animal kingdom were the primary source of danger, and of sustenance—the great human problem was to become linked psychologically to the task of sharing wilderness with these beings. An unconscious identification took place, and this was finally rendered conscious in the half human, half animal figures of the mythological totem-ancestors.[18]

In the latter stage religious myth occupied the centre of the mythical scene as it could place "the object of man's desires outside and beyond worldly goods and naturally lift the soul into regions far above the realm of the senses".[19]

And yet the modern world has witnessed the erosion of the pervasive power of religion and with it of religious myth. The beginning of this process coincided with what Levi-Strauss defines as the breaking point between scientific and mythical thought. This separation, Campbell argues, created a new world in which "there was no hiding place for the Gods from the searching of the telescope and the microscope".[20] In the modern world myth had to portray itself as based on scientific evidence.

Pressure was therefore created to misinterpret religious symbols as signs.[21] But this was a double-edged sword. Once religious mythology came to be perceived as pseudo-history, it was open to a new kind of criticism. "When people realise that it couldn't have taken place, they lose their faith and their religion, and then they are without the vocabulary of the communication with the transcendent and the rationality of a living human being."[22] This was the perfect moment for national mythology—which is grounded in historical myth, which "could be proven" or at least could be believed—to offer an attractive alternative language and to capture centre stage. Historical myth could fulfil the central functions of mythology, namely, to "ensure that the future will remain faithful to the present and the past",[23] and yet could be supported by scientific evidence. Hence it is not surprising to find that the emergence of nationalism coincides with the flourishing of archaeological research as well as with the extensive development of cultural institutions like museums, archives, census and maps.[24]

If this description is an adequate one, then nations should be seen not as historical communities but as communities whose members share a pseudo-history, or a set of practical myths constructed to serve practical concerns, undertakings or engagements. George contrasts such communities with what he calls "purely historical communities". The identity of the latter type of community lies in an historical, not a practical, past.

> This means its correlative present is not the practical present of transactions, reassurances, moral and other lessons, the satisfaction of wants and so on, which the practical past serves in various ways. It is, . . . a chosen present made up of survivals from the past which constitute the primary evidence from which the historical past of events is constructed, or rather, inferred.[25]

Historical identities, George argues, are composed of historical events exclusively: "nothing but such events connects together other historical events. The contingent connection between them, as antecedent and consequent, is that of continuity or contiguity."[26] Yet the distinction between purely historical communities, which grow out of historical events in a process that involves no practical intervention and fabricated communities, which are based on historical myths formulated in light of present purposes, is a very problematic one.

When we are engaged in historical research, Levi-Strauss wonders, "do we really do something scientific, or do we too remain astride our own mythology in what we are trying to make as pure history?"[27] McNeill goes even further when he claims that the historians' assaults on myth "are themselves based on myth: the faith that facts speak for themselves, that infinite detail somehow organizes itself into a meaningful patterns without the intervention of human intelligence, and that historical truth resides in faithful transcription of recorded words and deed ".[28] This kind of scepticism might be going too far, as there is at least one clear distinction between history and mythology that has to do with the motivations of the agents involved: whereas historians study the past in order to understand it, those who are involved in the creation of myths use the past in order to influence future events. This distinction does not imply that even the most well-meaning historians could detach themselves from their own values and beliefs, as the fierce debate between the "new historians" and the more traditional school of historians in Israel demonstrates. In this debate each side accuses the other of letting its ideology influence its scientific findings: the former group accuses the latter of harnessing its research to the purposes of the Zionist state; the latter accuses the former of serving anti-Zionist forces. Be that as it may, it seems safe to assume that both schools produce a history that, in one way or another, reflects their own normative tendencies.

What is true of professional historians is certainly true of the way history is used in the political sphere. National communities are thus a product of complex interaction between historical events and the interpretation of these events, which serves present purposes. No national community could thus be a purely historical one in George's terms.

This is especially true as nations are able to serve some of the functions Canovan attributes to them only if they are seen as having a long, and preferably glorious, past. If the nation is to be seen as part of the order of nature, if the national community is to be perceived as an extended family whose members share a common ancestry as well as a common future, and if national membership is to be experienced as a destiny transcending individuality, then nations must have a past. Hence, those nations that cannot fall back on a long and rich heritage seek to imitate those that can do so by "inventing", or rather "rediscovering", and "annexing history and cultures for their communities, in order to provide that cultural base without which no nationalism can attain widespread legitimation".[29] And yet it is important to remember that the fabrication of national history through myth is not peculiar to new nations: old nations also invent traditions, reinterpret their culture, reconstrue their history, forget differentiating features and embrace common characteristics in order to create the illusion of a "natural" unit that has a long and mostly glorious history and a promising future. Consequently, all national movements tend to cling to even the faintest evidence of historical continuity and to adopt strictly false beliefs in order to prove their antiquity and assert that the emergence of their nation was a matter of historical necessity—or, better still, that their nation was chosen by divine forces to fulfil a sacred mission. Hence there are more nations that claim that their people are a God-chosen people and that their land is holy than there are Gods.

True Lies

"A man", Kundera writes, "knows that he is mortal, but he takes it for granted that his nation possesses a kind of eternal life."[30] In these words he captures the message that national myths convey: nations are immortal; they transcend contingency, thus shifting finite human experience from the sphere of the mundane and contingent to the realm of the eternal. This notion of continuity is of particular importance in a secular era, in which identification with the nation is "the surest way to surmount the finality of death and ensure a measure of personal immortality".[31] National myth thus meets the need for continuity, for an assurance that in the midst of an ever-changing world some aspects of one's social life are stable.

The argument so far portrays a rather bleak picture: nationalism seems to be able to serve its social functions only at the price of spreading illusions, misrepresentations and falsehoods, concerning the very aspect on which its operative powers lie. This accounts for the tension between the antiquity and continuity of nations in the eyes of nationalists and their evident modernity and instability in the eyes of social scientists. National fictions are almost deliberately not seen, as life itself depends on a conspiracy not only to sustain the fictions themselves but also "to keep going the universal disposition to live by fictions, to enact them. The struggles between systems of fiction can be unremitting, but all systems are united by a common interest in fixing the world's loyalty to fictions and in keeping it fixed by struggle and sacrifice."[32] These tendencies, so forcefully described and objected to by Kateb, are demonstrated by the intentional disregard of nationalists for the truth-value of their claims. Nationalists have long understood, Smith argues, that the criterion for national dignity "is the felt antiquity of a community's ethno-history, *irrespective of its truth-content*". This is the bar at which they must make their appeal for national assertion. "The truth-content of unearthed memories is less important culturally and politically than their abundance, variety and drama (their aesthetic qualities), or their example of loyalty, nobility and self-sacrifice (their moral qualities) that inspire emulation and bind the present generation to the 'glorious dead'."[33]

Deliberate forgetfulness and misrepresentation of historical facts thus seem to constitute an important, and perhaps indispensable, feature of nation-building. And yet, despite the abundant evidence attesting that national identity is often based on false beliefs, few philosophical discussions touch on the implications of these findings. Miller is one of the few exceptions: whether a nation exists, he argues, depends on "whether its members have the right beliefs; it is not part of the definition that the beliefs should in fact be true".[34] For individuals to be able to cultivate national feelings, Miller argues, it is important that the story the nation tells itself about its past be generally believed, but it need not be historically accurate.

The will to believe, Kateb argues, is the worst of all the vices required to encourage group identity. "It is the most regrettable because it is a gross form of self-deception (a most murky vice) and, hence, a severe blow to one's integrity. The process of drowning out one's inner reproaches and accepting one's own lies . . . makes one an instrument of mendacity, and hence an instrument of immorality."[35] This statement seems to be far too inclusive: just as there may be cases in which self-deception is not a vice, there may also be cases in which it is justifiable to deceive others. If people consider a particular set of feelings a precondition for living a meaningful and satisfying life, and if they fear that inquiring into the nature of the beliefs that evoked these feelings might disrupt them, they have a reason, Heil argues, to hold the beliefs that support their feelings even though they have no other justification for doing so. We thus have no moral commitment to ground our feelings in true beliefs only. Moreover, there might even be practical grounds for taking intentional steps toward acquiring functional beliefs even if they are false.[36]

In this respect Heil follows Elster, who argues that, if a belief is valuable to a person in the light of his or her underlying goals, it would be rational for that person to set up mechanisms to ensure the acquisition and preservation of this belief from eventual rational scrutiny.[37] It could then be argued that, if national affiliations are crucially important to a person, there is nothing irrational in fostering them, as well as the false beliefs on which they depend.[38]

But having a reason to hold a false belief and being able to hold one are two separate issues. According to Williams, the most straightforward way of expressing one's belief in p is asserting that p. "To say 'I believe that p' itself carries, in general, the claim that p is true."[39] Hence, when agents claim that they hold certain beliefs, they seem to be claiming that these beliefs are true. How, then, can the claim that the development of national feelings depends on the agents' ability to believe their national history to be true be reconciled with the patent falsity of many of these beliefs?

It could be claimed that, although nationalism fosters false beliefs, it does so in a way that convinces innocent agents that these beliefs are true. This can explain the tendency of nationalists to invest a considerable amount of time and effort to "prove" their claims: they write history books, build monuments, celebrate memorial days, conduct archaeological excavations, establish museums and institute national education. They thus teach their fellow nationals to accept an official narrative entailing a manipulated and distorted version of the national history, with certain events consciously eliminated and others emphasized or invented. This version is presented as true, and individuals are encouraged to foster the image of their nation in its light.

Communist countries have often provided a lively example of such manipulations. Think, for example, of the role played by Stalin's *History of the Communist Party of the Soviet Union: A Short Course.* The historical conclusions of this manifesto are simple, Kolakowski claims: "The Bolshevik party, under the brilliant leadership of Lenin and Stalin, unswervingly pursued from the outset the faultless policy which was crowned by the success of the October Revolution. . . . Stalin was from the beginning an infallible leader, Lenin's best pupil, his truest helper and closest friend." Those who read the short course probably read it as a valid description of historical events and did not suspect that they were being manipulated.

Kundera illustrates the way a national myth was created in another Communist country—what used to be Czechoslovakia. In February 1948 the Czech Communist leader Klement Gottwald gave his famous address from the balcony of the palace in Prague. Alongside Gottwald stood his faithful comrade Clementis. "There were snow flurries, it was cold, and Gottwald was bareheaded. The Solicitous Clementis took off his own fur cap and set it on Gottwald's head."[40] Four years later Clementis was charged with treason and hanged. The propaganda section immediately airbrushed him out of history, and obviously out of all photographs as well. "Ever since, Gottwald has stood on that balcony alone. Where Clementis once stood, there is only bare palace wall. All that remains of Clementis is the cap on Gottwald's head."[41] In all such cases there are manipulators and manipulated individuals: the first do not believe in the story, and the latter do not doubt it (or do not dare to doubt it).

But there are other cases in which the distinction between the manipulator and the manipulated is much less clear. These cases raise questions bearing on the rationality of the "believing agents" themselves. These agents seem to know that their "national history" is false but decide to act as if it were true, consciously disregarding evidence to the contrary. The essence of the mythological point of view, Campbell claims, "is, 'It is as if' ".[42] This kind of behaviour, Freud claims, is both functional and rational. For example, "Even if we knew, and could prove, that religion was not in the possession of the truth, we ought to conceal that fact and behave in ways prescribed by the philosophy of As if—and this in the interest of the preservation of us all."[43]

But what does it mean to act "as if" your beliefs were true? One interpretation could be that you know that the belief conveyed by the myth has a directive purpose, and as this purpose fits your other projects or ends you are ready to accept it—in such cases myths are no more than a source of illustrative support for the set of beliefs and narrative you already hold to be sound. They are believed to be true

> not because the historical evidence is compelling, but because they make sense of men's present experience. They tell a story of how it came about. And events are selected for inclusion in a myth, partly because they coincide with what men think *ought* to have happened, and partly because they are consistent with the drama as a whole.[44]

Another possibility is that you accept the mythical story because it comes from a source that is, for you, an authority. As individuals may take different sources to be authoritative, they may recognize that there could be a variety of possible truths, "literal or not: sensory or everyday truth; truth as grasped religiously or philosophically. Perhaps still another kind of truth may be added: truth in the sense of balance, experience of wisdom."[45] Mythical stories could thus be followed out of respect for one of these sources: one's parents, one's national culture or tradition. This option is persuasively expressed by the words of Nathan, the hero of Lessing's 1779 play *Nathan the Wise*: "History must be accepted wholly upon faith . . . [and surely we rest this faith on those] who from childhood have given us proofs of love. . . . How can I trust my fathers less than you trust yours?"[46]

But the beliefs we inherit from our forefathers may not always be functional. We may grow to suspect the authority of our forefathers in some spheres but not in others. What are we to do when we come to suspect some aspects of our tradition while cherishing others? An interesting example that exposes the way individuals function when they are torn between information given to them by different authoritative sources comes from Ethiopia. Ethiopians believe that the leopard is a Christian animal and respects the fasts of the Coptic church. Nevertheless, they are no less careful to protect their livestock on Wednesdays and Fridays, which are fast days, than on other days of the week. "Leopards are dangerous every day; this [the Ethiopians] know by experience. They [the leopards] are Christians; tradition proves it."[47] Similarly, although the founding fathers of Zionism believed in the nationalist ethos of "a land without a people for a people without a land", they nevertheless armed themselves in order to counter the resistance of the land's Palestinian inhabitants. These examples seem to indicate that individuals know which authority applies to what issues. They may thus believe in a myth—because they accept the authority of the religious or national source who conveys the myth—and disbelieve it on the ground of their own experience or the experience of others whose authority they accept. Their actions in different spheres are thus directed by different beliefs regarding the same mythical story.

This obviously raises questions concerning the ways in which individuals compartmentalize their beliefs. How do individuals decide, in each particular context, which of their conflicting beliefs to act upon? How do they reconcile the internal conflicts resulting from contradictory beliefs? If it is indeed rational to act at times in accordance with false beliefs, might not this behaviour influence other fields of action and prevent the efficient achievement of other ends? If such "overflow" endangers rational behaviour, can individuals learn to direct their actions while relying on contradictory epistemic principles? Does this approach involve a measure of self-deception?

I do not attempt to answer these questions here but only very briefly summarize the argument. National attachment fulfils basic human needs; it does so by endowing individual life with meaning and fostering an illusion of fraternity so desperately needed in an age characterized by rapid social change, extensive geographical mobility and alienation. But it can do so only at the price of fostering false beliefs. This would be a terrible price to pay if it implied that individuals would lose altogether their ability to discern true beliefs from false ones and would thus be exiled for ever from the sphere of rational behaviour. And yet there could be another option, which is rather hard to define. It is based on the ability to adopt two parallel lines of reasons for action that are grounded in two kinds of epistemic proof: the first is grounded in national myth; the second, in scientific evidence.[48]

This suggests that individuals analyse the structure of their beliefs and know what kind of evidence they need in order to support the different beliefs they hold. This ability is beautifully summarized in Yehuda Amichai's poem *Like Sand Grains*:

When God in the Bible wants to promise
He points to the stars.

Abraham comes out of his tent at night
and sees lovers.
"Like sand grains on the shore," says God.
And man believes. Even though he knows
that saying: "like sand grains on the shore"
is no more than a metaphor.

Notes

1. *Arcadia* (London: Faber, 1993), p. 25.

2. H. Seton-Watson, *Nations and States* (London: Methuen, 1977), p. 3.

3. Especially as presented in my book *Liberal Nationalism* (Princeton: Princeton University Press, 1993) and in a recent paper "The Enigma of Nationalism", *World Politics*, Vol. 47, No. 3 (1995), pp. 418–440.

4. E. Hertz, *Nationality in History and Politics* (London: Routledge & Kegan Paul, 1944), p. 3.

5. I offer this definition and discuss it in greater detail in "The Enigma of Nationalism", pp. 424–427.

6. B. Anderson, *Imagined Communities*, 2nd. edn., (London: Verso, 1991), p. 7.

7. H. Seton-Watson, *Nations and States* (London: Methuen, 1977), p. 7.

8. A. Smith, *National Identity* (Las Vegas: University of Nevada Press, 1991), p. 14.

9. D. George, "National Identity and National Self-Determination", chapter 2 in this volume, p. 19.

10. Ibid., p. 16.

11. A group of friends can be identified only by referring to the feelings of the individuals involved. Some types of behaviour might indicate that some individuals are friends, but these individuals may be only pretending to be friends without bearing any affectionate feelings for one another. The opposite is also possible: individuals who feel friendly towards one another may agree to disguise their friendship. Hence, an external observer cannot be sure that X and Y are friends without referring to their feelings.

12. In the latter case there may be some overlap between the groups as some individuals may be citizens of more than one state.

13. J. Charvet, "What Is Nationality, and Is There a Right to National Self-Determination?" chapter 4 in this volume, p. 58.

14. Quoted in Canovan, "The Skeleton in the Cupboard", chapter 5 in this volume, p. 60.

15. Ibid.

16. J. Campbell, *The Way of Myth: Talking with J. Campbell* (Acton, CA: Shambhala Press, 1994), p. 38.

17. B. Malinowski, *Magic, Science and Religion* (Garden City, NY: Doubleday Anchor, 1954), p. 101.

18. J. Campbell, *The Hero with a Thousand Faces* (Princeton: Princeton University Press, 1968), p. 390.

19. That, Tocqueville argues, is true even of the most false and dangerous religions: A. Tocqueville, *Democracy in America* (New York: Harper & Row, 1966), p. 444.

20. Campbell, *The Hero with a Thousand Faces*, p. 387.

21. A *sign* according to Campbell is a reference to something that is known or knowable in a perfectly rational way. A *symbol* on the other hand does not refer to something that is known or knowable in a rational way; it refers to a spiritual power that is operative in life and is known only through its effects, (Campbell, *The Way of Myth*, pp. 31–32.)

22. Ibid., pp. 33-34.

23. C. Levi-Strauss. *Myth and Meaning; Cracking the Code of Culture* (New York: Schocken Books, 1979), p. 43.

24. See Anderson's extremely interesting discussion of these topics, in chapter 10 of the 2nd edn. of *Imagined Communities*.

25. George, "National Identity and National Self-Determination", p. 25.

26. Ibid.

27. Levi-Strauss, *Myth and Meaning*, p. 41.

28. In L. Thompson, *The Political Mythology of Apartheid* (New Haven: Yale University Press, 1985), pp. 21–22.

29. Smith, *National Identity*, pp. xxiv, xxx.

30. M. Kundera, *The Book of Laughter and Forgetting* (Harmondsworth: Penguin Books, 1980), p. 229.

31. Smith *National Identity*, p. 160.

32. G. Kateb, "Notes on Pluralism", *Social Research*, Vol. 61, No. 2 (1994), p. 19.

33. Smith, *National Identity*, p. 164.

34. D. Miller, "The Ethical Significance of Nationality", *Ethics*, Vol. 98 (1988), p. 648.

35. Kateb, "Notes on Pluralism", p. 19.

36. See Heil's discussion in J. Heil, "Doxastic Incontinence", *Mind*, Vol. 93, No. 1 (1984), pp. 56–70, and "Believing What One Ought", *Journal of Philosophy*, Vol. 80, No. 11 (1983), pp. 752–765.

37. See Elster's discussion in both *Ulysses and the Sirens* (Cambridge: Cambridge University Press, 1979) and *Sour Grapes* (Cambridge: Cambridge University Press, 1985).

38. This claim raises an interesting difficulty. Suppose I am the kind of person who desperately needs approval. It would then be rational for me to interpret other people's behaviour as indicating approval. Yet, would not awareness of this personality trait in myself cast doubts on this interpretation? I may be inclined to suspect that I have forced myself to interpret their behaviour in this way, because of my desperate need for approval. Ironically, I may then be less likely to believe that I have genuinely earned their appreciation. Similarly, knowing myself to be the kind of person for whom national feelings are immensely important must raise qualms about the nature of these feelings, and the beliefs on which they depend.

39. B. Williams, "Deciding to Believe", *Problems of the Self* (Cambridge: Cambridge University Press, 1973), p. 137.

40. Kundera, *The Book of Laughter and Forgetting*, p. 3.

41. Ibid.

42. Campbell, *The Way of Myth*, p. 180.

43. S. Freud, *The Future of an Illusion* (Garden City, NY: Doubleday Anchor, 1964), p. 57. Note that Freud refutes this view later on in his essay, but not because one cannot adopt the "as if" philosophy of action but because he thinks that civilization runs a greater risk if we maintain our present attitude to religion than if we give it up. So he questions not the plausibility of "as if" philosophy but whether religious beliefs would justify such behaviour.

44. In L. Thompson, *The Political Mythology of Apartheid*, p. 20.

45. S. Biderman and B. Scharfstein, eds, *Myth and Fictions* (Leiden, Brill 1993), p. 13.

46. In S. Fleischacker, *The Ethics of Culture* (Ithaca, NY: Cornell University Press, 1994), p. 117. An illuminating discussion of the issue of authority can be found in this excellent book.

47. P. Veyne, *Did the Greeks Believe in their Myths?* (Chicago: Chicago University Press, 1983), p. xi.

48. This could be one of the dialectical aspects of mythological thinking Levi-Strauss did not examine.

7

National Obligations: Political, Cultural or Societal?

Paul Gilbert

Loyalty is a sentiment, not a law. It rests on love, not on restraint.
—Roger Casement[1]

Introduction

These words from Roger Casement's speech from the dock provide my text. What is it to have obligations of loyalty as a member of a nation? What are such obligations grounded in? Casement, of course, was hanged for treason against the *British* crown, after conspiring to form a brigade of Irish prisoners of war in support of the 1916 Rising. It was to the British crown that he was deemed in law to owe allegiance. His point is that law cannot exact allegiance, and, in particular, cannot exact the kind of allegiance one owes as a member of a nation. He claims an obligation of loyalty to Ireland that cannot be captured by, and overrides, any political obligation he may be deemed to have to the existing—to a British—state. Yet this claim is contestable. Might not Casement's *national* obligations have simply consisted in political ones incurred as a member of that state? Certainly those who called him a traitor thought so.

In what follows I shall investigate whether a satisfactory account of national obligations can be given in terms of political ones, or, if not, what we can make of the notion that they depend upon sentiment. I shall be intolerably vague about what national obligations might in fact consist in,[2] though throughout the sort of obligations I shall have in mind are ones whose fulfilment is somehow expressive of loyalty. I shall simply assume that there are *obligations* in this area. If someone were to take Casement as denying even that, I shall have nothing to say here to confute them.

Civic Voluntarism and Obligations

It should at least be allowed that Casement is right to deny that the mere *presence* of a law requiring acts of allegiance or forbidding treachery can create political obligations. Given this, then the obvious move to make if one claims that national obligations are reducible to political ones is to hold that only the law of a *legitimate* political authority can create obligations. To say that the obligations created are political ones is to say that they are obligations to the state or other polity. These will include legal obligations, i.e. obligations to obey the law, which might be justified on other grounds, for example the utility of lawfulness. Political obligations go beyond these, however, precisely in requiring loyalty to the state, loyalty that is not expected of casual visitors to it,[3] who are none the less expected to behave lawfully, as are those who live in occupied territory. But loyalty can be demanded only by a state whose control of a territory is legitimate.

Casement's lack of loyalty to the British state can be excused, perhaps, on the grounds that British rule in Ireland at the time lacked legitimacy. The commonest way to argue for this sort of position would be to claim that Britain lacked the consent of the Irish people over whom it sought to exercise authority. It seems a small step to the conclusion that an appropriate[4] group of people who do consent to a certain state constitutes the *nation* over which that state exercises authority, so that the state is legitimate precisely when it corresponds to such a nation. In this case national obligations will just be political obligations to that state. It seems only a slightly larger step to the corollary that an appropriate group of people who would consent to an as yet non-existent state in their territory also constitutes a nation. Their national obligations comprise what would be political obligations were that state to exist. Just as then they would have a political obligation to support it, so now they have an obligation not to support the illegitimate state that exercises control in place of it, and perhaps to further the creation of a legitimate successor.

This picture, which I shall term the *civic voluntarist* conception of the nation and national obligation, is a species of those approaches that are civic in that they give a political account of nationhood and seek to represent national obligations as intelligible in terms of political ones. The voluntarist conception does this by utilizing two leading principles of liberal political thought. First, the principle of voluntary association allows everyone a right to enter whatever associations they choose.[5] A state that seeks to impose an unwanted association infringes this right and thereby lacks legitimacy. Second, the principle of voluntary obligation holds that people fall under obligations only when they choose to incur them.[6] A state that seeks to impose, through law, obligations that people have not chosen to incur through consenting to the state is not one to which they have a political obligation.

Both these liberal principles are, of course, open to objection. Arguably, the circumstances we find ourselves in may determine the associations we can permissibly enter. The obligations that these circumstances bind us to may be ones we do not choose to incur. These issues cannot be settled here. But their application to national groups and national obligations presents a more tractable problem. For those who do consent to a certain polity and acknowledge its obligations are very commonly reproached with mistaking their nationality and misplacing their sense of national obligation. The official position of Irish nationalists on Ulster Unionists is an obvious example. The point is that such a position is not evidently indefensible. And, though commonly at odds with the two liberal principles, it is not necessarily so. It may simply deny their applicability in determining the membership of nations, by contrast with the membership of states, and in deriving national obligations from political ones.

Civic voluntarism takes an oversimplified view of nationality and national obligation, making it hard to see how people could plausibly go wrong about them.[7] But "education" to correct such errors is the stock in trade of nationalist politics. How does it typically proceed? In the case of the Ulster Unionists, by alleging, for example, that their relations with the British are in fact relations of subordination and exploitation, while their relations with other Irish people are of an essential community of interest, not a conflict. I am not concerned with the facts here, only with the form of argument employed, which seeks to establish the real relations on which an acknowledgement of national identity and an informed political consent should rest. This is not to say that those who exercise their political consent otherwise than as their nationality would indicate are necessarily in error about it. They may consent to political arrangements that do not reflect their nationality for reasons of immediate or sectional interest. But civic voluntarism cannot at all easily account for this: it is blind to the reasons for political choice, and observant only of relationships as they are consciously and intentionally entered into by their participants.[8]

Civic Republicanism and Obligations

Both these points can be accommodated by a second approach to viewing national obligations in terms of political ones. It is an approach adopted by a strain of *civic republicanism*,[9] which sees political obligations as arising ordinarily[10] from a reciprocal exchange of duties between members of the polity in accordance with their civic roles. A legitimate state is a republic in which the performance of civic duties is actuated by concern for, and conduces to, the common good—the good of citizens as fellow members of the state.[11] On this approach, a nation[12] is formed by properly motivated performance of civic duties: it fails to emerge where this is not forthcoming and where private interest and exploitation replace it. National obligations are here coterminous with political ones for members of a legitimate state. Where the state does not function as a republic, the civic obligations people have are just the political obligations they would have had to a legitimate state, namely to work together for the common good and thereby to create a republic and a nation.[13]

Civic republicanism provides, I think, a much more promising account of national obligation than does voluntarism. It may, furthermore, provide an account that calls into question Casement's stark contrast between love and law as grounds for loyalty. For while acts of loyalty are part of my civic duty and my opportunities to avoid them are subject to restraint, still they are expressions of civic *friendship*.[14] The exchange of duties for the common good is just the kind of thing that characterizes friendship generally; the exchange of civic duties is simply the civic form of it.[15] The love of one's country that civic duty expresses just *is* love of one's fellow citizens.[16] It is an attractive but yet a problematic and unstable picture. The duties of citizenship arise, it must be remembered, within a state, whose function it is to enforce the laws that offer citizens the conditions for a good life, in particular the protection of their persons, lives and liberties.[17] The state has a determinate (though not immutable[18]) function, and the civic roles of citizens are correspondingly restricted. Political obligations arise from the obligations that attach to these roles. Civic friendship is thus limited in its possible expression to acts that are performed within these roles.

Membership of a nation, by contrast with citizenship, is not the holding of a role, since nations, unlike states, do not have determinate functions.[19] National obligations attaching to membership cannot, therefore, arise from the occupancy of such a role, and any national sentiment their performance evinces cannot be restricted by such occupancy. The problem here is one that surfaces in civic republicanism in a systematic uncertainty as to whether the friendship that binds citizens together really is, as I have characterized it, *civic*, or whether it is a wider ranging bond antecedent to and necessary to motivate citizenship,[20] or at least to motivate a form of citizenship that has the general welfare of fellow citizens at heart.[21] If it is the latter, however, the project of giving an account of nationality and national obligation in civic terms must be abandoned, and an alternative account of national sentiment must be found.

Yet if it is only the former, then doubts must arise as to the justice of regarding the relationship as truly *friendship*; for friendship would seem precisely to require a disposition to go *beyond* the strict requirements of duty. Conscientious and considerate reciprocation for a common goal may certainly express a kind of fraternity, but it could as well be a "fraternity of fear"[22] as a fraternity of affection. It might, perhaps, be replied in pessimistic mood that the patriotic virtues do betray just such an instability. Maybe there is no one source of motivation for national loyalty, and its open-ended character reflects this fact. Moved now by friendship, now by fear, the group imposes new duties, scents fresh betrayals. This, it may be said, is republicanism in action; but it can scarcely provide the kind of rational *grounding* for national obligation that republicanism seeks.

I tentatively conclude that an attempt to account for national obligations in terms of political ones will not work. What other alternatives are there?

Cultural Voluntarism and Obligations

It is now commonplace[23] to contrast civic accounts of nationality, which tie it to membership of actual or potential states, or similar polities, with ethnic accounts, which link it to pre-political, and usually cultural, group membership. On such accounts national obligations will turn out to be a species of cultural ones. What *these* might be is as slippery a question as what culture is. Rather than seeking to answer it directly, I shall proceed, in parallel to my earlier discussion, by distinguishing two kinds of *cultural* conception of nationhood and national obligation.

With liberal nationalism[24] now the subject of discussion, it should come as less of a surprise to start with *cultural voluntarism*. Here the two liberal principles mentioned earlier are at work again, but in a different way. This time a culture, rather than a polity, is regarded as the nexus of national association, and the obligations freely entered into are the ones required to sustain that culture.[25] On this kind of account a nation is a certain kind of cultural group characterized by the self-awareness and commitment of its members: national obligations proceed from their sense of membership[26] just because this implies their assumption of a voluntary commitment. This is the case whether their membership in fact originates in birth or in explicit allegiance.

Despite the last proviso, the picture of cultural attachment at work here is a curious one. To what extent *can* I choose my culture? Might not national obligations be imputed contrary to my choice, creating the same problems here as arise for civic voluntarism? And in any case, are *cultural* choices necessarily to the point in determining *national* loyalty or betrayal?

With respect to the first question, Yeats wrote as follows:

No people hate as we do in whom the past is always alive. . . . Then I remind myself that. . . . all my family names are English; that I owe my soul to Shakespeare, to Blake, perhaps to William Morris, and to the English language in which I think, speak and write; that everything I love has come to me through English. My hate tortures me with love, my love with hate.[27]

Yeats, the principal architect of the Irish Literary Revival, cannot *choose* to disown his English culture, however much he hates the English suppression of Irish identity. The cultural choices he can make do, indeed, reflect the obligation he felt to Ireland, an obligation that was for him, as Anglo-Irish, one of two apparent options. Yet his cultural choices do not *constitute* that obligation. Thus, those who make other choices can be reminded what their commitment *ought* to be. Their cultural choices, like their political ones, can, it may surely be argued, reveal an error as to where their national loyalties ought to lie.

We may have cultural obligations that are freely undertaken, but are they necessarily even a *part of*, let alone constitutive of, national obligations? The kind of cultural manifestation that is solemnly *willed* as that required of a patriot can easily seem comic:

> Old Scotia's jocund *Highland Reel*
> Might make an hermit play the deel!
> So full of jig!
> Famed for its *Cotillons* gay France is;
> But e'en give me the *dance of dances*
> An Irish jig.

> The slow *Pas Grave*, the brisk *Coupée*
> The Rigadoon, the light Chasée
> Devoid of gig,
> I little prize; or Saraband
> Of Spain; or German Allemande:
> Give me a jig.

So runs this nineteenth-century Irish ditty, until it reaches the ringing injunction:

> Why let us *laugh* and *dance* for ever,
> And still support with best endeavour
> The IRISH JIG.[28]

Is supporting the Irish jig even necessarily patriotic, let alone a national obligation? Is telling bedtime stories from one's own culture,[29] rather than from the "diversity of stories. . . . that could constitute the beginning of a truly multicultural heritage"?[30] Or is the latter, far from really being *multi*-cultural, just doing something characteristic of contemporary eclectic *American* culture, and thereby fulfilling an American national obligation? This, I suggest, would be a desperate response. There may well be a patriotic American intention in following the latter course, but it has nothing to do with fulfilling cultural obligations.

Cultural Contextualism and Obligations

I have already gone somewhat beyond a criticism of cultural *voluntarism*. But I now wish to turn to another culturalist account of national obligation, which I shall term, for reasons that will become immediately apparent, *cultural contextualism*. On this view a culture is not something I can *choose*, precisely because it constitutes "a context of choice"[31]—the "language and history [which] are the media through which we come to an awareness of the options available to us".[32] Nations are taken to be individuated by cultures so understood,[33] and a national obligation must be an obligation to sustain a culture as the necessary precondition for meaningful choice and self-respect. To lose one's own culture leads, instead, to anomie and alienation.

But why should the obligation to sustain a culture rest especially upon its members?[34] After all, cultural membership is a good which everyone has the same moral obligation to ensure as they do the other means necessary for leading a good life to which people have a right.[35] For the notion of a member's *national* obligations under a conception such as cultural contextualism, we need, I think, the idea of an obligation to *cherish* one's own culture. This is not an attitude we can normally have to another's culture; and to cherish is surely very near to love. To cherish one's culture is to see it as having a value to oneself and one's fellow members that may be inaccessible to others; it has nothing to do with a judgement of comparative merit.[36] Just so does one find a value in one's lover that others may not, and which does not reflect the outcome of a beauty contest.

The obligation to cherish one's culture springs from one's standing in an analogous relationship to it. One would not be true to it unless one undertook the obligation:[37] one's recognition of its value would be unresponsive —superficial or not fully sincere. While such a recognition comes, characteristically, through upbringing, there is no principled reason why it should not be acquired through other forms of acculturation. However acquired, it sets a value on the culture that demands transmission to others who can cherish it:[38] its prospective loss occasions the acutest pain. So, while those outside the culture have a general obligation to preserve it as the context of choice for its current participants, those participants have a special obligation to see that it survives.[39]

I find the kind of cultural contextualization developed here a tempting theory. My difficulty with it is in seeing how it can generate, as any cultural account surely must,[40] obligations to fellow members of the nation. If nationalism "conceives the natural object of human loyalty to be a fairly large anonymous unit defined by shared language and culture",[41] then the question is *why* sharing a language or culture should generate loyalty to fellow members of the unit so defined. Or to put essentially the same point in a different way, why should people who share a language constitute a *community*,[42] if a community involves reciprocal obligations between members? For though no doubt a language or a culture in fact require more than isolated individuals to survive, still it would seem that a language and a culture can figure in the lives of isolated individuals without any communal exchange involving them. It is one thing to value a culture, thought of in terms of language and history, quite another to value the social relationships they shape.[43] But it is the social relationships of a community that must surely be valued if I am to recognize obligations to my fellow participants in them.

It is not enough to suggest that a love of one's language, and of one's culture generally, can be understood only as an attachment to it as a fitting vehicle of one's social relationships.[44] It is true that I feel at home in my language for just such a reason, and the beauty that it has for me is inseparable from the joy of the relationships it mediates. But this move would be a perilous one for any culturalist. For it attempts to ground obligations to fellow members not ultimately in *culture*, but in the value of a community's social relationships. While we may admit that these relationships cannot be characterized apart from the culture that mediates them, there are still questions to be raised about the significance and value of the relationships which do not arise about the culture. A culture that makes possible good relationships also makes possible bad ones: a common context of choice can lead to bad choices as well as good ones.

Analogous considerations apply if it is argued that our national obligations derive from our history, which is an aspect of our culture: "because our forbears have toiled and spilt their blood to build and defend the nation, we who are born into it inherit an obligation to continue their work, which we discharge partly towards our contemporaries and partly towards our descendants".[45] Supposing the nation our forebears built to be culturally characterized, how does our obligation to them to maintain it derive from our cultural membership? For suppose, by contrast, that the nation was characterized in *civic* terms: could not the same sort of argument as to our obligations be mounted? I believe it could, and what this seems to show is that our obligations as to our culture derive from our social relationships rather than the reverse: the obligations that constitute those relationships cannot be derived from cultural membership. Indeed, history plays no essential role in generating them, since the relationships that I owe to my forebears for what they have done for me and for my posterity are no different in kind from the obligations I owe to my contemporaries for what they now do for me.

At this point there is, I think, a tendency for culturalists to fall back on the idea that we simply *do* have obligations to fellow nationals, culturally characterized,[46] which we cannot feel to others, or cannot feel nearly as well. We respond to fellow nationals because of their cultural characteristics, and this response is necessary to successful relationships of cultural obligation with them which do in fact sustain our culture. Perhaps there is some truth in this, although the extent of it seems to be very debatable. However, the fact that I responded sexually only to tall dark partners would do nothing to show that I *should* have a certain sort of relationship with them. Analogously, the fact that I disliked all except my fellow Englishmen could scarcely show why I should be a member of a "community of obligation"[47] with them alone. The only way to show that would be to demonstrate why such a community was, *ceteris paribus*, a good thing, and thus really did generate obligations. But then, these obligations derive from *further* features of the community which a common culture can promote, perhaps even its *civic* potential.[48] Even if a common culture provides the best, or only, form of national community, then, though I have national obligations in virtue of my culture, their *force* does not derive from this but from the benefits of the community.

I conclude that culturalism fares no better than the civic approach in giving an account of national obligation. Where else, though, can we turn? For the civic and culturalist approaches are characteristically presented as exhaustive alternatives for an account of nationhood, and our discussion does not suggest any way of combining them to overcome their separate defects.[49] Before proceeding, I want to take a step back and reflect upon this dichotomy.

Civic and Cultural Nationalisms

How does the dichotomy between civic and cultural nationalisms arise? Why should anyone ever have thought that such widely divergent accounts of the same notion could plausibly be offered? This is not a question requiring an historical answer which relates an account of what nations are to an explanation of their origins:[50] it is a question about the significance of such an account. What is the *point* of advancing a particular conception of nationality? To what purposes can it be put? The answer is, very evidently, a *political* point. In particular, claims to nationhood are made to support claims to the legitimacy of a certain state, or claims that the existing state structure is in need of replacement by one that better reflects alleged national identities; or, if statehood is not necessarily in question, at least the demarcation of some analogous polity is. National obligations of loyalty are commonly imputed in support of such political claims.

The uncertainty as to whether to discern *one* nation in the United Kingdom or several illustrates this point. After the Act of Union the new British state needed to foster a sense of national loyalty, which could be promoted only along civic lines.[51] John Wilkes was a scoundrel who took refuge from what he saw as the overweening power of that state in a fiercely *English* patriotism:[52] "my ruling passion", he wrote from prison, "will be the love of England". His patriotism was, in a broad sense, culturally based, stressing a history of English liberties (by contrasts with Scottish servility) and "plain English" (by contrast with "Scotticisms"). But it had the political point of insisting on a polity that respected English common law and custom in opposition to the encroachments of a British sovereign power. Such English national sentiments are, relatively recently perhaps, extinct. They have been superseded by nationalist movements in Scotland and Wales which have much clearer cultural bases just as they have clearer autonomist aims. Opposition to these aims is liable to be expressed in an assertion of civic Britishness.[53]

The *point* of classifying people into nations is a specific political one, and one that becomes possible only with the emergence of the modern state. The *methods* of classifying them are correspondingly modern, or, as one might say, modernist, and they relate to modern thought concerning the legitimacy of states. The civic approach insists on the necessity of political organization for effective social life and emphasizes either the voluntariness of civic association, or formal equality and fraternity within a republic. The culturalist approach attends to the boundaries of cultures supposedly demarcated by modern historical scholarship or scientific methods of ethnography. Thus, what may seem like a purely anthropological classification of nations is to be seen in the context of political programmes[54] and of sociological thought about the functionality of social and political institutions. The scientific study of cultures, like the pseudoscientific study of race, provides material for persuading people of where their *real*, and practical, loyalties should lie.

Each approach carries its own political dangers. The civic approach officially overlooks merely cultural differences between territorially concentrated groups, just as it does those of widely diffused groups like Jews or gypsies. But it is in danger of failing to recognize the claims of what we may think of as genuinely national minorities, like the Kurds in Turkey, Iran and Iraq. By conflating national obligations to political ones, it risks seeking to impose by law loyalties that cannot be felt in national *sentiment*. In contrast, culturalism recognizes two possible foci of loyalty—culture and state. But these are potentially in conflict, so that culturalism risks either attempting to eliminate or assimilate cultural minorities on the one hand,[55] or fomenting self-destructive fissiparity on the other.

We are often inclined to react to the situations that thus arise with a sense that *both* the civic and culturalist approaches have got things wrong, and to deplore the damage to societies that results. I say "societies" advisedly, for the sense we have is of national societies unrecognized by the two approaches or factitiously constructed by them. And this is not surprising, for each approach claims to give an account of what a national society *must* be like through the application of contrasting assumptions as to how its unifying social relations could be constituted—by civic or by cultural obligations of loyalty. But both sets of assumptions are, as I have sketchily indicated, the products of very general modernist patterns of thought. As such they are clearly contestable, though this paper obviously lacks adequate scope to contest them.

We can, however, explore an avenue that might lead to an alternative approach by pursuing the thought that classifications of nationhood have a political point, in particular in the legitimation of actual or proposed states. If a nation has, *ceteris paribus*, a claim to its own state or other polity, then, since that state will be able to impose political obligations, the nation has a claim to bind its members together through such political obligations. But what could ground this claim? Surely only that its members are already bound by national obligations, so that the political ones flow from and reinforce the national. We should ask, then, what kind of obligation could properly play this role, as a matter not merely of contingent fact but of logic. To answer this question would be to say what a national society, correctly understood, is like. The civic approach cannot do so, since it does not recognize any obligations as distinct from and underpinning political ones. Culturalism cannot either, since it offers at best an empirical account of how a common culture is necessary to political organization and is protected by it.

In the next section I shall conclude with a few tentative remarks as to how to tackle the question by returning to Casement's observations on loyalty as depending upon love.

Love and Loyalty

In Elizabeth Bowen's *The Last September*, set in the Irish War of Independence, an Anglo-Irish family, the Naylors, entertain English officers with whom they have both cultural affinities and a common civic allegiance. Yet when an officer captures the rebel son of one of their tenants, their reaction reveals unexpectedly different loyalties.

> "Oh, I say, Uncle Richard, Lesworth has captured Peter Connor."
> "I'm sorry to hear that", said Sir Richard, flushing severely. "His mother is dying. However, I suppose you must do your duty, We must remember to send up now and inquire for Mrs. Michael Connor. We'll send some grapes. The poor woman. . . . it seems too bad." He went off sighing into the library.
> Gerald was horrified. His duty, so bright and abstract, had come suddenly under the shadowy claw of the personal. "I had no idea", he exclaimed to Lawrence, "these people were friends of yours."[56]

"Friends" is, of course, as Gerald understands it, the wrong word for them. The English officer, Gerald, misunderstands the loyalty of the Naylors as indicative of a conflict between the claims of country and friends, public and private obligation, in which friends might be the winners.[57] Yet this is not the point: "the shadowy claw of the personal" extends, in this Irish setting, across a whole range of relationships that Gerald had only seen in clear-cut civic and cultural terms. But neither captures them: here the personal *is* the political.

How might we develop this kind of conception of the relationships eliciting national obligation? The image it evokes is a distinctly Burkean one: "to love the little platoon we belong to in society is the first link in the series by which we proceed towards a love to our country."[58] National society is demarcated by the limits to which this sort of small-scale relationship can be readily extended, by the limits to which others can be thought of as related to me in the same sort of way as the members of the little platoon. Two ideas are at work in such an account: one is of the possible scope of such a sentiment; the other, of national society as constituted by an interactive system of "little platoons". A coincidence is claimed between the scope of the sentiment and that system. Two questions arise. What is the relevant notion of *belonging* to the little platoon from which national loyalty arises? How is it extended and limited to the nation?

One kind of answer to the first question must be immediately rejected, though it may have been Burke's and is certainly that of many of his Conservative followers. Surprisingly perhaps, it surfaces in Bertrand Russell:

> Love of home and love of family both have an instinctive basis, and together they form the foundation of love of country considered as a sentiment. . . . A nation, unlike a class, has a definition which is not economic. It is, we may say, a geographical group possessed of a sentiment of solidarity. Psychologically it is analogous to a school of porpoises, a flock of crows or a herd of cattle.[59]

There may or may not be a "natural" attachment to our immediate circle, in the required sense of an attachment springing from our biological natures, rather than simply something occurring in the usual course of events. Whatever is the case, such a fact would do nothing to generate obligations, and, if obligations are necessary to love, would not constitute *love* of home and family, properly so called. For that, a value must be set upon them, such that it is, *certeris paribus*, better for people to love home and family than to hate them, better to be related in ways that allow others in the group to depend on them than to mistreat them, and so forth. It is, I suggest, in these elementary *ethical* facts that obligations within the small group are grounded, and membership of the group simply consists in being bound by them. But because of the value we set upon love of those around us, all that we need to do to *justify* our special obligations to them is to indicate that they are those we do love in this way, in circumstances where it is quite proper to do so.

How, to turn to the second question, does such a relationship get extended and yet limited? It cannot be, as Russell goes on to suggest, because of a feature that others share with my immediate circle, such as language, descent or culture.[60] That would no more justify adopting a similar attitude to them than the fact that another shared my lover's looks would justify a similar love towards them. But the fact that I *depended* upon them in the same sort of way, and vice versa, might surely do so. This is, indeed, the point of the dramatic redefinition of my "neighbour" accomplished in the parable of the Good Samaritan. The point is to get us to acknowledge the salient *facts* about our interdependencies, and thus to overcome the limitations of political and cultural prejudice—tasks that, in a less ambitious way than Christianity, the nationalist is also attempting to achieve.[61]

But why should such sentiments be *limited* at all, as in Christian and other universalistic ethical theories they should not? The interdependencies evoking social sentiments are those involved in sharing a common life; and the nationalist's assumption is that there are, for all practical purposes, boundaries beyond which others are living a different life, depending principally on others, not upon us, and vice versa. It need not be a different *kind* of life, but the customs that regulate their life, however similar to ours, derive their force from the fact that they are *their* customs, not ours; just as their goods and services have a relative value in their coinage, not ours. Indeed, a national currency is a better model for what distinguishes a nation, on this model, than a national language, since the national currency has a use in mediating many of the exchanges that together constitute national society, and is useless beyond it. Indeed, the dependencies involved in national society must be, in the broadest sense, economic; so Russell is wrong to rule out an economic definition of the nation.

This may seem unconscionably vague. Certainly I should like to be able to spell out more clearly the *formal* features of the interdependencies presumed in the notion of a national society. But that is, I suggest, as far as we should want to go in clarifying their character. For the *substance* of the interdependencies, the specific exchanges and mutual assurances that constitute national society, these are determined by the society itself—just as they are, we may notice, in any love relationship.[62] This is the grain of truth in the oft-repeated dictum that nations are self-defining.[63] The terms of that definition would, of course, be cultural. But extensionally equivalent interdependencies can be captured in different conceptual systems: the relationship of lovers does not *necessarily* change when they become politically correct "partners", rather than husband and wife. Membership of a national society demands a grasp of the required dependencies, but no particular cultural representation of them.

On this societal model political obligations do flow from and reinforce national ones, since the state exists, essentially, to regulate and safeguard a society. The obligations I owe to other members of that society include those that, where it is deemed appropriate, are enforced as political obligations.[64] When love is insufficient to motivate performance, the law takes over. But it cannot in general impose obligations where national sentiments are insufficient to motivate them, any more than it can create worthwhile relationships of interdependence,[65] rather than simply recognize and formalize them.

The model is, of course, a highly idealized one. Are there, one may ask, any actual national societies of the sort it postulates? Far fewer, perhaps, than states or separatist movements may suppose. And if this is so, then fewer people

will fall under genuinely national obligations than we thought. Within allegedly national states, areas of socio-economic interdependence are fragmented,
replaced by exploitation or neglect; and, internationally, the limits of societal
obligations seem increasingly hard to draw, with the demise of economic
autarkies and the globalization of economic relationships. The nation, as
understood on the societal model, may well be on its way out.

The model is idealized, but is it also an objectionably *ideal* one—a model
of how a nation *ought* to be, formulated against a specifically Western cultural
background which reflects, it may be said, the moral nostalgia possible only
within a particular Western history? There are two replies to this. One is to
concede the point but deny its force, by insisting that nationhood is, in any case,
a specifically Western notion. The other, and more heroic, would be to argue
that the notions of loyalty and love that the model displays are necessary to any
system that can be thought of as ethical, and bear the same relation to the law
in any that can be thought of as political. In this chapter I shall be happy to settle for the first.[66]

Notes

1. Quoted in (Frank) Lord Pakenham, *Born to Believe* (London: Cape, 1953),
p. 72.

2. Though there is a large measure of vagueness here anyway, dependent for its
resolution on the circumstances and aspirations of particular nations.

3. *Resident* aliens, by contrast, may be expected to demonstrate loyalty *outside* the
country. See M. Walzer, "Political Alienation and Military Service", in J.R. Pennock
and J.W. Chapman, eds, *Political and Legal Obligation* (New York: Atherton Press,
1970), pp. 401–420; G.P. Fletcher, *Loyalty* (New York: Oxford University Press,
1993), chapter 3.

4. "Appropriate" is intended to cover such requirements for statehood as territorial
compactness, etc.

5. See e.g. H. Beran, *The Consent Theory of Political Obligation* (Beckenham:
Croom Helm, 1987), pp. 34–42.

6. Or at least obligations to obey authority: see Beran, *Consent Theory,* pp. 50–53.

7. Except, implausibly, by being wrong about what others *do* consent to, which is
generally transparent.

8. The *big* problem with voluntarism is to know how to determine who "the people" are who decide on their national identity by a majority. Here I overlook this by
unrealistically assuming that their consent is unanimous and compactly distributed over
a single territory.

9. The account presented is an idealized one, owing several of its features to
Rousseau.

10. Non-members may have some obligation to the state as resident aliens, and
some others are viewed as having obligations under English law in return for the pro-

tection the crown affords them. In Britain this feudal notion of allegiance to the crown is the basis for national loyalty; I shall not discuss it further.

11. This is intended as a partial gloss upon "each of us contributes to the group his person and the powers which he wields as a person under the supreme direction of the general will" (Rousseau's *Social Contract,* bk. 1, ch. V1).

12. Civic republicanism is sometimes viewed as hostile to nationalism, which is seen as subversive of *citizenship.* Cf. C. Navari, "Civic Republicanism and Self-Determination", in M. Wright, ed., *Moral Dimensions of International Issues* (Aldershot: Avebury, forthcoming). But in the French Revolutionary tradition influenced by Rousseau, nationalism is central to it.

13. I suspect that the notion of an obligation existing in these circumstances springs from the idea that a *right* to a legitimate state exists, but I cannot pursue this line of thought here.

14. Interestingly discussed in A. Oldfield, *Citizenship and Community: Civic Republicanism and the Modern World* (London: Routledge, 1990), esp. pp. 20–24.

15. "Homonoia" or concord, as Aristotle calls it (*Ethics* 1167 a-b).

16. Rather than a love for the land, with which Rousseau contrasts it (cited by Oldfield, *Citizenship and Community*, p. 53).

17. *Social Contract*, bk. 1, ch. V1.

18. Since citizens themselves determine the function of their state.

19. This casts some doubt on D. Miller's notion of national identity as *active*: "In Defence of Nationality", in P. Gilbert and P. Gregory, eds, *Nations, Cultures and Markets* (Aldershot: Avebury, 1994), pp. 19–20.

20. See Oldfield's claim that concord is required "before they become citizens", in *Citizenship and Community*, p. 9.

21. Which is the (non-civic) position emphasized by Miller, "In Defence of Nationality", p. 22.

22. As Sartre calls it, *Critique of Dialectical Reason* (London: Verso, 1976), pp. 428–444.

23. See e.g. A.D. Smith, *National Identity* (Harmondsworth: Penguin, 1991), pp. 8–15.

24. In the sense of Y. Tamir, *Liberal Nationalism* (Princeton: Princeton University Press, 1993).

25. Ibid, pp. 87–90.

26. Ibid, p. 135.

27. Quoted in R.F. Foster, *Paddy and Mr Punch* (London: Allen Lane, 1993), pp. 304–305.

28. Sydney Owenson (1776–1859), "The Irish Jig", in A.A. Kelly, ed., *Pillars of the House* (Dublin: Wolfhound, 1988), pp. 35–36.

29. As Tamir implies, in *Liberal Nationalism*, p. 90.

30. S. Wolf, "Comment", in C. Taylor, *Multiculturalism and "The Politics of Recognition"* (Princeton: Princeton University Press, 1992), p. 82.

31. W. Kymlicka, *Liberalism, Community and Culture* (Oxford: Clarendon Press, 1989), p. 166. Tamir seems to fail to appreciate the force of this account in her criticisms of Kymlicka: *Liberal Nationalism*, p. 38.

32. Kymlicka, *Liberalism, Community and Culture*, p. 65. Note that on Kymlicka's account (which could be contested) *values* are excluded from the context as subject to revision and thus forming part of a culture's current "character".

33. Implied by Kymlicka, *Liberalism, Community and Culture*, p. 135; though see p. 179, n. 2.

34. Perhaps this question could be answered by holding that a division of labour is needed to sustain cultures. This does not seem to me to capture the *heartfelt* character of the cultural loyalties that people have.

35. As Kymlicka argues: *Liberalism, Community and Culture*, p. 177.

36. A point Taylor fails to appreciate in his discussion of the "presumption of equal worth" owed to all cultures. He holds this to imply that all cultures "have something important to say to all human beings", but that "it can't make sense to demand as a matter of right that we come up with a final concluding judgement that their value is great, or equal to others", *Multiculturalism*, pp. 66–69.

37. This is not to deny that one's culture could *lack* the value one supposed, and one would have no corresponding obligation. But as a member of the culture it will seem to me that I have it.

38. A culture may, for instance, be evangelistic or hermetic, depending upon its conception of who *can* cherish it, rather than vulgarize and devalue it.

39. This is, I think, an answer to the criticism Tamir makes of Kymlicka (*Liberal Nationalism*, pp. 40–41, n. 16), to the effect that his liberal account of the protection of minority cultures cannot capture the goal of cultural *survival* that their members have.

40. Thus, Taylor instances the well-being of fellow nationals as something that one has a national obligation to ensure: *Multiculturalism*, p. 88.

41. E. Gellner, quoted A.D. Smith, *The Ethnic Revival* (Cambridge: Cambridge University Press, 1981), p. 47.

42. As Tamir, Kymlicka and others *assume* they do.

43. See P. Gilbert "The Ethics of Secession", in Wright, *Moral Dimensions*.

44. I discuss this in "The Idea of a National Literature", in A. Baumeister and J. Horton, eds, *Political Theory and Literature* (London: Routledge, forthcoming).

45. Miller, "In Defence of Nationality", p. 19. For discussion see M. Freeman, "Nation, State and Cosmopolis", *Journal of Applied Philosophy*, Vol. 11 (1993), p. 84, who observes that we cannot inherit an obligation from forebears who committed genocide. (In citing Miller I do not mean to impute to him the brand of culturalism I am here considering.)

46. Note Gellner's description of nationalism as holding the culturally characterized nation to be the *natural* object of loyalty (cited in n. 41 above).

47. Miller's phrase: "In Defence of Nationality", p. 19.

48. As Rousseau seems to have thought. See F.M. Barnard, "Will and Political Rationality in Rousseau", in J. Lively and A. Reeve, eds, *Modern Political Theory from Hobbes to Marx* (London: Routledge, 1989), pp. 141–144. Barnard has an interesting discussion of Rousseau's comparison between patriotism and sexual love, touched on above.

49. Maybe we could regard a nation as a cultural group requiring a political organization, such that its national obligations derived from political ones, but these had to depend on cultural affinities. Such an account (perhaps similar to Miller's) might overcome the difficulties noted above, though it would be open to others, not least in explaining why such a group would be a worthwhile society and thereby generate obligations.

50. Contrast A.D. Smith, *National Identity*, p. 85.

51. See L. Colley, *Britons: Forging the Nation 1707–1837* (London: Pimlico, 1994); on Wilkes see pp. 105–117, from which the ensuing quotations are derived.

52. "Patriotism is the last refuge of a scoundrel" according to Dr Johnson's definition with Wilkes in mind, according to Colley.

53. The difficulty of the Ulster Unionists may stem in part from their attempting to combine such an assertion with a claim to cultural community with their fellow Britons—a claim that cannot be substantiated by participation in, for example, the English culture of the Anglo-Irish. But the difficulty arises from the political problem of securing both admission to a politically constituted state by allegiance and exemption from what they regard as a culturally grounded one by a claim to cultural difference.

54. A point I missed in P. Gilbert, "Criteria of Nationality and the Ethics of Self-Determination", *History of European Ideas*, Vol. 16 (1993), p. 515.

55. An extension of the old principle *cuius regio, eius religio*, as noted by R.W. Seton Watson, *Britain and the Dictators* (Cambridge: Cambridge University Press, 1993), pp. 343–344.

56. E. Bowen, *The Last September* (Harmondsworth: Penguin, 1983), pp. 91–92. The novel was first published in 1929.

57. The kind of conflict in English liberal thought epitomized in E.M. Foster's famous dictum, "if I had to choose between betraying my country and betraying my friend, I hope I should have the guts to betray my country", *Two Cheers for Democracy* (Harmondsworth: Penguin, 1965), p. 76.

58. *Reflections on the Revolution in France* (Harmondsworth: Penguin, 1968), p. 135. (Burke believes that our "public affections" can extend to "mankind", but only via a more ready extension to our country).

59. B. Russell, *Freedom and Organisation 1814–1914* (London: Allen and Unwin, 1934), p. 394.

60. His ensuing suggestion of common interests or common dangers is nearer the mark.

61. For a discussion of "the language of neighbours" as mediating relations between *citizens*, see S. Mendus, "Strangers and Brothers", in D. Milligan and W. Watts Miller, eds, *Liberalism, Citizenship and Autonomy* (Aldershot: Avebury, 1992), pp. 19–34.

62. See P. Gilbert *Human Relationships* (Oxford: Blackwell, 1991), pp. 120–123.

63. e.g. C.R. Beitz, *Political Theory and International Relations* (Princeton: Princeton University Press, 1979), pp. 106–107. It is only a *grain* of truth in a fatally flawed notion. See Gilbert "Criteria of Nationality", pp. 518–519.

64. Which is not to imply that a political obligation is imposed only on those who have corresponding national ones. However, the principles whereby nationals and resident aliens have the same political obligations are exactly the same on the societal models, as they would not be on the civic or culturalist ones.

65. As in the family and neighbourhood itself.

66. Noting only that the second, though more general than the first, need not presuppose the universalist aspirations of modernism: the ethical and the political, love and loyalty themselves, may be fragile social constructions.

8

Individuals, Nations and Obligations

Simon Caney

Nationalism is very much to the fore in contemporary European countries. One doctrine affirmed by nationalists is that individuals have special obligations to members of their nation. This doctrine thus stands opposed to an ideal of impartiality which insists that persons have the same obligations to everyone and should not favour their own. The question I wish to address in this paper is whether the nationalist claim that we have special obligations to members of our nation is justified. Most people would argue against the impartialist ideal that individuals have special obligations to members of their family or to their friends. My question is whether we also have special obligations to fellow nationals. And in the course of answering this question, I shall outline, and defend, a general account of special obligations.

To do this I shall in the next section present what I shall call the National Obligation Thesis and distinguish between two types of defence of special obligations (value-independent and value-dependent defences). Then in the following section I consider several value-independent defences of national obligations, finding each of them unconvincing. The third section then presents and defends an objection to value-independent defences of special obligations. The final section examines several value-dependent defences of national obligations; it defends this approach to special obligations but argues that it does not justify national obligations. None of the justifications of national obligations, I argue, is convincing.

National Obligations

Before the arguments for the National Obligation Thesis are considered, it is important to make several points about the claim that individuals have an obligation to members of their nation. These points concern the thesis's content, strength and the types of justification to be considered. With respect to its *content*, the National Obligation Thesis affirms that all members of a nation have an obligation to promote the well-being of other members of their nation. In terms of *strength*, it states that individuals have a *prima facie* and non-enforceable obligation. It is not incompatible with the claim that individuals have other (i.e. universal or familial) obligations, nor does it maintain that national obligations should always override other obligations. Finally, when considering *justifications of special obligations* (and in this case national obligations), five points should be made concerning the nature and types of justification available.

First, since special obligations arise when there is a special relationship between an individual and another or other individuals, it is important when defending special obligations to have a clear account of the way in which those concerned are said to be related. Special obligations arise when individuals A and B are related in a certain way to each other. The contention that there are national obligations therefore claims that an individual's membership of a nation constitutes such a relation. It is useful then to begin with an account of what a nation is. Defining a nation is notoriously problematic. One very common and, I think, the most plausible account maintains that a group of individuals constitute a nation if they define themselves as such and if they share a common culture and history.[1]

Second, it is worth distinguishing between two approaches to defending special obligations (and consequently national obligations), namely instrumental defences and intrinsic defences. Instrumental defences maintain that assisting fellow nationals is the best way to fulfil our universal obligations. National obligations are thus derived from a universal goal. Many utilitarians argue that we should help our friends and family because, and to the extent that, doing so maximizes the general goal of utility. Intrinsic defences of national obligations, by contrast, do not make special obligations parasitic on our universal obligations. In this paper I wish to focus only on intrinsic defences.

Third, we should also distinguish between two types of intrinsic argument, what I shall call value-dependent (VD) and value-independent (VI) arguments.[2] VD arguments assert that one can have a special obligation to a group to which one belongs only if that group is morally acceptable. Membership in a group might be morally acceptable because that group is just and fair, for example; or membership in a group might be morally acceptable because it promotes one's well-being. For example, one might argue that one has a special obligation to members of one's family because the family enhances one's well-being. VI arguments, on the other hand, state that we have obligations to members of a group to which we belong independently of the moral value of the group. For example, a VI defence of obligations to members of one's family might maintain that one should devote greater attention to one's family just because they are members of one's family and regardless of whether the family is a fair or in any other way commendable institution. As we shall see, most of those who have given an intrinsic defence of national obligations (i.e. George Fletcher, David Miller and Yael Tamir) have given VI arguments.

Fourth, discussions of special obligations often present a very Manichean position. Alasdair MacIntyre, for example, suggests that *either* we have special obligations to fellow nationals *or* we accept a completely impartial theory which allows no special obligations.[3] This picture is, however, inaccurate, for one might argue that we have impartial obligations and special obligations to some groups (families or friends) but not to others (race or nation).

Fifth, when appraising the claim that we have special obligations (in this case to fellow nationals), we should not confuse valuing "special obligations" with valuing loyalty. Someone who denies that we have national obligations might none the less admire someone who promotes the well-being of her fellow nationals on the grounds that she is keeping faith with her national identity. One might therefore praise that person's *loyalty* and her *commitment*.[4] Claiming that this action is morally commendable, however, is quite different from claiming that people have an obligation to do it. So even if one thinks that keeping faith with one's cultural attachments is morally laudable—and therefore wishes to reject a purely impartial approach—this does not show that one has a *special obligation* to be loyal to one's cultural attachments.

Value-Independent (VI) Arguments

Having explicated the National Obligation Thesis, I now wish to consider various arguments that have been given in defence of it. I shall begin with VI arguments. These arguments make the following claim:

(P1)   In virtue of his or her membership of a group, an individual acquires special obligations to members of that group.

David Miller, for example, states that

> the subject is partly defined by its relationships and the various rights, obligations, and so forth that go along with these, so these commitments themselves form a basic element of personality. To divest oneself of such commitments would be, in one important sense, to change one's identity.[5]

Given (P1), argue the VI proponents, it follows that

(C)   Those who are members of a nation have special obligations to the other members of their nation.[6]

To accept this argument, however, we need a defence of (P1). Various considerations have been adduced in defence of it, and in the remainder of this section I shall consider five such defences. In particular, I consider what might be called (a) the "self-recognition" argument, (b) the "self-fulfilment" argument, (c) the "motivation" argument, (d) the "intuitive" argument and (e) the "argument by analogy".

The "self-recognition" argument

In his book *Loyalty*, George Fletcher suggests what I have termed the "self-recognition" defence of (P1). He maintains that "we find the duty of loyalty . . . in the process of self-recognition".[7] Individuals, he argues, should affirm their personalities: "In acting loyally, the self acts in harmony with its personal history. One recognises who one is. Actions of standing by one's friends, family, nation, or people reveal that identity."[8]

Now Fletcher clearly believes that people should act "in harmony with" their identity and hence that people should be faithful to their national identity. The problem with this argument, however, is fairly obvious. Suppose that someone has a repellent social identity—he comes from a clan that has historically robbed and pillaged its neighbours. Then it would be a *non-sequitur* to insist that he has a duty to maintain this tradition in order to affirm his identity. Talk of acting "in harmony with" one's self sounds considerably less attractive in this type of example. Whether or not self-recognition is valuable is a function of the moral worth of that person's commitments and pursuits. The trouble then with the "self-recognition" approach is that it is quite unclear why one should follow one's social identity and frequently clear that one should not do so.

The "self-fulfilment" argument

On occasions Fletcher indicates a more extended defence of (P1) and suggests what I have called the "self-fulfilment" argument. That is, he argues that a completely impartial approach would be inappropriate since individuals have social attachments (including their membership of a nation) and being loyal to these is necessary for their well-being. As he writes,

> the historical self generates duties of loyalty toward the families, groups, and nations that enter into our self-definition. . . . *To love myself, I must respect and cherish those aspects of myself that are bound up with others.* Thus by the mere fact of my biography I incur obligations toward others. (Emphasis added)[9]

Fletcher's suggestion in this passage appears to be that, if someone does not keep faith with their social identity their well-being will suffer. If one sets one's attachments aside and acts on a purely impartial basis, one will not be able to love oneself. Self-fulfilment and self-realization require that one keep faith with one's cultural attachments.[10]

But two points can be made against this argument. First, the considerations it adduces do not show that individuals have special *obligations* to others. At most they show that individuals have a reason not to promote the interests of all impartially, but this is not the same as saying that one has special obligations to members of groups to which one belongs. To see this, suppose that someone fails to promote the well-being of a fellow national in a situation where there are no countervailing obligations and where the fellow national is in dire need. If one had national obligations, one would say that this fellow national had been let down, but the "self-fulfilment" argument does not establish this. Where one has an obligation (special or otherwise) to someone to perform an action A, the reason for doing A emanates from other people. The reason given by the "self-fulfilment" argument for not acting impartially, however, is not derived from *another*: rather, it is a self-derived reason to advance one's well-being. The reason is that *I* benefit.

Second, it is not true that to love oneself one needs to adhere to *all* of one's attachments. Someone might, for example, keep faith with their family and friends but not their nation and yet remain capable of loving themselves. Self-love and self-esteem thus do not require fidelity to all of one's attachments, and one can therefore not affirm one's national identity and yet remain capable of loving oneself. The "self-fulfilment" argument is thus unconvincing as a defence of (P1).

The "motivation" argument

Consider then the "motivation" argument. One might argue that, in contrast to impartial obligations, individuals are motivated to fulfil special obligations.[11] People are willing to assist those who belong to the same group as themselves but are far more reluctant to help others on the other side of the planet. Let us call this the psychological fact. Special obligations (including national obligations), it is suggested, are less utopian than impartial duties, and this should count in their favour.

Two points can, however, be made against this line of reasoning. First, it is difficult to see quite what the psychological fact is supposed to establish. On its own it does not establish that individuals have national obligations. Even if one supposes (what is in itself disputable) that one can have a moral obligation to do X only if performing X is not very strenuous, this is more forceful as an *objection to* impartial duties to all the members of the world than it is a *defence* of special obligations to fellow nationals. Suppose we take the psychological fact seriously and argue that it shows that global duties should be rejected: it does *not* follow from this that we have special obligations. That we (putatively) do not have impartial obligations to assist everyone in the world does not, of course, entail that we have special obligations. Moreover, just because individuals are (allegedly) willing to assist fellow nationals does not show that they have obligations to do so. Before we can accept the latter, we need a positive defence of special obligations. Surely, the psychological fact just shows that *if* people have national obligations *then* they are likely to be able to comply with them.[12]

Second, accepting the National Obligation Thesis, it should be noted, makes morality more onerous than denying it. The reason for this is that most of those who claim that we have national obligations also maintain that we have some global obligations.[13] (Let us call this the humanitarian nationalist position.) Now, if we compare this position with someone who accepts only the global principles that such humanitarian nationalists affirm (which I shall call the global position), it is clear that accepting that there are national obligations makes that person's morality more strenuous. An individual must comply not only with her global duties but must also with other (national) obligations as well. So if one really is concerned with not overburdening individuals with strenuous obligations, taking the humanitarian nationalist position would seem unattractive.

A nationalist might respond to this second objection by denying that accepting national obligations as well as global obligations increases the number of obligations that one has to fulfil. Rather, she might argue, accepting national obligations cancels out some global obligations. The two types of obligation do not get added together: rather, national obligations displace some global obligations. Consider, for example, a situation in which there is a finite amount of a medicine which can be used to save either a fellow national or a foreigner. In such a situation, the argument runs, accepting that one has a national obligation does not make more demands on one. One should simply, *ceteris paribus*, save the fellow national, and this overrides the impartial duty to help the foreigner. In other words, accepting national obligations does not mean that one has more obligations.

The problem with this response is that national obligations will not always cancel out global obligations. There are likely to be cases where an individual has satisfied his global obligations (however these are defined by the humanitarian nationalist) and yet has not performed all his national obligations. Such a position is explicitly affirmed by Yael Tamir.[14] In this case, the humanitarian nationalist position is more demanding than the global position. It affirms all the global principles affirmed by the global position and then adds some more. The humanitarian nationalist position is still therefore more demanding than the global position.[15] So the second objection still applies: accepting the National Obligation Thesis makes morality more onerous rather than less.[16]

The "intuitive" argument

A proponent of (P1) (and national obligations) might, at this point, argue that the arguments considered so far are misconceived. It is not possible to give arguments for (P1), and we do not need to do so. Rather, all that is required is that we draw on people's intuitive understanding that membership in groups implies special obligations. This I shall call the "intuitive" argument. David Miller takes this approach. In "In Defence of Nationality", he offers what he calls a "Humean" defence of national obligations and recommends a

> philosophy which, rather than dismissing ordinary beliefs and sentiments out
> of hand unless they can be shown to have a rational foundation, leaves them
> in place until strong arguments are produced for rejecting them. . . . In moral
> and political philosophy, in particular, we build upon existing sentiments and
> judgements, correcting them only when they are inconsistent or plainly
> flawed in some other way. . . . It is from this sort of stance (which I shall not
> try to justify) that it makes sense to mount a philosophical defence of
> nationality.[17]

(P1)—and also national obligations—need not be based on argument but simply on intuition.

This defence of (P1), however, suffers from two problems. First, the conception of moral philosophy on which it rests is highly questionable.[18] Persons' moral views and opinions frequently embody ignorance and illusion and are influenced by a bias towards people's own wants. People's judgements (on morality, but also on other areas of human life) are frequently distorted by wishful thinking, selective information and a lack of reflection. Moreover, people's intuitive judgements of strangers are particularly open to dispute since these are so frequently based on stereotyping, inaccuracy and self-interest.[19] Many cultures, for example, embody racist attitudes and judgements, but this does not establish the legitimacy of racism. Miller's methodology is therefore suspect.[20]

This point should not be misunderstood. My claim is not that a correct account of morality should eschew intuitions altogether. It is simply that we should not blindly treat people's intuitive beliefs as sacrosanct. A far more plausible account of morality is given by James Griffin, who suggests that some moral beliefs are given a privileged status and that some should be rejected.[21] Now there is not space here to indicate how such an account of morality would operate, but it is worth noting that the arguments made against simply following common opinions do not entail that a correct moral theory rejects all reference to any intuitions.

Moreover, Miller's approach faces a second difficulty: namely, that it is not clear that people's intuitive judgement is unequivocally that we have special obligations to fellow nationals.[22] Let us take the celebrated case devised by William Godwin: a house is burning down and one can save either one's mother or the archbishop Fenelon.[23] It seems plausible to argue that, *contra* Godwin, what one should do is save one's mother. Suppose, however, that the example is altered and one has the choice of saving a fellow national or a foreigner. It seems far from obvious that one should save a complete stranger who happens to be the same nationality. It seems implausible to claim that someone who saves a foreigner in this example has somehow failed in his duty. The intuitive argument is thus not very powerful.[24]

The "argument by analogy"

A proponent of national obligations and (P1) might respond to this objection by giving what I have called the "argument from analogy". This argument makes two claims. First, it states that (as was suggested above) we can have faith in some intuitions. One such intuition is the conviction—recognized by almost everyone—that individuals have special obligations to family and friends; to treat one's family and friends as one treats utter strangers is highly implausible. Second, the argument maintains that, since one has special obligations to some groups to which one belongs (one's family or one's friends), one therefore has special obligations to other groups to which one belongs (such as one's nation).

This type of argument is given by Andrew Oldenquist, who states that "[s]ince it is fashionable in some quarters to have contempt for patriotism, I shall defend the easier case of family loyalty, and assume that I have shown that whatever we can conclude about the one case we can conclude in principle about the other".[25]

How persuasive is this defence of national obligations? The main problem lies in the second step, namely the claim that if one has family obligations one also has national obligations. This relies on the assumption that the morally important properties of families which imply familial obligations are shared by nations. Of course, Oldenquist's case is not that families are identical to nations: rather, his claim is that they are *morally analogous*, that they share some morally valuable properties. But he has given us no reason to suppose that this is the case. He has provided us with no indication of what these morally valuable attributes are that nations and families are said to have in common. Perhaps the factors that mean that families and friends produce special obligations are absent in the case of a nation. Thus, we need more than Oldenquist supplies before we can conclude that national membership implies national obligations. (This issue will again be taken up in the final section.) Oldenquist's argument is therefore incomplete.

The Obnoxious Identity Objection

Having considered and rejected five defences of (P1), I now want to consider an objection that might be made against it. (P1), recall, states that individuals have obligations in virtue of their social identity. Someone's membership of a group, it is claimed, implies obligations to other members of that group. One powerful objection to this claim is that it produces quite implausible and morally unacceptable conclusions.[26] Consider the following example:

- A is a white racist. She is travelling through the desert and comes across two starving people—another racist (B) and a black (C). Both are in need of food and water: A only has enough for herself and one other. According to (P1), she has a *moral obligation* to give to B since they belong to the same group. (P1) stipulates that A should act along racist lines, and if she does not do so this is a moral failing given her membership of a racist culture.

Now, as is the case with members of a nation, members of a racist culture define themselves in terms of their membership. In addition, members of a racist culture, like members of a nation, share a common set of beliefs and shared norms of custom and behaviour. So, according to (P1), racists have a moral obligation to favour the well-being of other racists. The same point can be made about other cultural attachments: (P1) would conclude that anti-semites have moral obligations to favour other anti-semites; that WASPs should advance the well-being of other WASPs; that members of a high caste should promote the well-being of other members of their caste. Similarly, it would enjoin upper-class snobs to favour their own. This renders (P1) very implausible. Surely, given this objection, being a member of a group does not necessarily mean that one has obligations to other members of that group. Let us call this the *obnoxious identity* objection. To rebut it, what the nationalist needs is an explanation of why an individual's membership in a nation entails national obligations but her membership in a race or class does not entail analogous obligations.

Three responses might made to this objection.

One is made by George Fletcher, who argues that one's membership of a group does imply duties to the members of that group but that we also have impartial obligations and these may override the former obligations.[27] So a person's membership of a racist culture gives him a special obligation to promote the well-being of his fellow racists but this can be outweighed by other obligations (such as to respect life). This position is, however, still unacceptable. It misdescribes the situation: it is implausible to assert that a racist has a moral duty to fellow racists which can be overridden.[28] Rather, we think that the racist does not have any such obligation in the first place. Fletcher's emendation is therefore inadequate.

A second response to this objection is proposed by Samuel Gorovitz, who states that

(P1a) Membership of a group does not entail special obligations to further the well-being of other members of that group if doing so would violate others' basic rights.[29]

For example being a parent gives one no reason to kill someone who is bullying one's son because to do so would clearly violate that person's basic rights. On the other hand, suppose that one night you come across two separate individuals, one of whom is your sister and the other a complete stranger, who have both been robbed and are accordingly both penniless. Both ask you to give them a small amount of money so that they can take the bus home. Unfortunately, you only have enough money to help one of them. In such a situation, Gorovitz's proposal would suggest, very plausibly, that you should help your sister (on the assumption that the other individual does not have a basic right that you should give her money). Should (P1) therefore be replaced by (P1a)?

Unfortunately, (P1a) is an inadequate response to the *obnoxious identity* objection. It would conclude that people have obligations in cases where that is highly implausible. To see this, consider a variation on the last example given. Suppose that A, an anti-semite, is faced with the following situation: two penniless individuals who have just been robbed, namely, B (a fellow anti-semite), and C (a Jew), both ask him for a small amount of money. Again, A only has enough money to help one person. Now (P1a) says that one should put the interests of members of one's group before others unless doing so conflicts with the other's basic rights. In this case, not helping C does not violate C's basic rights. Furthermore, A and B belong to the same group. (P1a) therefore states that A has a moral obligation to act along anti-semitic lines. This surely is a *reductio ad absurdam* of (P1a).

A third proposal is made by David Miller. He is aware that saying that individuals have obligations in virtue of being a member of a group like a nation runs the risk of appearing irrational. He writes, therefore, that membership of a group cannot be deemed rational unless two further conditions are met:

(a) an individual's commitment to a group is based on a correct belief, namely that the group really exists (what I shall call the factual condition);

(b) an individual's membership of a group is compatible with her other commitments (what I shall call the coherence condition).[30]

Explicating (a), Miller argues that being a member of a group is rational if the group actually exists, that is, if there is a group of individuals who think of themselves as a group. He writes:

> I may have pledged my loyalty to a group of people, but it turns out on closer inspection that the group does not really exist as a group, in the sense that no one, except myself, takes his or her commitment seriously. My commitment is based on false assumptions and, once these are brought to light, it must simply evaporate.[31]

Miller's second condition, the coherence condition, states that a person's commitment to a community is appropriate only if the demands of belonging to this community are compatible with other commitments this person has. He writes:

> one can investigate the coherence of one's existing set of commitments—that is, the extent to which the understanding of personal identity provided by each is consistent with that provided by the others. For instance someone committed both to being a caring father and to being a ruthless tycoon might come to believe that this involved an incoherence—not in the relatively superficial sense that the two commitments might require incompatible actions on certain occasions, but in the deeper sense that he simply could not be both kinds of person at the same time; that the qualities needed to be a good father just could not be reconciled with those needed to be a tycoon. Having reached this point, he must then decide which of his two commitments really is the more fundamental.[32]

Now one might be influenced by Miller and according revise (P1) so as to incorporate these two conditions. We then arrive at the following claim:

(P1b) In virtue of his or her membership of a group, an individual acquires special obligations to members of that group where (a) the factual condition, and (b) the coherence condition both obtain.

Does (P1b) then escape the *obnoxious identity* objection? I do not think so. First, it is too loose a theory. There are cases where someone belongs to a group and satisfies both conditions, and yet we would not say that her membership of the group implies special obligations. Consider, again, a racist. He belongs to a racist organization dedicated to "purifying" the nation. This racist commitment thus satisfies the factual condition. Furthermore, suppose that this person's racism coheres with his other commitments. According to Miller's two conditions, this person has a moral obligation to put the interests of fellow racists above those of other races. This, again, is highly implausible.

Second the central problem with Miller's suggestion is that it is not concerned with the *moral value* of the community. He gives only formal conditions, but what is needed to explain why membership of some communities (like families or friends) implies special obligations whereas membership of other groups (like racist cultures) does not is attention to the moral worth of the groups in question. So what is needed before we can respond to the *obnoxious identity* objection is a belief that nationality is morally valuable. This brings us on to value-dependent defences of national obligations.

Value-Dependent Arguments

The most plausible defence of special obligations, I think, argues that obligations are part of a morally valuable relationship. Joseph Raz has defended obligations to one's friends in this way: "[t]he justification of the duties of friendship is that they make, or are part of, a relationship which is intrinsically valuable".[33] Raz does not elaborate on why friendship is morally valuable, but this is hardly a controversial claim. We regard friendship to be an important form of well-being and one ingredient of a fulfilling life. This is not to say that the good of friendship can not be overridden by other goods. It may conflict with other goods. A great philosopher's quest to write a profound philosophical treatise may lead him to lock himself away from others and become so preoccupied with his work that he thereby forgoes the good of friendship, and we may judge the choice to be a good one. This does not detract, however, from the claim that friendship is valuable. And since obligations are an integral part of this morally valuable relationship, we can conclude that friends have special obligations to each other.

Before considering whether this value-dependent approach implies that there are national obligations, it is worth stressing two advantages of a value-dependent approach. First, it avoids the *obnoxious identity* objection that afflicted all the VI arguments. In cases where someone is involved in a morally unacceptable relationship, a value-dependent approach denies that this relationship creates special obligations. Secondly, this approach explains why we think that people usually do have special obligations to friends and siblings since we think these are (normally) morally valuable relationships.

Does a VD approach justify the claim that there are national obligations? To answer this we must address the question of whether nations are morally valuable. Finding a plausible moral criterion that all nations satisfy is, it seems, very unlikely. Consider three possible defences of the claim that membership of a nation is morally valuable.

The well-being argument

First, one might argue that nations serve an important role. Human beings need to identify with a group, to be a part of a community, and membership in a nation satisfies this need. Fichte, for example, argues that human beings yearn to belong to something that will outlast them, and membership of a nation satisfies this longing.[34] Moreover, a nation, it is argued, is uniquely capable of satisfying this need. Families and friends are not permanent but nations are far less ephemeral and transient. This argument, however, does not show that all members of a nation have special obligations to fellow-nationals, because there are nations that have not contributed to a person's well-being. Whatever account of well-being one adopts, there are cases where membership of a nation has not advanced one's well-being. It may cause one shame, guilt or embarrassment. One's national identity can be a source of unhappiness. There is therefore no guarantee that one's membership of a nation does advance one's well-being.

The self-development argument

Consider a second argument, which maintains that nations are morally commendable. It is often argued that being a member of a nation enables one to develop. One needs a social environment to develop one's skills and become an adequately functioning individual. In particular, a national community enables one to develop. Consequently, the argument runs, one owes an obligation to the national community that has nurtured and supported one's personal development.[35]

Two powerful criticisms have been made of this approach. First, it is implausible to claim that a person's nation is especially important for a person's self-development.[36] The objection is not that people do not need a social environment to develop, but rather that it is unclear why the requisite culture must be a national culture. This is especially true given increased communication and international interdependence. A contemporary American's personality (i.e. his conceptual framework, his assumptions, talents and desires) for example, is deeply shaped by a culture that transcends America's borders. The culture that nurtured him, for instance, contains the English language (which is in turn derived from Greek and Latin), Arabic mathematics, Japanese technology, a religious outlook that originated from the Middle East, and a set of assumptions shaped by the Enlightenment and Western civilization in general. Nations are not separate discrete systems immune to influence: consequently, individuals are not simply (or even chiefly) the creations of a national culture.

Second, as David Miller points out, if any institution can be said to play a crucial role in the development of the individual, it is the *state*, not the *nation*.[37] States, for instance, frequently provide educational institutions, and these are highly important as influences on individuals' personalities. So even if we overlook the first problem, what the argument being considered is most likely to support is not national obligations but obligations to fellow citizens (by which I mean members of one's own state).

Given these two objections, the claim that one has an obligation to fellow nationals because one's nation plays an important role in one's self-development is implausible.

A Dworkinian argument

In *Law's Empire*, Ronald Dworkin argues that people have special obligations to members of the communities to which they belong when five conditions are satisfied. Moreover, Dworkin suggests, national obligations can be defended in this way.[38] Special obligations, for Dworkin, involve the following features:

(a) They are "special" and not universal. That is, they are owed to members of one's group.[39]

(b) They are "personal". That is, members of a community have special obligations to their *fellow members*, and not to the *group* itself.[40]

(c) They require us to advance the welfare of the members of the group: they express "concern".[41]

(d) The members of the group are committed to "*equal* concern for all members".[42]

Later Dworkin adds that

(e) Special obligations exist only when the group is not engaged in grave injustice.[43]

To elaborate on (e), Dworkin believes that if someone belongs to a group which satisfies condition (d) and is unjust but not heinously unjust, then that person has "special" obligations to promote the welfare of the other members of that group (i.e. features (a), (b) and (c)). On his view, there is a conflict between the special obligation and the obligation to act justly. If, however, a group is committed to *grave* injustice (however that is defined), then members of that group (even if (d) is satisfied) have no obligation *at all* to members of their own group. Dworkin's account is, we should note, a value-dependent account for two reasons: first, communities must satisfy condition (d); second, they must also be reasonably just.

Can this approach justify the National Obligation Thesis? There are two central problems with it as a defence of the claim that all members of a nation have special obligations to fellow nationals. First, it is evident that many nations have waged unjust wars and have exploited other nations: thus they do not satisfy condition (e). Similarly, it is clear that some nations violate condition (d). Consequently, members of these nations, according to Dworkin's criteria, lack special obligations to fellow nationals.

Dworkin's argument faces a second problem. According to Dworkin, one has a national obligation only if one's nation is not extremely unjust. Therefore, one needs to know whether one's nation violates just principles of distributive justice: we need an account of distributive justice. Now, in practice, it is fair to say that all nations favour their own. So before we can know whether Dworkin's condition (e) is met, we therefore need to know whether this practice of looking after one's fellow nationals is very unjust. Someone who believes that this practice is highly unjust would of course conclude that national communities do not satisfy condition (e). In other words, a Dworkinian defence of national obligations can work only if one asserts (or defends) the claim that the practice of favouring one's fellow nationals is reasonably just. This, however, is partly what is in dispute and it is a large assumption which requires considerable defence. Without making this additional assumption—which, to some extent, runs the risk of being circular and begging the question—a Dworkinian argument fails to justify national obligations.

The three VD defences of national obligations which have been considered are thus unsuccessful. There may be other arguments which purport to show that all (or most) nations are morally valuable, but such a position does not look promising. Since, in each of the three arguments considered, nations failed to satisfy the standards set by the respective VD approaches, one might lower the moral standards by which one judged nations, so that all nations satisfied the moral criteria. But it is hard to think of a moral standard *weighty* enough to generate special obligations and yet *weak* enough for all (or indeed, most) nations to meet.

Conclusion

To sum up, an examination of both value-independent and value-dependent defences of special obligations and, in particular, national obligations suggests two conclusions—one positive and the other negative.

The negative conclusion is that we do not have any reason to accept the nationalist doctrine that members of nations have an obligation to fellow nationals. The problem with value-independent defences is that (a) none of the arguments successfully defend national obligations and (b) they are all susceptible to the *obnoxious identity* objection. Moreover, none of the value-depend-

ent defences supports the National Obligation Thesis, and it seems highly
unlikely that any value-dependent approach could provide us with a blanket
endorsement of national obligations. The intrinsic justifications of national
obligations considered in this paper are thus unconvincing. Taking this position, it should be stressed, does not deny the communitarian contention
(affirmed by Sandel, among others) that human beings are social creatures
whose social setting profoundly influences their characters.[44] Denying the
nationalist contention does not imply that one must endorse a non-social conception of the self. Like nationalists, those who doubt the claim that we have
national obligations agree that we belong to communities like nations: they
simply question whether this social identity justifies national obligations. And
none of the arguments considered in this paper have managed to show that
their scepticism is misplaced and that we do in fact have such obligations.[45]

The positive conclusion suggested by the preceding arguments is that we
now have a general account of special obligations (namely the value-dependent
approach) which can explain both when we have special obligations and why
we do. It clearly needs to be developed further: we need to know, for example,
what criteria to apply to judge whether a relationship is morally acceptable.
None the less, what has been established is that the value-dependent approach
is the most appropriate way to justify special obligations. It is obviously
immune to the *obnoxious identity objection* which undermines VI approaches
and it has the virtues of being able to justify and explain our judgements that
we have special obligations to some (i.e. our friends) but not to others (i.e.
members of our race).[46]

Notes

1. For plausible accounts of the nature of nationality, which I broadly follow, see
B. Barry, "Self-Government Revisited", *Democracy and Power: Essays in Political
Theory*, Vol. 1 (Oxford: Clarendon, 1991); D. Miller, "In Defence of Nationality",
Journal of Applied Philosophy, Vol. 10, No. 1 (1993), and D. Miller, *On Nationality*
(Oxford: Clarendon, 1995), chapter 2.

2. For a different typology, see A. Oldenquist, "Loyalties", *Journal of Philosophy*,
Vol. 79 No. 4 (1982), section IV.

3. A. MacIntyre, "Is Patriotism a Virtue?" Lindley Lecture (Department of
Philosophy, University of Kansas, 1984), especially section II.

4. Even then there are limits to the extent to which we praise someone's integrity:
see G. Dworkin, *The Theory and Practice of Autonomy* (Cambridge: Cambridge
University Press, 1989), p. 41.

5. D. Miller, "The Ethical Significance of Nationality", *Ethics*, Vol. 98, No. 4
(1988), p. 650. See generally section II. For Miller's views see also his *On Nationality*,
chapter 3.

6. For this argument see G. Fletcher, *Loyalty: An Essay on the Morality of Relationships* (Oxford: Oxford University Press, 1993), pp. 16, 25, 38–39 and 57; R. Rorty, "Postmodernist Bourgeois Liberalism", in *Objectivity, Relativism, and Truth: Philosophical Papers*, Volume 1 (Cambridge: Cambridge University Press, 1991), p. 200; M. J. Sandel, *Liberalism and the Limits of Justice* (Cambridge: Cambridge University Press, 1982), p. 179; Y. Tamir, *Liberal Nationalism* (Princeton: Princeton University Press, 1993), p. 99. For this type of approach to the issue of political obligations, see J. Horton, *Political Obligation* (London: Macmillan, 1992), chapter 6, especially pp. 145–171. For a critical discussion of this type of approach, see C. Beitz, "Sovereignty and Morality in International Affairs", in D. Held, ed., *Political Theory Today* (Cambridge: Polity Press, 1991), pp. 250–254.

7. Fletcher, *Loyalty*, p. 57; see also pp. 77, 153, and other passages on p. 57.

8. Ibid, p. 25.

9. Ibid, p. 16; relatedly, see also pp. 25, 33 and, for a discussion of the harmful effects of disloyalty, pp. 86–87.

10. This sort of point is made in criticism of impartiality by B. Williams and J. Cottingham: see B. Williams, "Persons, Character and Morality", *Moral Luck: Philosophical Papers 1973–1980* (Cambridge: Cambridge University Press, 1988) and J. Cottingham, "Partiality, Favouritism and Morality", *Philosophical Quarterly* Vol. 36, No. 144 (1986), pp. 364–366. Relatedly, see Williams's well-known discussion of utilitarianism and integrity in "A Critique of Utilitarianism", in J.J.C. Smart and B. Williams, eds, *Utilitarianism: For and Against* (Cambridge: Cambridge University Press, 1973), especially pp. 110–118. Neither Williams nor Cottingham claims, however, that this point establishes the existence of special obligations. For Cottingham's cautious discussion of patriotism, see "Partiality, Favouritism and Morality", p. 372.

11. See, e.g. S. Gorovitz, "Bigotry, Loyalty, and Malnutrition", in P. G. Brown and H. Shue, *Food Policy: The Responsibility of the United States in the Life and Death Choices* (London: Collier Macmillan, 1977), p. 136; MacIntyre, "Is Patriotism a Virtue?" pp. 17–18; Miller "The Ethical Significance of Nationality", pp. 650–651; R. Rorty, *Contingency, Irony, and Solidarity* (Cambridge: Cambridge University Press, 1991), chapter 9, especially pp. 190–191, 198.

12. See also Beitz, "Sovereignty and Morality in International Affairs", pp. 252–253, and H. Shue, *Basic Rights: Subsistence, Affluence, and US Foreign Policy* (Princeton: Princeton University Press, 1980), chapter 6, especially pp. 146–149.

13. See, e.g. Miller, "In Defence of Nationality", p. 5 and Tamir, *Liberal Nationalism*, pp. 99, 100, 115. Neither, however, spells out the content of these global principles.

14. See Tamir, *Liberal Nationalism*, p. 100.

15. A second objection that a humanitarian nationalist might make is to relinquish (or weaken) their global principles. Two points can be made in reply to this claim. First, the nationalist taking this route has to explain why we should relinquish the global obligations rather than the national ones. Assuming that accepting both obligations is excessively onerous, we need to know why we should not reject national obligations. Nothing the "motivation" argument says explains why the global principles should be dropped: why not drop the national obligations? Second, we cannot accept the suggestion to weaken or water down the global principles espoused by the

humanitarian nationalist until we are told exactly what global duties will be left. For two important defences of global principles of justice, see C. Beitz, *Political Theory and International Relations* (Princeton: Princeton University Press, 1979) and Shue, *Basic Rights*.

16. My aim in this paper is not to defend impartial duties, but two points can be made in response to the oft-made criticism that impartial duties are unduly strenuous. First, how difficult it is to comply with an impartial morality depends on the *content* of that morality. If one says, for example, that each person has an (impartial) obligation not to murder or rape others, then this is not onerous. The charge that an impartial morality is unduly onerous is far more plausible if we suppose that it tells people to maximize the total amount of utility in the world. Impartial duties are not therefore necessarily strenuous. Second, to claim that duties to promote the welfare of needy people in other parts of the world are onerous is to present a biased picture. It may be strenuous on the affluent but not for the vast majority of the world who stand to benefit. Indeed, suppose one argues (as I would) that as a matter of justice needy people in Africa and Asia are entitled to a considerable redistribution of resources from affluent nations. The present unjust arrangement is extremely onerous for them and a juster world would impose far less strenuous obligations on them. For an interesting related discussion, see J. Waldron's critical discussion of libertarianism in *The Right to Private Property* (Oxford: Clarendon, 1990), pp. 267–271.

17. Miller, "In Defence of Nationality", p. 4. This sort of approach is also taken by Y. Tamir: see *Liberal Nationalism*, pp. 96, 99. J. Horton makes the same type of claim when discussing political obligations: see his *Political Obligation*, pp. 147–148, 173–175.

18. For two excellent critical discussions to which I am indebted see J. Griffin, "How We Do Ethics Now", *Ethics*, Royal Institute of Philosophy Supplement, Vol. 35 (Cambridge: Cambridge University Press, 1993) ed. A. P. Griffiths; and J. Raz, "The Claims of Reflective Equilibrium", *Inquiry*, Vol. 25 (1982).

19. See R. Nisbett and L. Ross, *Human Inference: Strategies and Shortcomings of Social Judgement* (Englewood Cliffs, NJ: Prentice-Hall, 1980), especially pp. 237–241. Nisbett and Ross argue that our faulty judgements result from intellectual (i.e. "cold") errors and they downplay motivational (i.e. "hot") explanations. For a fascinating account of Western misconceptions about other cultures see E. Said, *Orientalism* (London: Penguin, 1978).

20. This point is made by M. Freeman: see his "Nation-State and Cosmopolis: A Response to D. Miller", *Journal of Applied Philosophy*, Vol. 11, No. 1 (1994), pp. 82–83. Miller does say in the passage that I quote on p. 125 that moral intuitions may be rejected if "they are inconsistent or plainly flawed" ("In Defence of Nationality", p. 4). This last phrase, however, requires elucidation, and before we can endorse Miller's "intuitive" argument he needs to explicate the notion of being "plainly flawed" in a way which (a) is plausible and (b) supports the national obligations thesis.

21. See Griffin, "How We Do Ethics Now".

22. See also Freeman, "Nation-State and Cosmopolis", pp. 82–83.

23. W. Godwin, *Enquiry Concerning Political Justice* (Oxford: Clarendon, 1971), abr. and ed. by K. C. Carter, p. 71. In different editions of his work, Godwin changes the example slightly, substituting different members of the family.

24. It is true that people often care more about fellow nationals, but this is not the same as, nor does it entail, their having *obligations* to these fellow nationals. Suppose, for example, that someone cares about the plight of a group of people. This gives him a reason to promote their well-being, but, in itself, it does not give him an obligation to them. They do not have a claim on him.

25. Oldenquist, "Loyalties", p. 186: see too p. 187.

26. See A. Buchanan, "Assessing the Communitarian Critique of Liberalism", *Ethics*, Vol. 99 (1989), p. 874; and P. Singer, "Reconsidering the Famine Relief Argument", in Brown and Shue, *Food Policy*, pp. 42–43. For a contrary view see Tamir, *Liberal Nationalism*, pp. 101–102.

27. Fletcher, *Loyalty*, chapter 8, especially pp. 162–165 and pp. 170–172. See also Tamir, *Liberal Nationalism*, pp. 9–10, 102 and 115.

28. See, relatedly, Horton, *Political Obligation*, p. 156.

29. Gorovitz, "Bigotry, Loyalty, and Malnutrition", p. 137. Gorovitz, I should add, does not give a full account of our basic rights.

30. Miller, "The Ethical Significance of Nationality", p. 650.

31. Ibid., p. 650. Miller's factual condition, I should stress, does not state that all the beliefs held by a community must be true. He distinguishes between "beliefs that are constitutive of social relationships and background beliefs which support those constitutive beliefs": see "The Ethical Significance of Nationality", p. 655. An example of a *constitutive belief* is a Briton's belief that there is a group of people who think of themselves, as she does, as being British. Without this belief there would be no group of people who could be described as the "British nation". An example of a *background belief* is a belief that the Battle of Hastings took place in 1066 or that the Great Reform Act was passed in 1832. Now Miller's claim is that what is important for group membership not to be irrational, and for it to imply group obligations, is that people hold correct *constitutive beliefs* even if they hold false *background beliefs*. This is an interesting claim, but I shall not examine it here because even if we accept it (and Miller's second condition) they fail to rule out some unacceptable commitments.

32. Miller, "The Ethical Significance of Nationality", p. 650. There is a footnote after the word "occasions" in the penultimate sentence of this quotation: see p. 650, fn. 5.

33. J. Raz, "Liberating Duties", *Law and Philosophy*, Vol. 8 (1989), p. 20; see also pp. 18–19. S. Nathanson supports a VD account of national obligations but does not provide the criteria a nation must satisfy to be morally worthy: see his "In Defence of 'Moderate Patriotism' ", *Ethics*, Vol. 99 (1989), pp. 551–552. For a VD account of special obligations (which does not discuss national obligations) see M. Friedman, "The Practice of Partiality", *Ethics*, Vol. 101 (1991), especially pp. 820–821, and 835.

34. See J. G. Fichte, *Addresses to the German Nation*, ed. G. A. Kelly (New York and Evanston, Ill.: Harper and Row, 1968), pp. 113–118. See also A. Smith, *National Identity* (London: Penguin, 1991), pp. 160–163.

35. For this sort of argument see S. Weil, *The Need for Roots: Prelude to a Declaration of Duties towards Mankind* (London and New York: Ark Paperbacks, 1987), pp. 151–152. See also Fletcher, *Loyalty*, pp. 56–57, Tamir, *Liberal Nationalism*, pp. 96–98, and, more generally, C. Taylor's discussion of the significance of society (although not necessarily a national society) for self-development in "Atomism",

Philosophy and the Human Sciences, Philosophical Papers, Vol. 2 (Cambridge: Cambridge University Press, 1985).

36. See Miller, "The Ethical Significance of Nationality", p. 651, and R. Goodin, "What Is So Special about our Fellow Countrymen?" *Ethics*, Vol. 98 (1988), section IV.

37. Miller, "The Ethical Significance of Nationality", p. 652.

38. See R. Dworkin, *Law's Empire* (London: Fontana, 1986), pp. 206, 208. Dworkin's expression of support for national obligations is a little ambiguous, but even if he does not embrace national obligations we need to know whether his account of special obligations does justify national obligations.

39. Ibid., p. 199.

40. Ibid.

41. Ibid., p. 200.

42. Ibid.; see also pp. 200–201. Dworkin thus does not think that members of a caste-ridden society have special obligations to each other: p. 201.

43. Ibid., pp. 204–205. Unfortunately Dworkin does not give a full account of what he would take to be severe injustice although he does give one example (i.e. a society committed to racial homogeneity): p. 204.

44. See Sandel, *Liberalism and the Limits of Justice*.

45. Two additional points should, however, be made here. First, since there may be other intrinsic justifications of national obligations, we cannot conclude that no intrinsic justification could be successful. Secondly, even if all intrinsic justifications were unpersuasive, we cannot conclude that we have no special obligations to fellow nationals: instrumental justifications may be more successful (although I am sceptical about this).

46. This paper was presented to the colloquium on "National Rights and International Obligations" at the University of Newcastle, and to the Political Theory Workshop at York University. I am grateful to the participants at both occasions (and in particular to John Horton) for their comments. I am also grateful for the written comments of Derek Bell, Andrew Mason and Andrew Williams.

9

Territorial Justice

Hillel Steiner

It is a commonplace of political history that, at some times in some places, liberalism and nationalism have *not* been incompatible. More than that, they have been good friends—lending each other vital support, rejoicing in one another's triumphs, holding a shared view of who is the enemy and so forth. Nor, according to Onora O'Neill, has this affinity been merely coincidental:

> In a pre-liberal world, [a person's] social identity might be given by tribe or kin, it might not depend on those who share a sense of identity being collected in a single or an exclusive territory. Because liberal principles undercut reliance on pedigree and origin as the basis for recognising who count as our own, and who as outsiders, liberalism had to find some alternative basis for identifying who counts. Pre-eminent among these ways are the differential rights with respect to a given state that citizenship confers.[1]

Liberalism, she seems to be suggesting, has actually *needed* nationalism.

Why? Well, because its hallowed subjects—namely individual persons, each of whom it lavishly adorns with all manner of rights and liberties—find themselves badly in need of some salient form of social identity when they emerge from their various imperial subjugations, ancient and modern. For whatever severe oppression and disempowerment they for so long endured under those subjugations, one thing they did *not* thereby lack was a strong sense of social identity: a sense of identity underwritten by their being officially and principally regarded as members of this family or that clan. That particular form of strong social identity being lost to them in the emancipatory world of liberalism, its only plausible replacement is said to consist in their recognition as citizens, as persons possessing significant and fully fledged membership in a national group. And nationalism is the celebration of that membership.

So what we have here is essentially a psychological hypothesis with strong political implications. People are said to have a vital need to be socially identified—to be thought of as members of groups—and, moreover, groups whose membership is neither open-endedly inclusive nor primarily elective. Marx (Groucho, that is) once famously remarked that he wouldn't want to be a member of any club that would have him in it. On the present hypothesis, while I might *want* to be a member of a club that would have me in it, what I *need* is to be a member of one that has no choice in the matter.

Now it is certainly beyond my competence to assess either the authenticity of that need or its weight or the grounds for claiming that its incidence has been as widespread as O'Neill suggests. Nor do I intend to dwell on the quite serious degree of practical indeterminacy attending the suggestion that significant membership in a national group is the favoured, perhaps now the *only*, way of satisfying it. That indeterminacy is, these days, the unmistakable message of virtually every headline and news story emerging out of the former Yugoslavia, the former Soviet Union and countless other places around the globe. Just which national membership will bestow on a person the social identity he or she needs is a matter currently being decided, in those places, by repeated resort to distinctly illiberal means.

And this, of course, is the problem about the relationship between liberalism and nationalism. For whatever historical affinities they have shared, whatever services they may have rendered to each other along the way to the modern world, the tensions between them are, and arguably always have been, transparently obvious. Neil MacCormick, the liberal legal philosopher, speaks for many when he rather despondently records that

> Whether "nation" and "nationalism" are antithetical to or compatible with "individual" and "individualism" is a question of acute personal concern for me. I have been for a good many years a member of the Scottish National Party, and yet remain in some perplexity about the justiciability of any nationalistic case within the terms set for me by the other principles to which I adhere.[2]

More trenchantly, Ernest Gellner describes these tensions as "a tug of war between reason and passion".[3] Why? What's the problem here? Wasn't Hume surely correct to insist that reason is the slave of the passions and that conflict between them is therefore impossible?

We don't, I think, need to disagree with Hume in order to see what Gellner and MacCormick are getting at. Nationalism is associated with passion because its imperatives are inherently particularistic. "This measure is necessary", the nationalist will say, "because it best serves the interests of *my* nation. My nation (or as in earlier times, my tribe or my family) is what matters most. Its well-being is far more intimately connected to my own well-being and to my sense of who I am than are the sundry other considerations with which it may, and often does, conflict."

Liberalism, in contrast, is associated with reason because its imperatives are universalistic. It indiscriminately assigns rights to everyone. And it adamantly rejects any proposed differentiation of these assignments that invokes bottom-line premisses that unavoidably include terms like "me" and "mine".[4] "That this policy would be good for me and mine" cuts no *moral* ice with liberals, because moral judgements—judgements about what *should* be done—have to be drawn from bottom-line premisses devoid of any proper name or particular reference. Premisses containing such terms may well furnish reasons for *my* doing or having certain things, but they cannot—logically cannot—furnish reasons for *others* to let me do or have them. They cannot serve those others as justifications for measures that require their (passive or active) co-operation—co-operation that would therefore be non-rational.

Not, of course, that liberalism forbids the pursuit of self-interest, whether by individuals or groups. Indeed, the very wide scope it allows for such pursuits has, historically, been the main target of its fiercest critics, among whom nationalists of one stripe or another have figured quite prominently. But what liberalism does forbid are those pursuits of self-interest that cross the boundaries demarcating other persons' moral rights. And the liberal's problem with many nationalisms, past and present, is that they have engaged in just such boundary-crossings on a truly massive scale, especially though not exclusively in relation to members of other nations.

Is this at all avoidable? Can nationalisms be reconciled? And can they be reconciled in such a way as to render the many diverse values, which they severally embody, compatible with one another's and, ultimately, with individuals' moral rights? To ask these questions is to ask whether those rights are sufficient to yield a set of national and international norms which at once allow scope for nations to enact their respective value-sets *and* entail clear limits on how far those enactments may extend. And to answer this question, we need first to take a look at what those rights are.

In a recent book on rights, I have argued that at least a necessary condition for any set of rights to be a *possible* set—that is, to be realizable—is that all the rights in it are mutually consistent, or what I there call *compossible*.[5] The duties corresponding to those rights have to be ones that are jointly fulfillable and not mutually obstructive. By means of a rather extended chain of reasoning, which I certainly won't bore you with here, I try to show that this condition is satisfied only by a set of rights, each of which is (or is reducible to) a discrete property right—one that can be fully differentiated from every other right in that set and which therefore does not (in the language of set theory) *intersect* with any of them.[6] I further argue that, for a set of rights to be like this, it has to have a certain historical structure whereby each current right is one derived from the exercise of an antecedent right. The upshot of all this is that sets of mutually consistent rights are jointly and exhaustively constituted by a subset of ultimately antecedent or *foundational* rights and by the subset consisting of all the rights successively derived from those foundational rights.

Now let us apply these conceptual truths about rights in general to the specific case of liberalism. At the core of liberalism are three normative claims—claims that are not always as carefully distinguished from each other as they should be. The first and, in a way, least exceptionable of these is that foundational or non-derivative moral rights are held by *all* individuals. The second claim, hardly more controversial, is that these rights are the *same* for everyone. Of course, there are several liberalisms and, correspondingly, several competing conceptions of what these rights are. What I have tried to show in that book is that only one foundational right, the right to equal negative freedom, can generate a set of rights that satisfies the compossibility condition I have just described.

It is liberalism's third claim that expresses what is most distinctive about it and that brings it into sharpest contrast with many other moral and political doctrines. And this is that no moral right may be permissibly overridden, regardless of how much social benefit might be achieved by doing so. There are numerous ways of characterizing this inviolable status that liberalism assigns to rights: Ronald Dworkin says that *rights are trumps*;[7] Robert Nozick sees them as *side-constraints*, that is, as restrictions on how we may permissibly go about pursuing our other values;[8] John Rawls assigns them *lexical primacy*, by which he means that all their demands, even otherwise trivial ones, must be satisfied prior to the satisfaction of any other demands, however weighty these others might be.[9] Yet another way of characterizing the liberal status of rights is to see them simply as *personal vetoes*. Whichever characterization we prefer, they all point to the same thing: namely, that each person has a set of claims on the conduct of other persons—a set of claims that must not be traded off by political decision-makers and must therefore be honoured irrespective of the cost of doing so.[10]

I suggested, just before, that the foundation of these claims, the basic moral right from which all our other moral rights are derived, is a right to equal freedom. In my book, I argue that this right immediately entails two other near-foundational rights which are construed, in a quasi-Lockean way, as rights to self-ownership and to an equal share of the value of natural resources. In effect, it is the exercise of these two rights that then serially generates all the various other moral rights we can have or, more precisely, all the mutually consistent moral rights we do have.

And it is not hard to see that many of the types of right implied by these two have a pretty direct bearing on some of the more salient aspects of nationalism. For it is from the right of self-ownership that liberalism infers such more familiar rights as those against murder and assault as well as rights to freedom of contract and association. And it is the right to natural resources that not only forms part of the basis of legitimate territorial claims but also, and interestingly, generates related requirements for international distributive justice, about which I will have more to say presently.

Because our main focus here is on territorial claims, I am not going to dwell for long on the ways in which the liberal right of self-ownership constrains the permissible pursuit of national interests. Most of these ways are well enough known already. Rights against murder and assault have immediate restrictive implications for the conduct of nations' military activities, many of which implications have long been explored in the literature on just wars and enshrined in various international conventions. Rights to freedom of contract pretty straightforwardly underwrite free trade and proscribe all manner of restrictions on it. Rights to freedom of association crucially entail rights to freedom of *dis*sociation; that is, they prohibit the kind of conscription implicit in Berlin Walls. And, just as they allow free emigration, they symmetrically prohibit national restrictions on immigration since, whatever social benefits are thought to be secured by such restrictions, they amount to violations of the rights of those citizens who are willing to take outsiders in. So in all these cases, political decision-makers—even *democratic* ones—are morally disempowered from enacting such measures by virtue of the fundamental rights that liberalism assigns to each person: rights that it construes as enjoying constitutional status in any legitimate legal system.

Which brings us to territorial claims. I think it is fair to say that territorial claims, though not the *sole* objects of nationalist preoccupation, have probably excited more of its passion than any other type of issue. To be sure, even if nations' territorial claims had everywhere and always been compossible, there would still be lots of other things for nationalists to be exercised about: the preservation of their language and culture, the prosperity of their economy and so forth. And many kinds of measure designed to advance these concerns are, as I have just indicated, not permitted under liberal principles. But perhaps the simplest and most encompassing measure deployed in behalf of these and other national concerns is, and always has been, the assertion of exclusive claims to territory, to portions of the earth's surface along with the supra- and subterranean spaces adjacent to them. Indeed, the assertion of such claims, if not always their recognition by others, is one of the essential criteria for distinguishing nations from other types of social group. And liberal principles have a very direct bearing on these claims.

The first and most important feature of this bearing is that, for liberalism, all legitimate group claims must be aggregations of—must be reducible without remainder to—the legitimate claims of individual persons. This means that a group's legitimate territorial claims can extend no further than the legitimate territorial holdings of its members or their agents. How do persons acquire legitimate titles to territory? Basically, there are two ways: first, by those titles being transferred to them voluntarily by the previous legitimate title-holders; but second and more fundamentally, by their staking claims to land that is not already claimed by others.

Now, readers of Locke and the voluminous literature exploring these Lockean arguments will be intimately acquainted with all the complexities implicit in that second stipulation. Locke himself explores the possibility of deriving claim-stakers' entitlements *solely* from their rights of self-ownership, suggesting that claim-staking consists in their investing some of their self-owned labour in portions of as-yet-unowned land. But even he acknowledges that this "first come, first served rule" cannot be the whole story on establishing legitimate land titles. (I will return to this problem presently.)

Yet for him, for liberals generally and perhaps for many others as well, it remains an important *part* of that story. So any piece of land currently right-fully belongs to whomever it has been transmitted by an unbroken series of vol-untary transfers originating in the person who first staked a claim to it. Any interruption of that pedigree, say by unredressed acts of conquest or expropria-tion, invalidates that current title no matter how innocently its current holder may have acquired it. And, needless to say, in our slowly liberalizing world of today, much applied philosophy literature and much litigation in American, East European, Australasian and other courts are deeply immersed in trying to figure out which current persons or groups are or are not in possession of legitimate titles to the land they claim on this basis. But however complex many of these enquiries have already proven to be—requiring, as they often do, massive amounts of historically remote data—those liberal principles do yield two rather concrete and highly topical inferences concerning nations' territorial entitlements.

The first of these is the endorsement of a right of *secession*. For, although Locke himself (for reasons that remain mysterious) balked at embracing this conclusion,[11] it is very clearly implied by his principles. That is, precisely because a nation's territory is legitimately composed of the real estate of its members, the decision of any of them to resign that membership and, as it were, to take their real estate with them is a decision that must be respected. Emigrants are not, under liberal principles, necessarily condemned to leave with only the shirts on their backs and whatever they can cram into their suit-cases or foreign bank accounts. Of course, nations may, if they choose, expel members, engage in certain forms of "ethnic cleansing", etc. But what they may not do is expropriate legitimate landowners or evict their tenants. Jurisdiction over land, like jurisdiction over persons, is a purely voluntary affair for consis-tent liberals and it is thus predicated on the agreement of all the parties con-cerned.

The second inference about national territorial entitlements, and the one that I personally find the more interesting of the two, engages issues of *international distributive justice*. I find it more interesting because, historically at least, liberalism has had conspicuously little to offer by way of a systematic account—one firmly anchored in its own basic premisses—of what wealth transfers some nations owe to others. Indeed it is a notorious feature of political theorizing in general that the questions it tends to address are posed at the level of polities taken separately, as if these were hermetically sealed units, with only occasional genuflections in the international direction when it comes to matters of trade and migration and war and peace. But the logical reach of basic liberal rights, although it certainly encompasses these matters as we have just seen, also extends well beyond them. Why? How?

I said previously that, even for Locke, the "first come, first served rule" is not the whole story on persons acquiring legitimate titles to as-yet-unowned land. This rule, you will recall, is derived by him from our near-foundational right of self-ownership. But that right is itself only one of the two types of right immediately implied by our most fundamental right, the right to equal freedom; the other one is a right to an equal share of natural resource values. Rights to equal freedom imply *both* of these rights, rather than only the first, in order to prohibit claim-stakers from engrossing too much and thereby leaving others with little or no freedom at all. Locke himself says that claim-stakers, in appropriating a piece of land, must leave "enough and as good" land for others.[12] But as many writers in the Lockean tradition have long appreciated, this "enough and as good" restriction is badly in need of some amplification if it is to sustain the freedom entitlements of countless persons who are generationally differentiated.

Accordingly, and again for reasons that would take too long to detail here, some of these writers have interpreted this restriction as a requirement that each person's entitlement, rather than being one in kind—an entitlement to literally an equal portion of land—is one to cash: that is, to an equal share of the *value* of land. This interpretation neatly accommodates the problem of generational differentiation and also takes account of the fact that, for a host of reasons, land values vary over time. The idea, then, is that landowners thereby owe, to each other person, an equal slice of the current site value of their property: that is, the gross value of that property *minus* the value of whatever labour-embodying improvements they and their predecessors may have made to it.[13] Hence the validity of their titles to that land vitally depends upon their payment of that debt.

This has immediate implications for what some nations justly owe to others. Liberalism's basic individual rights being ones of universal incidence, the equality of each person's land-value entitlement is necessarily *global* in scope. Everyone everywhere has a right to an equal share of the value of all land. To respect people's basic liberal rights, whether here or abroad, not only do we have to refrain from murdering or assaulting them, but also we must not withhold payment of their land-value entitlements.

Just what those entitlements amount to is obviously going to depend on how many people there are and what the current aggregate global value of land is. Neither of these magnitudes poses insuperable computational problems. We pretty much know, or can know, how numerous various populations are. And people who own or purchase pieces of real estate usually have a fairly shrewd idea of what those sites are worth. Evidently the ownership of an acre in the Sahara Desert is of a different value, and consequently attracts a different payment liability, from the ownership of an acre in downtown Manhattan or the heart of Tokyo. Similar things can be said about real estate in the Saudi oil fields, the Amazon rain forests, the Arctic tundra, the Iowa corn belt, the Bangladeshi coast and the City of London. No doubt the values of these sites tend to vary with such factors as technological change, population shifts and changing consumption patterns, as well as depletions of extractable resources and discoveries of new ones. But whatever relative variation there might be among these values, there is every good reason to suppose that their aggregate secular trend is unlikely to be downwards. Mark Twain was not giving his nephew unsound advice when he said: "Buy land, son; they're not making it any more."

Since nations' territories are aggregations of their members' real estate holdings, the validity of their territorial claims rests on the validity of those land titles. So nations wishing to sustain the legitimacy of their jurisdiction over these bits of real estate have to ensure that those titles retain their validity. And since states claim exclusive entitlement to the use of force in their societies, including the enforcement of debt payments, it falls to them to ensure that those land-value payment liabilities are met. To put it in a nutshell, liberal principles demand that *states pay rates.*

In my book, I describe the total revenue yielded by such payments as a *global fund.*[14] Each nation therefore has an equal *per capita* claim on this global fund. And its operation, we might reasonably speculate, would serve to establish a variety of benign incentive structures informing relations both within and between nations.[15] So I will conclude by briefly mentioning three of them.

First, the global impact of such a fund is bound to be strongly redistributive, since the differential incidence of its levies, in conjunction with the *per capita* parity of its disbursements, pretty much guarantees a substantial reduction in international (as well as national) economic inequalities. These international inequalities have always played a not unimportant role in generating high levels of demand for emigration. Under the regime of the global fund, poorer nations, being its net beneficiaries, would find fewer of their members leaving to seek their fortunes abroad. Second, the operation of such a fund might be expected to foster greater willingness to compromise in international boundary disputes (over land whose legitimate title-holders are difficult to identify) by attaching a price-tag to any instance of territorial acquisition or retention. And third, the existence of such a fund would give nations stronger *dis*incentives to engage in such odious practices as ethnic cleansing and forced expatriation, since their receipts from the fund would thereby decline with their loss of those members. Indeed, nations might well come to cherish each of their members all the more—to provide them each with a strong sense of social identity—for being sources of guaranteed income!

In short, the whole world might become a bit more liberal, both domestically and internationally. Now, wouldn't that be a Good Thing?[16]

Notes

1. O. O'Neill, "Magic Associations and Imperfect People", in B. Barry and R. Goodin, eds, *Free Movement* (Hemel Hempstead: Harvester Wheatsheaf, 1992), p. 118.

2. N. MacCormick, *Legal Right and Social Democracy* (Oxford: Oxford University Press, 1981), pp. 247–248.

3. E. Gellner, *Thought and Change* (London: Weidenfeld & Nicolson, 1971), p. 149.

4. "Unavoidably", in the sense that the only unconditional objection that the nationalist can offer to any counter-proposal (for a reversed differentiation, or none at all) is that it is contrary to *his/her* particular nation's interest.

5. Cf. H. Steiner, *An Essay on Rights* (Oxford: Blackwell, 1994), especially chapter 3.

6. That is, the set of physical components (spatio-temporal locations, material objects) involved in performing the obligatory action correlatively entailed by any right does not intersect with the corresponding set entailed by any other right. I describe this compossibility requirement as implying that all rights are *funded*.

7. R. Dworkin, "Is There a Right to Pornography?" *Oxford Journal of Legal Studies*, Vol. 1 (1981), pp. 177–212.

8. R. Nozick, *Anarchy, State and Utopia* (Oxford: Blackwell, 1974), pp. 28–33.

9. J. Rawls, *A Theory of Justice* (Oxford: Oxford University Press, 1972), pp. 42 ff.

10. These claims may, of course, be traded off by the persons vested with them: right-holders can *waive* their rights, thereby extinguishing the duties correlatively entailed by them.

11. J. Locke, *Two Treatises of Government*, ed. P. Laslett (Cambridge: Cambridge University Press, 1967), p. 364.

12. Ibid., pp. 306, 309, 310. That is, the individual right involved is the *negative* one, that no one else appropriate more than an equal portion of natural resources. J. Waldron, *The Right to Private Property* (Oxford: Oxford University Press, 1988), pp. 209–218, however denies that Locke actually intended this "enough and as good" formula as a restriction on just appropriation.

13. These values are conceived as periodized ones, that is, as the current *rental* value of the assets involved. The value of labour-embodying improvements is excluded from the calculation of this liability because persons' rights of self-ownership imply unencumbered rights to the fruits of their labour, i.e. provided landowners' liabilities have been met.

14. For reasons not germane to the concerns of this paper, the sources of the revenues constituting this global fund consist of *more* factors than only land values; cf. Steiner, *An Essay on Rights*, chapter 8.

15. Cf. N. Tideman, "Commons and Commonwealths", in R. Andelson, ed., *Commons without Tragedy* (London: Shepheard-Walwyn, 1991), for a more extended discussion of some of these incentive structures.

16. This chapter has benefited from the comments of Simon Caney, Tim Gray and Peter Jones. An earlier version appeared under the title "Liberalism and Nationalism" in *Analyse und Kritik*, Vol. 17 (1995).

10

Environmental Rights and National Sovereignty

Helen Batty and Tim Gray

Introduction

As we near the end of the twentieth century, one of the most pressing challenges facing humankind is that of environmental degradation. While the system of sovereign states divides the world into discrete entities with fixed boundaries, it is now widely recognized that we live in an ecosystem that is highly complex, interconnected and not respectful of such boundaries. The actions of one state may cause environmental deterioration in another state, or, alternatively, the actions of one state may contribute to patterns of global environmental change with adverse implications for all. Since the state has traditionally asserted a right both to national self-determination and to exploit its natural resources as it sees fit, it must be asked how far such rights are contributing to environmental deterioration and whether they should be limited by the assertion of moral claims to protect the environment.

In this chapter, we argue that this environmental predicament gives rise to international obligations which challenge some fundamental normative assumptions about national sovereignty. In particular, we examine the argument that there is a human right to an adequate environment which all states must recognize and guarantee, both domestically and internationally. The basis of that environmental right and its possible implications are the central issues discussed here.

The chapter develops as follows. First, we examine the justifications of national sovereignty and self-determination. Second, we consider the possible foundations of a moral claim to environmental protection and, since contemporary moral debate is dominated by the discourse of rights, we discuss the possibility of establishing this claim as the human right to an adequate environment and show that, although it is persuasive at first sight, any such environmental right is theoretically problematic. Finally, we conclude by suggesting that the language of rights is not appropriate to the environment and that, while there may be a *duty* to protect the environment, there is no corresponding *right* to an adequate environment.

Justifications for State Sovereignty

According to Krasner, "sovereignty is a system of political order based on territory", the defining principle of which is that "external actors are denied any authoritative powers within a given territory".[1] The principle of state sovereignty may be defended on three grounds. First, it may be justified on the grounds of the right to national self-determination. Since this right is closely connected with the possession of territorial land and the associated right to dispose of that land's natural resources, the right to national self-determination is particularly susceptible to challenge from environmental claims. The possession of territory is usually considered intrinsic to the definition of political communities. In the words of Gambles,

> The natural resources of the political community are constitutive of the community, which does not need to justify its possession of them . . . the political community and its territory are organically linked. The widespread notions of motherland and fatherland seem to confirm this link . . . the very concepts of diaspora and irredentism point to exceptions that prove the rule, signifying the powerful sense of deprivation, insecurity, and incompleteness felt by political communities who have lost their land. It is the separation of a political community from its territory which requires justification, not the opposite.[2]

Although an environmental right would not entail the separation of a political community from its territory, it would seriously undermine the right of the community freely to dispose of its territorial resources.

The right to national self-determination and the right to dispose of natural resources have been particularly emphasized in the post-colonial period. As Hurrell and Kingsbury note, "For many peoples of the post-colonial world, the achievement of statehood was the condition of political emancipation."[3] Significantly, the 1966 UN Covenants on Civil and Political Rights, and on Economic, Social and Cultural Rights, reinforce the concept of state sovereignty at the expense of the environment, declaring that "All peoples may, for their own ends, freely dispose of their natural wealth and resources."[4]

Yet the very notion of the nation-state seems inherently flawed in that few, if any, state boundaries coincide with those of single, coherent nations. Some nations, such as the Kurds, have no state, while many states, such as the United Kingdom, contain diverse nations. Thus, if the right to state autonomy were founded upon the right to national self-determination, most if not all states would fail the empirical test since there is no adequate "fit" between nation and state. There is a vast literature on this issue of national self-determination, making it unnecessary to pursue the debate here.

Moreover, even when state and nation coincide, it is by no means self-evident that the state "owns" the territory it occupies, together with all the resources within that territory. For example, the fact that North Sea oil is located within UK or Norwegian territorial waters is a matter of luck, and carries no moral right of ownership. Rather than belonging to these states, it could be argued that the oil belongs to the region as a whole or even to the world community.

The second justification for the right to national sovereignty is instrumental: that the maintenance of national sovereignty is vital for the continuation of peace between states. Unless the principle of national sovereignty is firmly upheld, it is claimed, states could invade other states on any pretext, and interstate conflict would become widespread. A new form of imperialism—in this case environmental or eco-imperialism—could occur. This fear has already been expressed by some Third World countries, who have accused the North of using environmental arguments as justification for interfering with their domestic affairs. This is said to have occurred either to prevent the South from competing with northern products (on grounds that cheaper southern exports are produced in environmentally damaging ways) or to ensure that the Third World continues to operate as a "sink" to absorb the global waste emitted by the North.

It is also held that the principle of state sovereignty maintains peace within states. Unless they are secure from external intervention, they will be vulnerable internally to groups that threaten to trigger external intervention to protect them. Environmental standards forced upon southern states by the international community could topple a regime that rests on fragile legitimacy. Intervention entails the violation of domestic authority and thereby undermines the legitimacy of a regime, and many southern states are acutely vulnerable to such international pressures. However, the claim that sovereignty is necessary to the maintenance of peace, both within and between states, seems to be undermined by the extent of inter- and intra-state war throughout the twentieth century. Far from promoting peace, the assertion of national sovereignty seems to have been the source of unprecedented conflict.

Moreover, even if it is empirically true that state sovereignty promotes international peace, how does this generate a moral right to state sovereignty? First, it confuses two different arguments: that it is a good thing if states are self-determining, and that states have a right to self-determination. Second, it presupposes that international stability is always of overriding moral value, but sometimes such stability may be purchased at the cost of violating more important values. For example, the policies towards the Kurds adopted by the states of Turkey, Iraq and Syria may help to secure stability, but they are morally pernicious policies.

The third justification for national sovereignty is based upon the notion of justice. Environmental intervention in southern states by northern states is held to be unjust because southern countries have been driven into environmentally harmful activities largely as a result of the North's hegemony and exploitation through its structural adjustment policies which have forced southern countries into monoculture and cash crops in order to pay foreign debts. Moreover, by far the greatest cause of past and present global environmental degradation has been the over-consumption of energy and resources of the northern countries. Southern countries argue that the North therefore has a moral duty (a) to provide compensation to the South for any environmental policies it seeks to persuade the South to adopt, and (b) to cut its own over-consumption patterns.

This argument for just compensation has been incorporated in several global environmental conventions—such as the Climate Change Convention and the Biodiversity Convention—to the extent that they require northern countries to transfer both funds and technology to the South to enable it to meet its obligations under the Conventions. Such agreements represent co-operative strategies between mutually respecting nation-states which are much more just than coercive strategies which undermine such respect. However, many northern states deny that they are solely responsible for parlous environmental conditions in the Third World, and argue with some justification that corrupt, incompetent and authoritarian regimes must share the blame for these conditions.

The Limits of Sovereignty

For some commentators, however, the concept of national sovereignty is a fiction. Camilleri and Falk, for instance, cite growing interdependence in the spheres of economics, technology, security and the environment as evidence of diminishing state sovereignty. They suggest that the authority of the state is being progressively undermined because it is unwilling or unable to deliver the goods, and as a consequence its legitimacy is being eroded. They convincingly portray sovereignty as both an impediment to action and a contributing cause of environmental problems. "A world comprised of sovereign states suggests a particular organisation of politics and treatment of nature. And whilst the official rationale for that organisation may be couched in terms of human needs, a sharp tension is developing between this method of addressing human needs and the understanding of the needs and organisation of the biosphere."[5]

The notion of state sovereignty as a moral good, then, is not without its critics. Increasingly, claims are being made that "sovereignty is no longer sovereign, the world has outgrown it. The exclusivity and inviolability of state sovereignty are increasingly mocked by global interdependence."[6] The claims of critics such as Camilleri and Falk may be empirically based, but they nevertheless demand a reassessment of the normative underpinnings of the notion of sovereignty. We must now turn to the concept of an environmental right: how far does it rest on grounds that are morally superior to those of state sovereignty?

The Concept of an Environmental Right

Environmental degradation poses a grave threat to the quality—and, ultimately, the continuation—of human life. Although some environmental problems are localized and can therefore be addressed within the boundaries of the nation-state, many of the more urgent problems are transnational or global in nature. Significant problems result from the use of resources that are not confined within territorial boundaries, such as the polar land mass, the oceans, the air and the stratosphere. The global commons cannot always be subject to the imposition of artificial boundaries and thus they necessarily stand outside the jurisdiction of national rights. Even the use of resources that are clearly demarcated within boundaries, such as the Amazonian rainforest, are now recognized to have consequences that transgress those national boundaries. This raises the issue of whether individuals are entitled to assert a right to protect themselves against the actions of other nationals which are causing damage to their environment and thereby threatening their personal health and well-being. If such a right could be justified, it would pose a direct threat to sovereignty, since the assertion of such rights of citizens in one state could challenge the way in which another state was using or abusing its natural resources.

The concept of an environmental right has been established in a number of state constitutions. For example, "in the late 1960s, several [American] states amended their constitutions to affirm the 'environmental rights' of their citizens, which include the right to a natural and clean environment".[7] Section 27 of chapter 3 of the Constitution of South Africa states that "every person shall have the right to an environment which is not detrimental to his or her health or well-being".[8] That such rights have found their way into state constitutions is indicative of the perceived seriousness of environmental degradation in the latter part of the twentieth century. However, these are rights that appear to be held by the citizen against his or her own state, and which therefore do not address the issue of transnational environmental problems and the possible limits of national self-determination. The notion of a *universal* human right to an adequate environment, however, was articulated in the Stockholm Declaration on the Human Environment in 1972, the first principle of which stated that "Man has the fundamental right to freedom, equality and adequate conditions of life, in an environment of a quality that permits a life of dignity and well being."[9] This suggests that people have environmental rights in virtue of being human rather than in virtue of being citizens of particular states. A similar principle appeared in the Brundtland Commission Report in its summary of proposed local principles for environmental protection: "All human beings have the fundamental right to an environment adequate for their health and well-being."[10]

The notion of an environmental right raises a number of vexed issues. What, for example, does it entitle the right-holder to? Is the right-holder necessarily an individual, or can there be group environmental rights?[11] If there are environmental rights, who is to be accountable for their implementation? (The complex nature of environmental degradation clearly entails problems for the proof of environmental harm and the location of its source.) Most importantly, can an environmental right be held to trump the right of a nation to make use of its own resources? And is the language of rights the most appropriate conceptual language to employ in addressing this problem? Or can we employ some other kind of moral claim by which to limit the right to national self-determination with regard to the exploitation of natural resources, and thereby protect the environment?

Let us consider seven objections to the idea of an environmental right.

First, it is not apparent upon what philosophical basis these assertions of an environmental right are founded. It clearly differs from the normal conception of a human right in that it is a right to a shared resource. Does it, then, require a fresh philosophical foundation, or does it share that of human rights in general? Can the standard justifications for human rights be applied to the environment?

Although we will not here enter into a discussion of whether universal human rights are in themselves justifiable, it is worth briefly considering a few of the justifications most frequently given, and whether the concept of an environmental right can be justified on similar grounds. The argument from human worth or dignity could, for example, be successfully employed, since, without an adequate environment in which to live and work, individuals are deprived of their dignity and self-esteem. However, humans can adapt to almost any environment, and thus an adequate environment is not necessarily a crucial aspect of an individual's self-worth, except in the most dire circumstances of acute environmental degradation.

The argument from self-ownership to environmental rights—that since I own myself I possess the right not to have my living environment controlled by others—seems inappropriate in that (deep green) environmentalism is distinguished by its opposition to all concepts of ownership of resources. If I have a right to a clean environment, it is not—as Locke might maintain—because I own myself, and therefore own things with which I mix my labour. Even if I own myself, I do not own my environment. Indeed, for deep greens, it is precisely because people do not own their environment that they are not permitted to despoil it.

The argument from need might be invoked in support of an environmental right. The most basic of human needs—air, food and water—are dependent upon an adequate environment, and without these humans cannot survive. Thus, an adequate environment, too, is a fundamental human need. However, while the concept of need clearly carries a greater moral force than, say, the concept of desire, it may be an insufficiently discriminating concept to generate a right. The concept of need begs the questions, how much environmental protection does one need, and how adequate is adequate? Without an answer to questions such as these, as Jones says, the assertion of rights to such goods becomes mere rhetoric. There is also the problem of how needs have arisen; if, for example, they are perceived to have been self-induced, this affects our moral response to that need.[12] It may be that an environment is a basic good yet not a basic right.

The concept of rights based upon need also raises the problem of the assignability of duties: just who is responsible for meeting those needs and fulfilling those rights? Indeed, as Jones argues, needs-based rights may not be duty-imposing at all. Such rights can be rights to and over a set of resources rather than rights "against" others. "In so far as people have a right to a set of resources which are essential for meeting their needs, needs-based redistribution should be seen as a means by which people are allocated the resources to which they are entitled and not as a process in which some perform duties of (legally coerced) giving out of deference to the needs of others."[13]

An argument from Rawls's "original position" has been used by Beitz to derive an environmental right. Beitz in his *Political Theory and International Relations* attempts to modify the Rawlsian conception of domestic justice to argue for a global principle of distributive justice. Rawls seems to assume that the provision of primary goods can be met within the state, and that his principles of justice need apply only within this political boundary. Contractors in the original position are assumed to be members of a sovereign state, and it is as citizens of a state that they choose their principles of justice. This, however, assumes that the state is the most appropriate unit within which to draw up a (hypothetical) contract. Yet, given the interdependent nature of environmental problems—and the fact that the distribution of natural resources is "arbitrary from the moral point of view"—it would seem appropriate for the contractors to want to formulate principles of international distributive justice. Thus, the relevant moral community to which a theory of justice applied would be the entire human race and that would result in a radical alteration in the demands of Rawls's difference principle.[14]

Beitz's notion of international distributive justice raises the question of intervention with sovereign states to protect environmental rights. Beitz believes that the non-intervention principle is not an "amoral" principle, but is rooted in a substantive conception of how the world should be arranged: that is, as a system of sovereign states. According to Beitz's conception of global distributive justice, however, there are no compelling reasons to abstain from judgements regarding the justice of the domestic political and economic institutions of others, since the principle of national self-determination is not primary: principles of justice are seen to apply primarily to the world as a whole and then derivatively to states. Beitz holds that the principle of non-intervention does not apply equally to all states, but is dependent on the justice of domestic institutions: if domestic institutions are not just, then intervention may be justified.[15] Since Beitz's account of international distributive justice includes the benefits gained from natural resources as well as those gained from social co-operation, it suggests that intervention might be justified if grave environmental injustice has occurred.

One difficulty with Beitz's argument is that it does not make clear how a grave environmental injustice is to be defined. If an environmental right is to be asserted, it must be capable of definition, if only in order to determine in what circumstances it could be violated. Beitz's argument does not provide that definition. Another difficulty is that the Rawlsian original position test might not produce agreement on an environmental right. If the original "contractors" pondered the likelihood of their belonging to a Third World country, they might well choose a developmental right rather than an environmental right, since their aversion to poverty could be greater than their aversion to a damaged environment.

The second objection to the idea of an environmental right is that, even if we can find an adequate justification for such a right, the right itself may be otiose. It may be argued that the concept of a human right to an adequate environment is simply redundant, in that an adequate environment will be virtually guaranteed if all existing human rights are secured. Alternatively, the objection might be that, if not all the existing human rights are secured, adding to them the idea of an environmental right will be useless, since it will never be prioritized above any of the conventional human rights. As Aiken rhetorically asks, is it

> a stringent enough right ... to ... carry some weight in the forum of conflicting claims? Could it be made strong enough to override rights to procreate, rights to own and use property in certain ways, economic "freedom" rights ...? Could public support for this right reach the intensity required to pressure governments into adopting policies which enforce this right?[16]

The third objection poses the question, is the proposed environmental right a liberty right or a welfare right? A human right to an adequate environment could demand either negative or positive action from the duty-bearer. It could, for instance, demand that a certain party should abstain from polluting behaviour or, alternatively, that it should actively pursue a course of action that will limit or correct environmental damage. As Aiken, asks, "Is such a right a welfare right (for example, an entitlement to safe water which may require treatment of naturally contaminated water) or a liberty right (for example, your right is violated only if other responsible agents knowingly pollute your drinking water)?"[17]

In answer to this question, we suggest that the concept of an environmental right would be primarily negative in that it would require humans to abstain from actions that damage the natural environment (and, ultimately, human life). However, given the degree of environmental degradation that presently exists, a negative claim-right would not, in many cases, be sufficient to provide for an adequate environment: rivers and seas are already polluted and lands have been deforested and subject to desertification. Those persons who are adversely affected by such environmental damage may be said to have already had their negative claim-right to an adequate environment violated. Consequently, they may be said to hold a *corrective* positive-claim right: that is, they hold a right that demands positive action by others to correct the infringement of their negative claim-right and to restore the environment to its former unviolated condition.

Whether or not the duty to fulfil a positive claim-right would fall upon the party that has violated the negative claim-right is however debatable. If the polluter-pays principle were to apply, this would indeed be the case, since the culprit is held directly liable. However, it is possible that some other body, such as a local or regional authority, may have to carry out the corrective procedure, particularly if those responsible for the infringement are not easily identifiable.

The notion of a *corrective* positive claim-right seems to be a particularly notable feature of an environmental right. Normally the infringement of a right creates a right to compensation: that is, a right to receive a good that is of comparable value to the good that is being compensated. In the case of the environment, it is unlikely that the damage done could be personally rectified to the individual or individuals whose right has been violated, and thus it would be pointless to award compensatory money to this end—as, for instance, might occur in the case of a car accident. It is more likely that either the culprit(s) must rectify the environmental damage they have caused, or that funding would be provided for some regional authority for the same purpose.

It is significant that this concept of compensatory action suggests that there is some recognition of inherent worth in the environment itself, for it demands that nature must be restored and protected, not merely that humans must be compensated. Of course it might be possible to provide as compensation an adequate human environment that is highly artificial—rather than "natural"—yet we may suppose that most people would consider this to be unacceptable. A satisfactory human environmental right, then, seeks to protect and preserve nature itself. This suggests that a human environmental right must incorporate the aesthetic or spiritual needs of human beings within its concept of what is "adequate"; or, somewhat paradoxically, that we are perhaps concerned with something more than a human right, in that there is some recognition of intrinsic value in the natural environment. This would entail some other moral imperative in order effectively to limit environmental degradation, since severe and irrevocable harm can be done to the environment without posing a direct threat to human life or transgressing a human environmental right.

The fourth objection is that the concept of an environmental right is further complicated by the problem of specificity. Jones holds that we cannot make duties to "unassignable individuals"—"duties directed at some diffuse public benefit"—as creative of rights,[18] yet most (anthropocentric) environmental protection seeks to benefit unassignable individuals. For example, it would be problematic to specify which particular individuals or groups of individuals were having their environmental right violated by the manufacture and use of CFCs, since the effects of ozone depletion are diffuse. Similarly, the effects of global warming are difficult to specify and may even advantage rather than disadvantage some groups or nations, since a warmer climate may bring new and better agricultural yields.

It may be said, however, that we have a moral obligation to limit the levels of CO_2 emissions because this will benefit humanity—by reducing the risk of global climate change—whereas not to do so could be severely harmful to humanity. Thus, while we may have a duty to refrain from environmentally damaging behaviour, these duties are often " 'due from' specific individuals without being 'due to' specific individuals",[19] and therefore will not necessarily give rise to rights. A question that needs to be addressed, then, is whether the duty to not damage the environment is "a duty to benefit individuals severally . . . or whether it is a duty designed to benefit individuals only as members of an undifferentiated collectivity".[20]

Moreover, the concept of an environmental right also lacks specificity in relation to the duty-bearers. For example, a group of citizens may assert a right to be protected from the consequences of a thinning ozone layer, but against whom is such a right held? Since those who contribute to the depletion of the ozone are manifold, and no discrete entity can be identified as being wholly responsible, it may not seem feasible to ascribe a right that entails correlative duties.

It seems, therefore, that a number of environmental problems are not sufficiently specific to warrant the assertion of a right. Yet, with regard to the problem of acid rain, for instance, both the right-holders and the duty-bearers are potentially assignable; thus, it may be possible to identify those industries in Britain that produce acid rain, and those in Scandinavia that are adversely affected by it. We must, therefore, differentiate between different types of environmental problem; some are amenable to the assertion of a right, others are clearly not, and in the latter cases some other type of moral claim must be asserted in order to limit the exploitation of national resources.

The fifth objection is that the idea of an environmental right raises issues relating to future generations. Much of the concern surrounding contemporary environmental degradation is focused on what the consequences of such degradation may be *in the future*. Thus, for example, we are familiar with scientific predictions as to the likelihood of rising global temperatures in the twenty-first century, and the adverse consequences these would have for many peoples. Such projections of future environmental scenarios raise the question of whether those generations of the future that are likely to suffer as a result of our environmentally significant behaviour in the present can be said to have a right which we have a duty to uphold. This is an issue that may be peculiarly relevant to an environmental right, since the denial of, say, political rights to one generation does not necessarily entail its denial to the next generation, yet the denial of an adequate environment to one generation could jeopardize its adequacy for ever.

The question of whether a member of a future generation can be deemed a holder of a right is clearly determined by our understanding of what "rights" are.[21] For those, like Steiner, who maintain that rights must entail choice, beings who are unable to exercise choice—including animals, infants, the dead and the unborn—cannot be said to have rights.[22] A benefit theory of rights, on the other hand, allows that future generations can have rights, since a right can be held by anyone who is thought capable of benefiting.[23] Since future generations can clearly be harmed by the way in which we currently treat the environment, so too would they benefit by our limiting the current extent of degradation, and thus it could be argued that the unborn do indeed possess the right to an adequate environment. Certainly, if the concept of an environmental right does not encompass protection of the environment for future generations, it would appear to be an inadequate concept to employ to safeguard the environment. There must surely be some kind of moral duty upon present generations to consider the consequences of their present actions for future people and to modify their behaviour accordingly. This point is clearly made by Derek Parfit:

Suppose that I leave some broken glass in the undergrowth of a wood. A hundred years later this glass wounds a child. My act harms this child. If I had safely buried the glass, this child would have walked through the wood unharmed. Does it make a moral difference that the child whom I harm does not now exist? On one view, moral principles cover only the people who can *reciprocate*, or harm and benefit each other. If I cannot be harmed or benefited by this child, as we can plausibly suppose, the harm that I cause this child has no moral importance. I assume that we should reject this view .

. . Remoteness in time has, in itself, no more significance than remoteness in space.[24]

Even if future generations can be said to be holders of rights, how many future generations must we consider? Rawls in his *A Theory of Justice* argues that the contractors in the original position, as representatives of family lines, would select a "just savings principle" which would restrict present persons' levels of consumption in order to provide for the next generation. However, Rawls's just savings principle is inadequate as an environmental ethic, since many contemporary actions of environmental significance, such as the dumping of nuclear waste, will have consequences that will extend much further into the future than merely the next generation. In the evocative words of Myers, "Were environmental problems to strike us like a heart attack, we would rush our ecosystems into intensive-care units and have them restored. Instead they are like a cancer, quietly undercutting our foundations, unseen and unresisted, until they eventually burst forth with deep damage all too apparent."[25]

This "problem of temporal distance", as Norton calls it,[26] poses a significant challenge to the concept of an environmental right. If one does not allow that future generations can be holders of rights, then neither future generations nor the environment itself will be adequately protected by an environmental right. Yet if one does allow that future generations can be holders of rights, "there seems no way to avoid expanding the moral reference class on and on to a bewilderingly endless and indefinitely expanding class of claimants", and ultimately, "present human life comes under attack".[27]

There is also the issue of gauging the relative value of resources for different generations. For instance, we may curb our use of finite fossil fuels in order that they may service future generations for longer; yet it may be that in the future an efficient form of alternative energy will be harnessed and that fossil fuels will not be as vital a resource for future generations as they are for the contemporary world. Similarly, a new way of disposing of hazardous waste more efficiently may be invented, rendering present efforts to deal with it largely redundant. However, Luper-Foy argues that

> it is a reasonable guess that resources which we want will always be wanted, and pollutants which we deplore will always be deplored, though not necessarily with the same intensity or for the same reasons as before . . . The upshot is that we do not need much information about the future to know that our descendants would want as large as possible a share of the world's natural resources and as low a rate of pollution as possible.[28]

The sixth objection to be considered is that the concept of an environmental right raises the issue of group rights. Although the environment is a shared resource and it is therefore likely that individuals will be asserting their right to an adequate environment together with other individuals who are similarly affected—i.e. as members of a group—it seems problematic to ascribe rights to groups. The collection of individuals who are asserting their environmental rights will not necessarily comprise a single integral entity—unlike a religious community, for example—and "a group can be conceived as possessing rights *qua* group only if it is conceived as a single unified entity".[29] Rather, it seems likely that a group asserting its environmental rights would be an *ad hoc* collection of individuals, brought into (perhaps temporary) association through the environmental circumstances in which they find themselves. However, it may be that discrete entities, such as nations or cultural groups, seek to assert an environmental right:—should we then ascribe to them a *group* right? This does not seem feasible in that the formation of the group is merely contingent upon adverse environmental conditions. Although the Norwegian nation may suffer the effects of acid rain caused by Britain, the fact that it is Norwegian is not in itself significant. The question arises, then, can all Norwegians claim compensation from Britain, or only those who can demonstrate direct personal damage?

The seventh and final objection is that the concept of an environmental right raises the practical question of what, if any, action should be taken if a state fails to fulfil its obligation to secure this right. Does an environmental right carry sufficient moral weight to warrant intervention in the affairs of another state? Even if we do consider an environmental right to hold the status of a universal human right, we must recognize that, to date, the record of interventions in states to protect other human rights is not encouraging. As Krasner points out, "states have been reluctant to accuse other states of human rights violations because of the danger that their own sovereign control would be undermined".[30] Even if we can establish a convincing basis for an environmental right, therefore, can we reasonably expect states to enforce it against one another? It might be argued that sanctions (such as trade boycotts) could be enforced against recalcitrant states, and that such sanctions have succeeded in reversing human rights violations (e.g. in South Africa). But in the case of environmental rights, would not such measures carry the risk of further environmental damage?

Conclusion

Many of the above arguments raise the question of whether the language of rights is appropriate in relation to the environment. The language of rights has become the lingua franca of contemporary moral debate, for understandable reasons. As Jones points out, "In coming to think of these things as rights, we shift them out of the realm of the merely desirable and into the domain of the morally essential. It is not surprising therefore that people have taken so readily to expressing their deepest concerns in terms of rights."[31] But we have seen that the notion of an environmental right is highly problematic, especially with regard to environmental problems which have diffuse causes and effects. While this cannot render such problems less significant, it does suggest that the language of rights may not be wholly appropriate to the challenges posed by environmental degradation. And, given the gravity of such challenges, this in turn suggests that we should perhaps reconsider our reliance upon the notion of rights. Perhaps, rather than questioning whether the right to national self-determination can be limited by the human right to an adequate environment, we should question our reliance upon the language of rights itself and broaden the discourse of moral debate beyond the realm of rights.

Such a broadening of the discourse could take either an anthropocentric or a non-anthropocentric form. The anthropocentric form would take us beyond a conception of rights, which is individualistic and atomistic, towards a conception of duties, which emphasizes community and interdependence. As Aiken notes,

> Senator Albert Gore wondered if the cause of Americans' failure to even recognise that there is "a crisis facing the global environment" might not be "because we have reduced our ability to recognise wrongs to those categories which are reserved to describe transgressions against individual rights". Maybe, he suggests, we need a more relational or communitarian, albeit humanistic, moral theory which recognises responsibilities without requiring a reduction to rights claims.[32]

The non-anthropocentric form would embrace the theoretical paradigm of deep green philosophy, and take us beyond the anthropocentric realm of human rights to consider whether nature herself can be said to have intrinsic value. Here the language of rights seems particularly redundant. A deep green theorist, Robyn Eckersley, has recently asserted that, while there is "no a priori reason why legal rights cannot be ascribed to nonhuman entities", nevertheless, this "is neither necessary nor ultimately desirable".[33] To declare a river or a plant to be a right-holder seems absurd, especially—as Eckersley points out—if one endorses "a *contractarian* notion of rights, whereby a right must be accompanied by a correlative duty".[34] Even if we employ a non-contractarian theory of rights which does not necessarily entail reciprocal duties,

> there is still something strained and ungainly in the attempt to extend to the nonhuman world political concepts that have been especially tailored over many centuries to protect *human* interests. This highlights the need to search for simpler and more elegant ways of enabling the flourishing of a rich and diverse nonhuman world without resorting to the extension to the nonhuman realm of peculiarly *human* political and legal models of justice, equality, and rights.[35]

The notion that there is a right to an adequate environment is thus highly anthropocentric: that is, it endorses "the belief that there is a clear and morally relevant dividing line between humankind and the rest of nature, that humankind is the only or principal source of value and meaning in the world, and that nonhuman nature is there for no other purpose but to serve humankind".[36] If we reject such anthropocentrism, then we must reject the idea of an environmental right. However, this does not entail that we must abandon any duty towards the environment: on the contrary, it may enhance that duty, by indicating where the responsibility lies. The concept of a right to an adequate environment tends to highlight the duties of *others* to provide *us* with an adequate environment—i.e. it shifts the onus of responsibility elsewhere. But the concept of a duty to care for the environment emphasizes the fact that the responsibility lies with ourselves. We each must take responsibility for our own actions and their environmentally significant consequences.

This emphasis on our duty towards, rather than our right to, the environment reflects the perspective of deep (or transpersonal) ecology, which seeks to contribute to "the cultivation of a new worldview, a new culture and character, and new political horizons that are appropriate to our times".[37] On this view, we have duties and obligations to recognize and preserve that which has inherent value, and to prioritize giving and interconnectedness over claiming and independence. While such human duties do not currently possess the moral standing of human rights, they seem to be more appropriate to the issues of international environmental obligations. In short, it is more convincing to argue that we all have a moral duty to care for the environment than to claim that we each have a human right to have the environment protected for us. In relation to the environment, the language of duties is more appropriate than the language of rights, since the environment is more of an ethical than a jurisprudential issue.

Forsaking the language of rights for the language of duties, our final conclusion is that the apparent conflict of values between state sovereignty and the right to an adequate environment is misconceived. The truth is that state sovereignty is defensible only on condition that it is consistent with principles of justice, and that principles of justice include due respect for the environment. In short, we have a duty to uphold the state, provided the state fulfils its duty to protect the environment.[38]

Notes

1. S. D. Krasner, "Sovereignty, Regimes and Human Rights", in V. Rittberger and P. Meyer, eds, *Regime Theory and International Relations* (Oxford: Clarendon Press, 1993), p. 142.

2. I. Gambles, "Global Distributive Justice: Rawls, Realism and the Priority of the Political Community" (unpublished paper delivered at the British International Studies Association Conference, Newcastle upon Tyne, December 1990), pp. 40–41.

3. A. Hurrell and B. Kingsbury, *The International Politics of the Environment* (Oxford: Clarendon Press, 1992), p. 7.

4. W. Aiken, "Human Rights in an Ecological Era", *Environmental Values*, Vol. 1, No. 3 (1992), p. 193.

5. J. A. Camilleri and J. Falk, *The End of Sovereignty? The Politics of a Shrinking and Fragmenting World* (Aldershot: Edward Elgar, 1992), p. 195.

6. J. Chopra and T. G. Weiss, "Sovereignty is no Longer Sacrosanct: Codifying Humanitarian Intervention", *Ethics and International Affairs* , Vol. 6 (1992), p. 104.

7. J. P. Hays, *Beauty, Health, and Permanence: Environmental Polices in the US, 1955–85*, (Cambridge and New York: Cambridge University Press, 1987), p. 485.

8. In T. Allen, "National Perspectives on the Environment and Fundamental Rights" (unpublished paper), pp. 1–2.

9. Brundtland Commission Report, *Our Common Future* (Oxford: Oxford University Press, 1987), p. 330.

10. Ibid., p. 348.

11. Allen, "National Perspectives on the Environment and Fundamental Rights", pp. 5–6.

12. P. Jones, *Rights* (Basingstoke: Macmillan, 1994), p. 156.

13. Ibid., p. 155.

14. Ibid., pp. 101–106.

15. C. Beitz, *Political Theory and International Relations,* (Princeton: Princeton University Press, 1979), p. 92.

16. Aiken, "Human Rights in an Ecological Era", p. 200.

17. Ibid., p. 195.

18. Jones, *Rights*, p. 28.

19. Ibid.

20. Ibid.

21. Ibid., p. 67.

22. H. Steiner, *An Essay on Rights* (Oxford: Blackwell, 1994).

23. Jones, *Rights*, pp. 67–68.

24. D. Parfit, "Reasons and Persons", quoted in Steiner, *Essay on Rights*, p. 59.

25. N. Myers, *Ultimate Security: The Environmental Basis of Political Stability* (New York: W.W. Norton, 1993), p. 28.

26. B. G. Norton, "Environmental Ethics and the Rights of Future Generations", *Environmental Ethics*, Vol. 4, No. 4 (1982), p. 332.

27. Ibid., p. 333.

28. S. Luper-Foy, "Justice and Natural Resources", *Environmental Values*, Vol. 1 (1992), p. 56.

29. Jones, *Rights*, p. 183.

30. Krasner, "Sovereignty, Regimes and Human Rights", in Rittberger and Volker, *Regime Theory and International Relations*, p. 164.

31. Jones, *Rights*, p. 4.

32. Aiken, "Human Rights in an Ecological Era", p. 196.

33. R. Eckersley, *Environmentalism and Political Theory: Towards an Ecocentric Approach* (London: UCL Press, 1992), p. 57.

34. Ibid., p. 58.

35. Ibid.

36. Ibid., p. 51.

37. Ibid., p. 63.

38. We are grateful to Simon Caney and Peter Jones for their helpful comments on an earlier draft of this chapter.

11

Cultural Pluralism, Universal Principles and International Relations Theory

Chris Brown

Introduction

The notion that there is a potential conflict between universal and particularist principles in the normative grounding of relations between political communities is well established in the literatures of political theory and international relations theory, and in the practices of international society. Andrew Linklater has traced the ways in which thinking about the obligations that individuals have in their capacities as "men" as opposed to the obligations they have as members of particular communities—"citizens"—evolved from the medieval period, through the writings of the international lawyers to the seminal contributions of Kant and Hegel.[1] Others have carried the story through to the present using Kantian and Hegelian ideas as devices for structuring the debate.[2] Post-Rawlsian writing on justice has addressed the issue extensively, partly because of a lack of satisfaction with the way in which Rawls himself handled the matter.[3] Recent work on "duties beyond borders" addresses similar themes.[4] And, as Mervyn Frost has demonstrated, the "settled norms" of international society contain an inbuilt tension between the universal and the particular.[5]

However, a great deal of this literature has assumed that the contest between the universal and the particular takes place in a context where dramatic cultural differences are not particularly relevant. The thinking referred to above is thinking generated in a European context, and for most of the last half millennium Europeans have been in a position to think about these issues without too much need to take into account large-scale cultural differences.[6] Europeans (and their descendants in the Americas, Africa and Australasia) have, of course, frequently come into contact with non-Europeans, but have been in a position to regulate that contact on their own terms, either via conquest and, in extremis, genocide, or by the imposition of their own standards, if necessary by force—as with the notion of "standards of civilisation".[7] For this reason, the contest between universal and particularistic principles has been cast, for the most part, in terms that assume that what is at stake is essentially the degree to which it is morally acceptable that state policy should reflect the self-interest of the community/state rather than the general interest of mankind—the further assumption being that there is at least a potential for conflict here, but no particular problem in seeing these two conceptions of interest as commensurable. Cosmopolitan writers have argued that the frame of reference ought to be universal interests, while others have made the case for the primacy of the national interest, but on neither side has the possibility that communities might embody different and fundamentally incommensurable conceptions of the good received much attention.

Changes in the world over the past half-century suggest that this neglect is no longer satisfactory. In this period we have experienced the end of Empire and of what K. M. Panikkar refers to as the "Vasco Da Gama Epoch" of Asian history.[8] It is, clearly, still the case that many of the institutions and norms of international society—beginning with the most basic institution, the territorial state—reflect the European origins of the system, but it is equally clear that it can no longer be assumed that these institutions and norms are compatible with those prevailing in the domestic societies that collectively make up this wider society.[9] In the immediate post-colonial era it may have been the case that elites in the non-European world still took many of their political ideas from European sources, but this is clearly no longer something that can be taken for granted. The reassertion of non-European ideas in the world of Islam, in India, in the Confucian societies of the East and the "tribal" societies of Africa seems to be a consistent feature of contemporary world politics. This is not to suggest that the older politics of universal and particular has disappeared: clearly it has not, and in such forms as the debate over international distributive justice, this older politics continues without any necessary reference to cultural concerns. Instead, what we have here is a new factor overlaying rather than replacing previous debates, which, of course, makes things even more complicated.

These last sentences contain a number of generalizations about cultural pluralism which clearly might be considered to require more in the way of justification than they have been given. However, I do not propose to offer such justification because to do so would require more space than is available. Instead, I propose simply to assume that cultural pluralism is a fact about contemporary international relations, and to ask what the implications of this fact are. The reason I adopt this procedure is because most of those who appear to deny the fact of cultural pluralism are actually, in practice, denying *not* the fact of cultural pluralism but rather its relevance to normative international relations theory. Since, as will be apparent, it is perfectly possible to make this latter denial while accepting that cultural pluralism is a real feature of contemporary world society, there is no great need to investigate in detail the existence of the problem.[10] What, then, are the implications of cultural pluralism? Put differently, how might normative international relations theory cope with cultural pluralism? I suggest there are a number of possibilities here, ranging from an argument for a morally acceptable version of cultural imperialism to a postmodern celebration of relativism and difference. The rest of these chapters will examine these possibilities.

Cultural Co-existence and the Norms of International Society

The first approach that merits consideration denies relevance to cultural pluralism on the grounds that we have available in the norms of international society a set of principles which are not culturally specific, but, on the contrary, offer a basis for co-existence between states and cultures. This approach draws some sustenance from the so-called "English School" of international theory which has always combined a rejection of realist amoralism in international relations with an insistence on the importance of allowing states to develop in their own ways.[11] It also has some affinities with the approach to international justice adopted by Rawls in *A Theory of Justice* in so far as it stresses procedural rather than substantive concerns.[12] However, the English School has a tendency to bring into play "the traditions of Europe" at key moments of the argument and is not perhaps the ideal source for an approach to cultural pluralism, while Rawls is equally restrictive in his concerns, at least in his earlier formulations.[13] Instead, the best source for this approach is, I believe, the theory of international society developed by Terry Nardin.[14] Nardin's approach is based on a distinction elaborated by Michael Oakeshott.[15] In his original argument, Oakeshott distinguishes between "enterprise" and "civil" association, the former being essentially voluntary and non-political, the latter being concerned with the general arrangements of a society and the only true form of a political association. Nardin takes from this the idea that civil association is the only form of association compatible with freedom of the individual and translates this into an account of international society which guarantees the individuality of the states of which it is composed. International society works as a "practical association"—renamed because "civil" has inappropriate connotations and because of the importance of practices of international society such as diplomacy and international law—but fails as a "purposive" association because the members of international society cannot be presumed to share any purposes other than those required to co-exist in peace and (procedural) justice.[16] There is a major role for purposive associations internationally, exemplified in bodies such as the GATT, NATO and the EU, but membership of such associations is voluntary. There is no requirement that states *qua* states must be members of these institutions, but all states that wish to be considered as such must abide by the practices of international society.

Pluralism is the key value here; as Nardin expresses the point, international society as a practical association is

> an association of independent and diverse political communities, each devoted to its own ends, and its own conception of the good. The common good of this inclusive community resides not in the ends that some, or at times even most, of its members may wish collectively to pursue but in the values of justice, peace, security and co-existence, which can only be enjoyed through participation in a common body of authoritative practices.[17]

As a matter of fact, these authoritative practices originated in the European state system, but matters of origin are of no significance here. Since the practices in question do not presuppose any particular conception of the good, there is no reason to be concerned by their origins. Potential clashes between the universal and the particular can be avoided so long as the universal element in the system is restricted to those practices that presume nothing other than a commitment to the values listed above. In principle, cultural pluralism and relativism do not pose a difficulty to international society. On the contrary, the constitutive rules of international society presuppose that there will be such pluralism, although it should be noted that Nardin writes of "states" and "political communities" and not, generally, of cultures; there is clearly a potential problem here, since the state/culture fit is obviously in many cases non-existent.

Nardin's approach is generally fruitful but not problem-free. Two types of problem seem clear. In the first place, the idea that states will respect the boundaries between practical and purposive associations seems implausible. A number of different kinds of "purposive" universalizing tendencies are clearly present in the system and seem unlikely to disappear. The (Western-led) movement to establish "international human rights" as part of the practices of international society clearly involves a blurring of the practical/purposive distinction.[18] The (Third-World-led) demand for a New International Economic Order involves the idea that the world ought to be engaged in a project to eliminate poverty, which, equally, is clearly not a requirement of practical association.[19] There is a general point here. States that take part in universal organizations such as the United Nations are always going to use these bodies to pursue their political ends, and it is unlikely that they will be open to the argument that by so doing they are committing some kind of philosophical error. Much the same point has been made with respect to the original Oakeshottian notion of civil association—the notion of politics it espouses is not one that appeals to the citizens involved, who insist on attempting to use what they take to be political means to pursue ends which Oakeshott would regard as non-political, such as social justice.

But there is a more fundamental problem with Nardin's formulations. Is it actually the case that the value of the practices of international society can be divorced from their origin in the way that he presumes? There is an analogy here with the later Rawls's "justice political not metaphysical" and his notion of an "overlapping consensus" in support of that distinction.[20] In both cases the assumption is that the distinction between procedural and substantive matters is not culture-specific, that a distinction between political and metaphysical is universally applicable. This is doubtful. Clearly, some "states" that are members of international society do not want to see themselves as "states" in the sense that this term has been used in a European context. They may well take whatever they can get in the way of international rights, but they may not accept that this involves corresponding duties, because they do not see themselves as similar entities to the states with which they have to interact. Thus, revolutionary states generally do not consider themselves bound by the same rules as non-revolutionary states, and this is particularly the case when the revolution in question involves cultural/religious issues, as in, for an obvious example, the Islamic Republic of Iran.[21] It might be that such states are, for the moment, very much the exception not the rule, but it seems reasonable to assume that in future there will be an increasing number of exceptions.

In summary, the idea of international society as practical association does seem to offer a possible reconciliation of the universal and the particular, but only on two conditions. First, states (and groups, individuals and so on) have to be willing to circumscribe their ambitions quite severely—accepting that there are many areas of international relations that are outside the scope of political action. Second, the range of particularisms that practical association can tolerate is limited to those willing to accept the distinction between practical and purposive in the first place; it is unlikely that this will be a universal trait.

Human Emancipation, the Acceptable Face of Cultural Imperialism

The idea of international society as a practical association attempts to remove the potential contradictions between universalism and particularism by stressing co-existence. An alternative resolution might be found by denying the value of the particular, that is by asserting the superiority of universal values over particularisms. Since any possible universal position represents a generalization of a local, particularist, position, this would amount to the assertion that one particular view of the world deserves to be treated in this way because of its superiority to the alternatives—because, that is, it represents the equivalent of a "view from nowhere", the basis upon which a universal position can be grounded. Obviously, the unthinking assertion of the superiority of one way of life over another would be a morally unacceptable instance of cultural imperialism. What is under consideration here is whether a morally acceptable form of cultural imperialism is a possibility.

A case can be made for viewing European thought since the Enlightenment as based upon exactly such a claim. The value attributed by the Enlightenment to science, reason and freedom was clearly not intended to be limited in its scope to Europeans: Kant's Critical project was based on transcendent —universal and necessary—categories; Hegel historicized reason and offered an explanation as to why Enlightenment was a product of Europe, but there is no assumption that its greatest achievement, the rational, ethical state, is for Europe alone; Marx's sequence of "modes of production" famously involves the rather suspect idea of an "Asiatic" mode which is almost outside of history, but, as his writings on colonialism make embarrassingly clear, capitalism's role in Asia is to prepare that continent for a place in the universal social-ist/communist future being shaped in Europe.

The point about each of these positions is not that they consciously espouse and justify an assumption of cultural superiority, but rather that they work on the basis that categories such as "reason", "freedom" and "truth" are acultural. Even that part of the tradition that stresses the historicity of these categories re-institutes a universal basis one way or another—via Spirit in the case of Hegel, or, uneasily, via Spirit's materialist equivalent in the case of Marx.[22] To describe this as a morally acceptable form of cultural imperialism may, or may not, be fair comment, but it is a description that would be denied by the foun-ders of the Enlightenment project of emancipation. From their point of view, what they were doing was pointing to the impact of universally valid forms of knowledge on the human condition; they believed their philosophical positions to be no more culture-bound than was the natural science that, for the most part, they took as the model for justified knowledge claims.

This is cast in terms of the founders of the Enlightenment project, but much the same points can be made with respect to its modern defenders, who include neo-Kantians, neo-Hegelians, Anglo-American theorists of justice and German proponents of discourse ethics and critical theory. Writers as diverse as Onora O'Neill, John Charvet, Mervyn Frost, Brian Barry, Jürgen Habermas and Charles Taylor continue to assert the possibility of a universal ethical posi-tion.[23] The problem these writers have to face is that the foundations upon which their predecessors built are no longer available. For Hegel, *Geist* was something real, and when he described its movement in history he did not see himself as developing a metaphor: modern neo-Hegelians cannot and, for the most part do not, claim this sort of support. Kant's moral theory was based on the Categorical Imperative explicitly to avoid having to produce a Humean the-ory of the "moral sentiments"; his successors today, such as Rawls, try to com-bine Hume and Kant because they do not have this escape route. Habermasian discourse ethics attempts to create a substitute for a "foundation" in the notion of open debate in the ideal speech situation, but the extent to which it succeeds is clearly open to question.[24]

Moreover, the analogy with the natural sciences that served the classical writers of emancipation so well is no longer readily available. Over one hundred years ago Nietzsche remarked in this context that "physics too is only an interpretation and arrangement of the world . . . and not an explanation of the world", and this perspectivism anticipated much of the philosophy of science of the second half of the twentieth century.[25] Even setting aside the apparent celebration of irrationalism in the work of Paul Feyerabend, the attempts of Thomas Kuhn and Imre Lakatos to preserve the idea of a special status for scientific knowledge have not proved successful in the *political* sense in so far as even these writers have often had to see their work used to justify a perspectivist approach to knowledge.[26] Once the credentials of natural science are impugned in this way, it can hardly be used as the model of reliable knowledge. Of course natural science *works*—but then so does witchcraft, in its own terms, as Winch among others has insisted on telling us.[27]

None of this makes it impossible to argue for the higher cognitive adequacy of Western thought, but it does make it difficult to cast such an argument in ways that are not vulnerable to the charge of cultural imperialism. If one is going to suggest that one particular local viewpoint is the appropriate basis for a universal position, one is obviously vulnerable to the charge that this constitutes an artificial limiting of the number of ways of being fully human—a charge directed against Kant by Herder two hundred years ago[28]—*unless* one can demonstrate that there is something special about the viewpoint to be universalized. However much most Europeans may believe this to be true, actually demonstrating the point is no longer simple and straightforward, if it ever was. The "incredulity towards metanarratives" described in Lyotard's *The Postmodern Condition* undermines the possibility of asserting the superiority of a particular point of view in terms that are compelling to those not already convinced.[29]

International Multiculturalism Versus the Culture of Human Rights

This latter reference to the work of Lyotard raises the possibility of a change of tack. Classical and modern theorists of emancipation rely on their ability to demonstrate the universal applicability of their metanarrative as a way of overcoming the problem of moral pluralism. Perhaps this is an impossible project and instead one should simply accept the implications of cultural pluralism and relativism and abandon the attempt to arrive at universal principles. Instead, one could simply celebrate "difference" as a value in itself, much along the lines of the "multiculturalist" movement in the United States—making sensitivity to the particular the supreme virtue.[30] The only "universal obligation" that is appropriate to an international multiculturalism would be the obligation to allow different cultures to develop in their own ways by not imposing universal obligations upon them.

The area of contemporary international relations where this attitude would have the most implications would be that of international human rights protection. Clearly, documents such as the Universal Declaration of Human Rights adopted by the UN General Assembly in 1948, or the International Covenants on Human Rights adopted in 1966, do not correspond to the demands of a multicultural understanding of international obligation.[31] Instead, they essentially privilege a particular form of political life. When Saudi Arabia abstained on the vote on the Universal Declaration in 1948, it was ostensibly on the grounds that the freedom to change religion (Article 18) was incompatible with Islam; but it would have been more accurate to acknowledge that the whole Declaration amounted to a root-and-branch condemnation of the Saudi way of life. The willingness of states to sign up to (though often not to ratify) later Declarations and Covenants is more a tribute to the impotence of these legal documents than it is to their effectiveness in establishing international standards. The recent UN Conference on Human Rights in Vienna in 1993 more or less gave up the ghost on the original notion of the concept, asserting that, although certain rights were undoubtedly universal, they must be interpreted in their local contexts. From a universal perspective, this is hardly reassuring.

In a broader sense than human rights, one can see the emergence of an argument here analogous to that developed recently by Iris Marion Young.[32] Oversimplifying massively, her point is that sometimes in order to maximize the rights of individuals it is necessary to maximize group rights, because some of the most important features of individuals stem from their membership of groups. To promote a notion of justice that involves denying the relevance of difference in the name of equal treatment for all is to disregard, for example, the right of a native American to be recognized as a native American—and this may be the most important feature of this individual as an individual. Thus, group and individual rights are not incompatible.

There is, however, a fairly obvious problem here. What is to be said to, say, the Indonesian dissident who does *not* wanted to be treated in accordance with the particular notion of human rights characteristic of that society, but wishes for protection in the light of his or her status as a human being rather than as an Indonesian?[33] Such a person may be granted one kind of individuality as a citizen but would prefer not to take up the offer. In a way, this version of pluralism comes quite close to the version espoused by the international society approach to international relations. It is, in effect, the other side of the coin—whereas in international society as a practical association *states* are obliged to obey the rules of co-existence and are to be discouraged from raising matters of universal obligation that go beyond such rules, in international multiculturalism *individuals* have rights only as members of a group, and have no opportunity to assert universal rights. In each case the restrictions seem intuitively unsatisfactory and politically implausible.

Moreover, in this kind of multicultural world, what would be the basis for principles of international distributive justice? Would the more wealthy parts of the world really be likely to accept an obligation to assist the poorer areas to develop their sense of individuality if, as seems quite possible, this sense of individuality was expressed in ways that the rich did not approve of? The strongest claim for international redistribution—in all conscience not very strong, it would seem, judged by its success rate—is that of universal obligation expressed in some kind of Kantian, neo-Kantian or utilitarian terms.[34] Take away the possibility of arguing in these terms and it becomes less and less possible to put together a coherent set of reasons why the rich are to be taken to be obligated to assist the poor.

Unless, that is, one is prepared to regard such an obligation as simply a matter of "sentiment". This is the tack taken by Richard Rorty in his recent Amnesty Lecture, "Human Rights, Rationality and Sentimentality"—in the context of human rights rather than redistribution, but the argument can be generalized.[35] In this lecture Rorty speaks of a "human rights culture". It has to be recognized that there are no foundations for rights on a universal basis; rights are associated with particular kinds of communities—basically, bourgeois and liberal—and with the cultures of such communities, and there is no universal community that generates a universal culture of human rights. There is nothing beyond the community—"it is impossible to think that there is something that stands to my community as my community stands to me, some larger community called 'humanity' which has an intrinsic nature".[36] This would seem to put the Indonesian dissident referred to above in real difficulty, since his or her community simply does not possess a suitable human rights culture—unlike, for example, the civil rights worker in the American South in the 1960s, who could, and did, root an appeal for an extension of civil rights in conventional understandings of the culture expressed in the US Constitution and American tradition.

The difference between Rorty and other postmodernists on this subject is that Rorty believes there is at least some mileage in the idea that we can enlarge the scope of the civil rights culture—promoting an enlarged sense of fellow feeling by appealing to the "sentiments" through story telling, drama and other rhetorics appropriate to a sentimental education. Moreover, as a "postmodern bourgeois liberal"—his own, playful self-description[37]—Rorty has no qualms about promoting this enlarged sense of fellow feeling. If he could undermine cultures that do not stress human rights, he would—unlike the international multiculturalists. But—like the multiculturalists, but unlike most more conventional bourgeois liberals—he does not believe that the promotion of a human rights culture could be grounded on an account of how the world really is, much less on an account that would provide assurance that those who deny basic rights are destined to get their comeuppance if they do not mend their ways.[38]

Rorty is particularly interested in human rights, but similar sorts of argument could be constructed in favour of international redistribution. The plight of the wretched of the earth is indeed, at times, pitiful, and such as to appeal to the sentiments of the comfortable and well-to-do. From Rorty's perspective only such a sentimental appeal could be effective. It is not clear to me whether all this is to be regarded as a brilliant response to the subject of this chapter or as a clever evasion of the question. What *does* seem to be clear is that, if one is to take seriously the arguments of pluralists, relativists and international multiculturalists, Rorty's is the only account of the universal and the particular that manages to give any political substance to the former.

Half-Way Hotel Rooms and Non-Relative Virtues

The various positions examined in this chapter so far cover a range of possible ways of dealing with universal obligation and cultural pluralism. International society theorists look to universal procedural rules as a way of coping with different notions of the good; justified cultural imperialists refuse ultimately to accept that there are such different notions; multiculturalists assert the inevitability and value of "difference", while Rortyans consider themselves entitled to privilege one particular culture even though they acknowledge that their decision to do so cannot be defended without reference to the sentiments. What these positions have in common is an either/or quality. Cultural relativism is, or is not, a problem. Universal principles can, or cannot, be defended. What the final writers to be examined below have in common is that they attempt to find some kind of middle way between the universal and the particular, to refuse the choice between extremes.

In a recent paper, "Objectivity and Social Meaning", Michael Walzer rather resignedly notes the frequency with which he is accused of disdaining objectivity.[39] This is because his approach to distributive justice and other such topics puts so much stress on the social construction of meanings, and thus appears to deny the possibility of an objective model against which social meanings can be judged.[40] The burden of his work is that social criticism is most effective when delivered from inside a particular culture as an interpretation of that culture by one of its own members, rather than as a denunciation from the outside.[41] This position has something in common with the relativists discussed above, and is open to the same kind of criticism, namely, what happens if "a long history of social construction has somehow gone awry"?[42] That is to say, while Walzer has no difficulty demonstrating that, for example,

Nazism was an aberration in terms of Western culture, there could be other circumstances where social meanings that we might want to describe as obnoxious are not aberrations but are deeply embedded in a culture and accepted by its participants.

In his "Objectivity and Social Meaning" essay, Walzer appears to argue that there is ultimately no answer to this problem; but in what I believe to be his best book, *Interpretation and Social Criticism*, he does offer an answer of a kind. There he posits prohibitions—of murder, deception, betrayal, gross cruelty—that constitute "a kind of minimal and universal moral code".[43] He backs up the idea with a very helpful analogy. If we take a culture and its social meanings as a "home", a thickly constituted environment which is (socially) constructed overtime as a comfortable place within which to live, then a minimal and universal moral code would also be socially constructed in the way that one might invent "the minimally decent accommodations of a hotel".[44] One would not wish to live in the thin environment of an hotel—on his argument, one could not actually survive in this environment—but any actual home that did not meet the minimal stands for decent accommodation demonstrated by a hotel would not be a proper home. This provides a kind of constraint on the range of acceptable social meanings, and a basis for criticizing worlds that are not one's own.

It would be wrong to suggest that this actually *solves* the problem of a potential clash between the universal and the particular. Apart from anything else, Walzer's universal prohibitions are described in language that is itself open to interpretation. What is "gross" cruelty? Murder is unlawful killing, but what is "unlawful"? The example Walzer comes up with of an obvious breach of the universal code in the context of a long history of social construction gone awry is that of Aztec human sacrifice, and while this may seem convincing it is also too extreme to be of much practical use. Even the most rigorous opponents of the idea of universal human rights generally support the Genocide Convention. Such relatively easy cases tell us little about the more common, routine oppression of our world. However, the advantage of Walzer's formulation is that it does provide a kind of entry point to an argument—and by stressing that the hotel room is as much of a human construction as a home Walzer avoids the charge of sneaking foundationalist thought back into the argument. Indeed, from a Rortyan perspective, the idea of a universal and minimal moral code might be a valuable rhetorical contribution to a sentimental education.

Another approach to the problem of universal obligations as against local values that attempts to avoid an either/or choice is the neo-Aristotelianism of Martha Nussbaum.[45] Nussbaum is concerned to engage in the rational criticism of local traditions, but she is also attracted to the ethics of virtue. The difficulty is that, for the most part, those who reject

> general algorithms and abstract rules in favour of an account of the good life
> based on specific modes of virtuous action . . . [generally take this to be] con-

nected with the abandonment of the project of rationally justifying a single norm of flourishing life for all human beings and a reliance, instead, on norms that are local both in origin and application.[46]

Nussbaum's general point is that Aristotle, usually thought to be the most important figure within the ethics of virtue, did not see things in these terms, and produced a non-relative account of the virtues. Her account of Aristotle's method is that, first, he isolates a sphere of human experience that figures in more or less any human life, in which human beings will have to make at least some choices; then he asks, what is it to choose or respond well or badly within that sphere? This produces a "thin account" of each virtue, namely that it is "whatever being stably disposed to act appropriately in that sphere consists in".[47] This then needs to be given concrete specification in order to produce a full account of the virtue. Thus, for example, in the sphere of "fear of important damages esp. death", the appropriate virtue is "courage" but what courage means in any particular circumstances, facing any particular choices, obviously needs fleshing out.[48]

This general approach precludes the possibility of arguing, as relativists wish to, that any particular society does not contain anything that corresponds to a particular virtue, or that any particular agent could argue that it would be a matter of choice whether any particular virtue played a role in his or her life. The spheres of human experience are part of all lives in some way or another:

> Everyone has *some* attitude, and corresponding behaviour, towards her own death; her bodily appetites and their management; her property and its use; the distribution of social goods; telling the truth; being kind to others; cultivating a sense of play and delight, and so on. No matter where one lives one cannot escape these questions, so long as one is living a human life.[49]

Obviously, arguments are possible about the ways in which a thin account of the virtues could be turned into a thick account, and opinion will vary as to whether any particular set of arrangements does the job properly. Ethical theory considers such matters; the point is that different sets of arrangements are always commensurable because they necessarily relate to the same list of spheres of human experience. There will be a range of social arrangements that do provide thick accounts of the virtues, and there is no suggestion here that there is one best such account—but there are social arrangements that are not adequate, and even among the adequate accounts comparison and argument are possible. The key point is that this will *not* be a matter of judging one society by the standards of another; nor are we dealing with criteria that exist outside of human existence—there is no view from nowhere. Instead, actual common human experiences form the foundations—Nussbaum uses the term "grounding experiences"[50]—upon which a basis for ethical theory arises.

In "Internal Criticism and Indian Rationalist Traditions", Nussbaum and Sen show how this approach might be applied to an examination of a particular culture, and in "Non-Relative Virtues" Nussbaum defends the approach against its critics. Interestingly, in terms of the arguments examined in the rest of this chapter, the key criticism is generally that the range of possible human experiences is greater than is anticipated by Aristotle's or Nussbaum's model. Thus, the "virtues" remain tied to a particular conception of the world, albeit quite a broad one, rather than being, as claimed, derivable from universal experiences. Nussbaum's defence is that, while acknowledging that it is not possible to work with uninterpreted experience, it is still possible to identify features of our common humanity on the basis of which debate can occur. It seems to me that Nussbaum's strongest point is that she has "solved" the universalist–particularist debate by the classic method of redefining the terms of the argument—and her "essentialism" would appear anti-essentialist to many conventional defenders of the Enlightenment project. In any event, it seems clear that this is the most elaborate and sophisticated attempt to avoid a downright choice between universal and particular obligations currently available.

Conclusion

This paper has come some way from a consideration of the norms of international society, and it would be good if it were possible to tie things together in a neat way, showing what implications particular views on the universal and the particular have for particular normative positions; but to do this would require another chapter—several more chapters—and, in any event, would somewhat miss the point. It is clearly not the case that each of the approaches examined above is addressing the same agenda. On the contrary, each brings with it its own agenda, its own conception of what is, or is not, a problem. For example, to take the basic issue of relativism, a writer such as Richard Rorty would deny that there is actually a problem here. On his account, such a "problem" could arise only if the possibility existed of non-relative knowledge. Since on his account this possibility does not exist, the problem of relativism simply disappears. As he would see it, we are only raising the issue in the first place because we have not understand this.

Others are actually addressing the same set of problems, or can be made to do so, but even here it does not seem sensible to search for a "solution"—at least not yet. We have here a subject that is in its infancy. The whole area of normative international relations theory has only been subjected to systematic exploration in the last twenty-five years—which, of course, is not to say that writers before the modern age have nothing to say about these matters—while the normative implications of cultural pluralism have received even less attention than such a time span might imply. As I hope this chapter has demonstrated, there is a great deal of relevant work going on in this area, but it would be a mistake to think we have yet gone very far down the road towards the provision of adequate theory. Moreover, some of the most promising areas—such as Nussbaum's work—are the farthest away from conventional international relations thinking on the subject, and the task of integrating this work into the broader field of normative international relations theory will be particularly difficult in such cases. All of these are reasons for caution, reasons for not attempting yet to close off particular avenues of inquiry. For the time being, a substantive conclusion would be a procedural error.

Notes

1. A. Linklater, *Men and Citizens in the Theory of International Relations* (London: Macmillan, 1982).

2. See, e.g C. Brown, *International Relations Theory: New Normative Approaches* (Hemel Hempstead: Harvester Wheatsheaf, 1992); J. Thompson, *Justice and World Order: A Philosophical Inquiry* (London: Routledge, 1992).

3. See, e.g. C. R. Beitz, *Political Theory and International Relations* (Princeton: Princeton University Press, 1979); T. Pogge, *Realising Rawls* (Ithaca NY: Cornell University Press, 1989); and B. Barry, *Treatise on Social Justice*, Vol. 1, *Theories of Justice* (Hemel Hempstead: Harvester Wheatsheaf, 1989), Vol. 2, *Justice as Impartiality* (Oxford: Oxford University Press, 1995). Rawls's thinking on the matter has evolved somewhat since J. Rawls, *A Theory of Justice* (Oxford: Oxford University Press, 1971); see his "The Law of Peoples", in S. Shute and S. Hurley, eds, *On Human Rights* (New York: Basic Books, 1993), pp. 41–82.

4. See S. Hoffmann, *Duties Beyond Borders* (Syracuse, NY: Syracuse University Press, 1981), and the ECPR workshop with this title which generated a special issue of *Ethics*, Vol. 98, July (1988).

5. M. Frost, *Towards a Normative Theory of International Relations* (Cambridge: Cambridge University Press, 1986), p. 121. A norm is "settled" when "it is generally recognised that any argument denying the norm (or which appears to override the norm) requires special justification".

6. The qualifiers "dramatic" and "large-scale" are used here to signal that I recognize that it would be a mistake to exaggerate the degree of cultural uniformity exhibited *within* Europe.

7. See G. C. Gong, *The Standard of "Civilisation" in International Society* (Oxford: Oxford University Press, 1984) and, for a general introduction to the subject, H. Bull and A. Watson, eds, *The Expansion of International Society* (Oxford: Clarendon Press, 1984).

8. K. M. Panikkar, *Asia and Western Dominance: A Survey of the Vasco Da Gamma Epoch of Asian History 1498–1945* (London: George Allen and Unwin, 1953).

9. Whether the term "international society" is now, or has ever been, appropriate is examined in C. Brown, "International Theory and International Society: The Viability of the Middle Way", *Review of International Studies*, Vol. 21, No. 2 (1995), pp. 183–196.

10. Of course, this would be a perverse procedure if it were plausible to argue that cultural pluralism is a figment of someone's imagination (mine?) and that, in fact, the world is self-evidently culturally one. I know no plausible argument to this effect.

11. For non-specialists, the best way into the English School is an exchange between S. Grader and P. Wilson: S. Grader, "The English School of International Relations: Insight and Evidence", *Review of International Studies*, Vol. 14, No. 1 (1988), pp. 29–44, and P. Wilson, "The English School of International Relations: A Reply to S. Grader", *Review of International Studies*, Vol. 15, No. 1 (1989), pp. 49–58. The key works of the School, revealing both virtues and faults, are H. Butterfield and M. Wight, eds, *Diplomatic Investigations* (London: Allen and Unwin, 1966); H. Bull, *The Anarchical Society* (London: Macmillan, 1977); and M. Wight, *Power Politics*, 2nd edn. (Leicester: Leicester University Press/RIIA, 1978).

12. See Rawls, *A Theory of Justice*, pp. 378 ff. Rawls Mark II in, for example, "The Law of Peoples" takes a different tack.

13. For English School Eurocentricity see particularly M. Wight's essays in *Diplomatic Investigations*, and the conclusion to his *Power Politics*, p. 293.

14. T. Nardin, *Law, Morality and the Relations of States* (Princeton: Princeton University Press, 1983) and "International Ethics and International Law", *Review of International Studies*, Vol. 18, No. 1 (1992), pp. 19–30. For a more extensive examination of Nardin's approach, see C. Brown, "Ethics of Co-existence: the International Theory of T. Nardin", *Review of International Studies*, Vol. 14, No. 3 (1988), pp. 213–222.

15. M. Oakeshott, *On Human Conduct* (Oxford: Oxford University Press, 1975).

16. A practice is "a set of considerations to be taken into account in deciding and acting, and in evaluating decisions and actions": Nardin, *Law, Morality, and the Relations of States*, p. 6. "Practical association" is a helpful coinage, but the change from "enterprise" to "purposive" association has caused much confusion, since practical associations also have purposes, albeit of a different nature from those of purposive associations.

17. Nardin, *Law, Morality, and the Relations of States*, p. 19.

18. Thus, for example, while a state that denies a well-founded and "practical" practice such as diplomatic immunity can plausibly be seen to be undermining its own claim to statehood, it is difficult to see how, for example, the denial of equality of the sexes, or religious freedom, is similarly self-undermining for the state.

19. Although some redistribution to give all states the capacity to act as international "citizens" might be acceptable.

20. See J. Rawls, *Political Liberalism* (New York: Columbia University Press, 1993).

21. In general, the way in which Islam has been elected as the "Other" to the West is to be deplored, but the behaviour of Iran over the US hostages and later the death threats to Salman Rushdie makes clear the contempt with which its present rulers regard the practices of international society.

22. Such an equivalent might be the realization of "species-being" in the Young Marx—but did the Middle Aged Marx continue to see things this way? For an argument that he did, see D. McLellan, *Marx before Marxism* (London: Macmillan, 1970).

23. See e.g. O. O'Neill, *Constructions of Reason* (Cambridge: Cambridge University Press, 1989); J. Charvet, *A Critique of Freedom and Equality* (Cambridge: Cambridge University Press, 1981); M. Frost, *Towards a Normative Theory of International Relations* (Cambridge: Cambridge University Press, 1986); B. Barry, *Treatise on Social Justice*, Vol. 1, *Theories of Justice;* J. Habermas, *Moral Consciousness and Communicative Action* (Cambridge: Polity Press, 1992); C. Taylor, *Sources of the Self* (Cambridge: Cambridge University Press, 1989).

24. Habermas's work is particularly interesting because he is so clearly conscious of the challenge of anti-foundationalism; see "Morality and Ethical Life: Does Hegel's Critique of Kant Apply to Discourse Ethics?" in Habermas, *Moral Consciousness*, pp. 195–216, and J. Habermas, *The Philosophical Discourses of Modernity* (Cambridge: Polity Press, 1987). The best collection on this subject is the engagingly titled work by A. Honneth, T. McCarthy, C. Offe and A. Wellmer, eds, *Cultural–Political Interventions in the Unfinished Project of Enlightenment* (London: MIT Press, 1992).

25. F. Nietzsche, *Beyond Good and Evil*, trans. R. J. Hollingdale (Harmondsworth: Penguin, 1971), p. 26.

26. See e.g. the egregious use of the phrase "inter-paradigm debate" in the discipline of international relations, the purpose of which is to suggest the incommensurability of the different perspectives identified; for example, M. Banks, "The Inter-Paradigm Debate", in M. Light and A. J. R. Groom, eds, *International Relations: A Handbook of Current Theory* (London: Pinter, 1985), pp. 7–26. Of course, from a Kuhnian viewpoint one could not have an inter-paradigm debate since only one paradigm can exist at any one time, but this is a by-the-by.

27. For example in P. Winch, "Understanding a Primitive Society", most conveniently available in F. Dallmayr and T. McCarthy, eds, *Understanding and Social Inquiry* (Notre Dame, Ind.: University of Notre Dame Press, 1977), pp. 159, 188.

28. See F. M. Barnard, *Herder's Social and Political Thought* (Oxford: Clarendon Press, 1965).

29. J. F. Lyotard, *The Postmodern Condition* (Manchester: Manchester University Press, 1986), p. xxiv.

30. However, it should be said that international multiculturalism need not imply domestic multiculturalism and *vice versa*. It is quite possible to believe that one should be intolerant of variation within one's society while promoting such diversity internationally.

31. For texts see I. Brownlie, ed., *Basic Documents in International Law*, 3rd edn. (Oxford: Clarendon Press, 1983).

32. I. M. Young, *Justice and the Politics of Difference* (Princeton: Princeton University Press, 1991).

33. The position with respect to an East Timorese who is Indonesian only as a result of conquest involves oppression of, perhaps, a worse kind—but this is a different point.

34. See e.g. O. O'Neill, *Faces of Hunger* (London: Allen and Unwin, 1986): C. R. Beitz, "Cosmopolitan Ideals and National Sentiment", *Journal of Philosophy*, Vol. 80 (1983), and P. Singer "Famine Affluence and Morality", *Philosophy and Public Affairs*, Vol. 1, No. 1 (1972).

35. See R. Rorty, "Human Rights, Rationality and Sentimentality" in Shute and Hurley, *On Human Rights*, pp. 111–135.

36. R. Rorty, *Contingency, Irony and Solidarity* (Cambridge: Cambridge University Press, 1989), p. 59.

37. R. Rorty, "Postmodern Bourgeois Liberalism", in R. Rorty, *Objectivity, Relativism and Truth: Philosophical Papers*, Vol. 1. (Cambridge: Cambridge University Press, 1991).

38. See Rorty, "Human Rights, Rationality and Sentimentality", p. 130.

39. M. Walzer, "Objectivity and Social Meaning", in M. Nussbaum and A. Sen, eds, *The Quality of Life* (Oxford: Clarendon Press, 1993), p. 164. This collection is, quite simply, the best available on the subject of the tension between cultural pluralism and universal obligation, although the fact that it is ostensibly a collection about development economics may cause some to overlook its virtues.

40. His most important statement is M. Walzer, *Spheres of Justice* (New York: Basic Books, 1983).

41. See M. Walzer, *Interpretation and Social Criticism* (Cambridge Mass.: Harvard University Press, 1987) and M. Walzer, *The Company of Critics* (London: Peter Halban, 1989).

42. Walzer, "Objectivity and Social Meaning", p. 173.

43. Walzer, *Interpretation*, p. 24.

44. Ibid.

45. From an international relations perspective, the best sources of her work are M. Nussbaum, "Non-Relative Virtues: An Aristotelian Approach", in Nussbaum and Sen, *The Quality of Life*, pp. 242–267, and M. Nussbaum and A. Sen, "Internal Criticism and Indian Rationalist Traditions", in M. Krausz, ed., *Relativism: Interpretation and Confrontation* (Notre Dame, Ind.: University of Notre Dame Press, 1989), pp. 299–325.

46. Nussbaum, "Non-Relative Virtues", p. 243.

47. Ibid., p. 245.

48. Ibid., p. 246.

49. Ibid., p. 247.

50. Ibid.

12

International Human Rights: Philosophical or Political?

Peter Jones

One of the most common objections brought against human rights thinking is that we live in a world characterized by diversity of value. Theories of human rights necessarily ascribe rights universally to all humanity. Some people find that universalism implausible given the plurality of cultures, ideologies and religious beliefs to be found among human beings. Others find it objectionable. They see the assertion of human rights as an exercise in cultural (usually Western) domination or an all too convenient excuse for some states to meddle in the affairs of others.

The human rights theorist can remain unmoved by these objections. Human beings, he might reply, have certain rights merely in virtue of being human, and systems of value that fail to recognize that should be cast aside. The doctrine of human rights should be a fighting doctrine. Historically, both it and its predecessor, the doctrine of natural rights, were developed not merely to interpret the world but to change it. It would be a strange state of affairs if a moral theory could be faulted merely because it had not already been embraced and acted upon by everyone everywhere.

Yet so abrupt a reply seems inadequate. If a theory of human rights aims to be sensitive to the needs and well-being of human individuals and to respect their beliefs and identities, it can hardly be so cavalier in its dismissal of systems of value that give meaning and purpose to people's lives. A theory of human rights must challenge some values if it is to have any content of its own, but it must also extend a measure of respect to the sincerely held beliefs and values of individuals and communities if it is to remain true to its own spirit. Somehow, then, a theory of human rights needs to accommodate diversity rather than merely to reject it.

Diversity is not confined to the world beyond human rights. It is also a feature of human rights thinking itself. Philosophers present very different moral explanations of why human beings have rights. Some ground human rights in Kantian conceptions of the person, others in the logic of moral agency or in claims of self-ownership. Some appeal to human nature or to natural law, while others assert the self-evidence of human rights. Still others offer rival theological accounts of human rights. Not surprisingly, these different theories about why human beings have rights often issue in different catalogues of the rights they have. Even when theorists appear to agree, closer inspection often reveals that they have different understandings of the status and content of human rights. Human rights theory has also therefore to find some way of coping with the diversity within its own ranks.

In spite of this lack of unanimity, the idea of human rights has achieved great popularity. With the exception of its potential rival, the right of national self-determination, perhaps no idea can claim such widespread international acceptance. When governments are charged with abusing human rights, their typical response is to declare their innocence rather than to deny that human beings have rights.

What the theory of human rights seems to need, then, is a formulation that renders human rights compatible with these various forms of diversity, but one that retains for human rights a significance and a content worthy of the place they have come to occupy in our political thinking. John Rawls has recently tried to meet that need by developing a conception of human rights that all members of the international community should find acceptable. He articulates a specifically "political" conception of human rights designed to give due weight to rights of national self-determination and to accommodate a plurality of cultures and doctrines. It is his political conception of human rights that I examine in this essay.[1]

Political Conceptions and Comprehensive Doctrines

In his *Political Liberalism*, Rawls presents a theory of justice that is "political" in a special sense. A "political" conception is distinct from what he calls a comprehensive doctrine. Comprehensive doctrines include philosophical, religious and moral doctrines. Rawls describes them as "comprehensive" because paradigmatically they aim to provide comprehensively for how we should live. In fact, a doctrine need not be fully comprehensive in scope to be the kind of doctrine that he calls comprehensive. An ethical or religious doctrine may provide for some rather than for the whole of life but still count as comprehensive for Rawls's purposes. Comprehensiveness refers to the nature of a doctrine rather than merely to its range, and that is why he can speak, without contradiction, of "partially comprehensive" doctrines.

In modern democratic societies, people subscribe to a wide variety of different and conflicting comprehensive or partially comprehensive doctrines. Consequently, if we were to base a theory of justice for those societies on a comprehensive doctrine, that theory would also be a source of controversy and dispute. What a democratic society needs is a conception of justice that is independent of any comprehensive doctrine so that its citizens can accept that conception in spite of their doctrinal disagreements with one another. Rawls's "political" conception of justice is designed to meet that need.

His conception of justice is political in three respects (*PL* pp. 11–15). First, it is concerned to provide only for the basic structure of a society, that is, for its main political, economic and social institutions. It is a moral as well as a political conception, but it is a moral conception designed only for, and that applies only to, a society's basic structure. It therefore contrasts with comprehensive moral doctrines, such as utilitarianism, which provide for political life only by way of providing for life in general.

Second, it is a "free-standing" conception—it is worked out independently of comprehensive doctrines. It is not itself a comprehensive doctrine and it is not derived from a comprehensive doctrine. Some comprehensive doctrines may endorse the political conception, but it does not depend upon their endorsement for its content or rightness.

Third, it is articulated in terms of "certain fundamental ideas seen as implicit in the public political culture of a democratic society" (*PL* p. 13).[2] Rather than relying upon controversial doctrinal claims, a political conception draws upon a society's "fund of implicitly shared ideas and principles" (*PL* p. 14).

Rawls takes several of those shared political ideas and "works them up" into a conception of justice appropriate for a democratic society. The main ideas he draws upon are those of persons conceived as "free and equal citizens" and of society conceived as "a fair scheme of co-operation" and as "well-ordered". By applying the principles of practical reason to these ideas, he eventually comes up with his celebrated two principles of justice. These principles are therefore political rather than doctrinal in character and can be embraced by democratic citizens independently of their diverse doctrinal commitments.

Why does Rawls think that we should adopt this political approach to doctrinal diversity? In part, he is motivated by the goal of stability. True stability for Rawls is achieved by neither coercion nor deception but only when the citizens of a society willingly accept and comply with its institutions. Only then is a society "well-ordered". Since the citizens of modern democratic societies subscribe to different and conflicting comprehensive doctrines, a doctrinal conception of justice cannot secure that stability. They need a conception of justice that is independent of, and therefore not in competition with, their comprehensive doctrines.

But Rawls is not concerned only with stability. It is also important that the principles he develops for a democratic society can claim to be "just" for that society. Two ideas fundamental to the notion of a democratic society are that it should be a fair scheme of co-operation, and that its members should be accorded the status of free and equal citizens. Rawls's principles are just because they are evolved by a fair procedure of construction from those fundamental ideas; his political principles of justice secure fair public arrangements for democratic citizens who wish to pursue, either individually or in groups, the different conceptions of the good that stem from their different and incompatible doctrines.

A Political Law of Peoples

In his lecture on the law of peoples, Rawls aims to extend his political approach to the international arena. Given the plurality of doctrines present in democratic societies, an international conception of justice based upon a comprehensive doctrine would be no more acceptable to the citizens of those societies than a doctrinally based intranational conception of justice. In addition, Rawls holds that the law of peoples must extend beyond liberal democratic societies. It should also embrace what he calls well-ordered nonliberal societies. Those nonliberal societies are based upon comprehensive doctrines, and different nonliberal societies are based upon different doctrines. For that reason too we need a law of peoples that is independent of any particular comprehensive doctrine.

Thus, he constructs a law of peoples, including an account of human rights, that is "political" in the same special sense as his conception of justice for democratic societies. First, just as his political conception of justice is a moral conception designed only for a limited subject, a society's basic structure, so his conception of international justice is designed only for "the society of political societies" (*LP* p. 48) and for the law that is to govern that international society.

Second, his account of the law of peoples, including his account of human rights, is "free-standing". Like his political conception of justice, it is derived independently of any comprehensive doctrine.

Rawls is less explicit about what, for international purposes, equates with the third feature of his political conception of justice—its use of fundamental ideas implicit in the public political culture of democracy. The parallel would seem to be certain ideas about the form that international relations should take which are common to the community of well-ordered societies.[3] These may or may not amount to a "political culture", but they do provide us with some shared principles upon which we can draw in constructing a political conception of international justice. Two of those shared ideas replicate ideas implicit in a democratic political culture: that the international society of peoples should constitute a "fair scheme of co-operation", and that it should form a "well-ordered society". However, at the international level, "peoples" replace "persons" as the relevant units of political life; even so, we should ascribe to peoples in the international arena the same "free and equal" status that we should ascribe to individual citizens in a democratic society.

Why should the law of peoples assume this "political" form? Rawls would presumably give the same two-fold answer that he gives for his political conception of justice.[4]

First, an effective law of peoples should be stable and should secure stability of the right sort. That is, it should be able to gain the support of all reasonable peoples and it can do that only if it does not conflict with their comprehensive doctrines. Only a political law of peoples can provide the basis of a well-ordered international society.

Second, Rawls is in pursuit of a "just" law of peoples, and only a politically constructed conception of justice can provide a just law appropriate for a society of political societies each of which has its own internal conception of justice. As I have already indicated, Rawls believes the law of peoples should encompass well-ordered nonliberal societies committed to comprehensive doctrines along with liberal societies committed to none. If liberal societies were to impose their principles upon nonliberal societies, they would be guilty of an injustice directly analogous to that of individuals' imposing their comprehensive doctrines upon other individuals. Any such imposition, Rawls claims, would be inconsistent with liberalism itself. It would also negate the free and equal status of peoples. That status requires the same sort of toleration of peoples in international relations as it requires of persons in democratic societies.

Rawls employs the same contractual apparatus to develop a just law of peoples as he uses to construct just principles for a domestic society (*LP* pp. 53–4, 60, 64–5; cf. *TJ* pp. 377–9). For international purposes the contracting parties in the original position represent peoples rather than individuals. We are to suppose that those representatives will act rationally; that is, they will do their best to promote the fundamental interests of the peoples they represent. However, the constraints imposed by the original position ensure that the law of peoples selected by those rational representatives will also be "reasonable". That is achieved by giving all parties in the original position an equal standing, reflecting the equal status of peoples. It is also secured by using the veil of ignorance to deprive them of information that would unfairly influence their decisions. Thus, any particular party in the original position will be ignorant of the size of the territory or population of the society he represents or its strength relative to other societies or the extent of its natural resources or its level of economic development. He will also be unaware of whether he is acting on behalf of a hierarchical society committed to a comprehensive doctrine or a liberal society committed to none.[5] That is the apparatus we should use to devise a just law of peoples, and a law so devised will be just because it derives from a fair procedure of construction.

Rawls accepts that his approach to the law of peoples might be described as "liberal" given the independence and equality it accords peoples. But, he argues, that should not make it unacceptable to nonliberal societies since it is "liberal" only at the level of peoples. A nonliberal society, which does not accord persons a free and equal political status, can consistently attribute a free and equal status to peoples (*LP* pp. 65, 79–80).

It is also worth noting that Rawls, in shaping the law of peoples to accommodate well-ordered nonliberal societies, does not understand himself to be making a concession to imperfection. On the contrary, the ideas and reasoning that I have described belong to what he calls "ideal" theory (*LP* p. 60). Someone who subscribes to liberalism as a comprehensive doctrine may well believe that the world would be a better place if all societies were liberal (*LP* p. 81). But that belief does not figure in Rawls's political reasoning. His political conception of international justice is designed neither to challenge nor to affirm the truth of any comprehensive doctrine, including the truth of comprehensive forms of liberalism. But it is designed to show that it would be unreasonable and unjust for any society to impose its comprehensive doctrine or its domestic conception of justice upon any other society.[6]

The content of the law of peoples that Rawls derives from his approach is, for the most part, just what we might expect it to be: the independence of peoples is to be respected; they have the right of self-defence but no right of war (i.e. aggression); they have a duty of non-intervention; they are to observe treaties; and so on (*LP* p. 55). Rawls also claims, with less obvious justification, that a system of international law constructed in this way would require peoples to honour human rights. It is upon that claim that I shall focus in the remainder of this chapter.

A Political Conception of Human Rights

At first sight, Rawls's approach to the law of peoples seems unlikely to generate human rights. Consider the fundamental ideas from which it works. All of these centre on peoples rather than persons. The goal is to arrive at an international community that is consistent with the free and equal status of peoples, that secures a fair scheme of co-operation among peoples, and that constitutes a well-ordered society of peoples. Nor is there anything in Rawls's procedure of construction to direct us towards the rights of individual human beings. The parties in the international original position aim to promote only the interests of peoples *qua* peoples. They are constrained in the way they do that by the equal standing enjoyed by the contracting parties and by the veil of ignorance, but neither of those constraints does anything to deliver rights for individuals. If a theory adopts peoples as the relevant moral units of international political life, it is hard to see how it can deliver an international concern for the rights of individual human beings.

In fact, Rawls's constructivist theory of international justice plays only a very limited role in his account of human rights. As I shall indicate, the individual rights that figure in his law of peoples are rights to which all of the relevant societies are already committed as individual societies; they are rights that all well-ordered societies recognize quite independently of their being parties to an international arrangement. All that Rawls's hypothetical international contract adds is a reason for treating those rights as "human" rights. Thus, if we are to make sense of Rawls's account of human rights, we must confront two questions:

1. Why should well-ordered societies, taken severally, be committed to a common set of rights?
2. Why should those societies wish to make individual rights matters of international concern rather than limit their concerns to the rights of their own members?

Before taking up either of those questions, it is worth pausing to consider what Rawls understands a human right to be. For Rawls, the adjective "human" indicates only that a right is one that peoples must recognize and respect in their dealings with one another. Rights are "human" in the international arena and nowhere else. Their being "human" signifies that they are rights that societies must honour if they are to be "members in good standing of a reasonable society of peoples" (*LP* p. 42). The international community should regard as legitimate only regimes that respect human rights, but, if a regime does honour human rights, it should be immune from external interferences such as military force or economic sanctions (*LP* p. 71). But that is all that human rights are: a set of standards that peoples (not persons) have good reason to adopt and to follow in their relations with one another.

This parsimonious conception of human rights departs significantly from the conventional conception. In moral and political philosophy, human rights have generally been conceived as rights possessed by human beings as such and as rights that must therefore be respected in all the various contexts and circumstances in which human beings find themselves. Of course, those rights are likely to be of greater significance in some contexts than in others, simply because in some contexts people have greater need of the safeguards they provide. That is why they are most commonly asserted as constraints upon political power. But that is a contingent matter. Human rights as such attach to human beings as such.

But that is not Rawls's understanding. His human rights are not rights that regulate relations between individuals, nor are they rights that regulate relations between individuals and non-state associations. Nor even are they rights that citizens possess in relation to governments or states in purely domestic contexts. Attaching the adjective "human" to rights signifies no more than that they are rights that states or peoples justly ascribe to individuals solely for international purposes. Recall that Rawls's conception of the law of peoples, and his conception of human rights as part of that law, are "political" conceptions, and that part of what makes a conception "political" is its applying to a limited political subject. His principles of international justice are not the international dimension of a set of moral principles that are general in scope; they are not even principles that apply to every dimension of political life: rather, they are principles constructed specifically for the society of peoples. Likewise, Rawls's human rights are not part of a general moral theory of the rightful treatment of human beings. They figure only in his just law of peoples, and accordingly their role is limited to regulating relations between peoples.[7]

That does not mean that the rights that Rawls lists as human rights can be disregarded or infringed in intranational contexts. Rawls seems to suppose that in "smaller" contexts the moral demands made by human rights are subsumed within other principles of justice. In particular, although part of the role of human rights is to enable the international community to limit the internal sovereignty of governments, the domestic constitutional constraints that limit a government's authority may include and go beyond those rights. In the sort of liberal democratic society for which Rawls provides in *Political Liberalism*, those constraints include his second principle of justice, which provides for fair equality of opportunity and for the difference principle—subjects that fall outside the compass of his human rights. They also include constraints imposed by the rights that appear in his first principle, some of which also figure as human rights but some of which do not, such as full rights of free expression and liberty of conscience and full rights of political participation.

Rawls therefore breaks with the long-standing tradition in political thought which identifies rights that properly constrain the authority of governments and societies as universal natural or human rights. There is no place in Rawls's political theory for rights that individuals possess just as human beings and which, morally, they hold in advance of, and take with them into, political society—so that the limits of political authority are set by those morally pre-determined rights. Rather, the rights that citizens hold in relation to their own societies are rights that they hold only as members of those societies. The rights appropriate to a liberal society form part of a conception of justice that is both political and constructivist, while those appropriate to a nonliberal society will be sanctioned by the comprehensive doctrine to which the society is committed. Accordingly, different societies will afford their members different rights.

Rawls finds all of those differences acceptable provided that the relevant societies are well-ordered. He does suppose that there is a set of basic rights that all well-ordered societies will recognize, but even those count as human rights only when they are taken up by the international community. Consequently, Rawlsian human rights should figure in the foreign policies of states but have no role in their domestic lives.

Basic Rights and Well-Ordered Societies

How, then, does Rawls derive human rights—granted his limited conception of what these are—from his "political" approach to international justice? As I have already suggested, the answer is, in part, that his rights do not issue wholly and simply from his constructivist account of international justice. The rights that he describes as "human" are a sub-set of the rights already acknowledged by well-ordered societies in their domestic political lives. Why then should we suppose that liberal and nonliberal well-ordered societies will, severally and independently and because they are well-ordered, accord a common set of rights to their members?

In *Political Liberalism* (*PL* p. 35), Rawls describes a well-ordered society as one characterized by the following features:

(i) all its members accept, and know that one another accepts, the same principles of justice,

(ii) its basic structure is publicly known, or with good reason believed, to satisfy those principles, and

(iii) its members have an effective sense of justice and generally comply with the society's institutions which they regard as just.

Thus, a society is well-ordered when its members share a common conception of justice and comply with their society's institutions because they believe those institutions conform with that conception. Part of Rawls's case for the political conception of justice that he constructs for liberal democratic societies is that it is a conception that enables those societies to be well-ordered.

However, Rawls does not believe that good order can be found only within liberal societies. A "hierarchical" society based upon a comprehensive doctrine can also be well-ordered.[8] It is well-ordered if its system of law imposes moral duties and obligations upon all persons in its territory, if that system is guided by a common good conception of justice, and if the judges and officials who administer the system genuinely and not unreasonably believe it to be guided by a common good conception. By a "common good conception of justice" Rawls means "a conception that takes impartially into account what it sees not unreasonably as the fundamental interests of all members of society" *(LP* p. 61).

A hierarchical society is necessarily not a democratic society, but Rawls holds that, if it is to be well-ordered, it must constitute "a reasonable consultation hierarchy" (*LP* p. 62). Thus, although its members are not regarded as free and equal citizens and do not enjoy full liberal rights of free expression, there are ways in which they can make their voices heard, and those in power are obligated to take their dissent seriously.[9]

Rawls insists that a hierarchical society that is well-ordered in this way will respect basic rights such as rights to subsistence and security, rights to liberties such as freedom from slavery and from forced occupation, the right to personal property and rights required by the rules of natural justice. Rawls's model of a hierarchical society is one committed to a comprehensive doctrine, typically a religious faith, so that it does not clearly separate church and state. Even so, if it is to be well-ordered, it must extend religious toleration to its members. It will accept a measure of liberty of conscience and freedom of thought and it will not persecute any of its members for their religious beliefs. It will also afford them the right of emigration (*LP* p. 63). Thus, there are some rights that will be recognized by both liberal and nonliberal well-ordered societies, and it is those rights that the international community can adopt as human rights (*LP* pp. 62–3, 68, 70).

How is a society's acknowledgement and respect for these rights bound up with its well-ordered character? Although Rawls presents respect for rights as a feature of a well-ordered society, he signals that that respect somehow follows from the other features of a well-ordered society;[10] but the nature of that linkage is far from clear. There seem two possibilities. One is that, as a matter of fact, no population would find the non-recognition of these rights acceptable, so that in reality there never has been, nor would there be, a people that accepted the legitimacy of a social order that did not recognize these rights. The other is that a conception of justice that failed to incorporate basic rights would not qualify as a common good conception, so that, even if an entire people did embrace that conception of justice, Rawls would not describe their society as well-ordered. I consider each of these in turn.

Sometimes the primary element in Rawls's notion of a well-ordered society seems to be acceptance of its principles and institutions by the society's own members. He describes a well-ordered society as one that is legitimate "in the eyes of its own people" (*LP* pp. 43; also pp. 61, 79, 80). It would clearly be inappropriate for Rawls to use a specific conception of justice as the test of a regime's legitimacy since he allows that different societies can reasonably subscribe to different conceptions of justice.[11] By contrast, the approval of a society's arrangement by its own population is a much more accommodating standard and one that accords with the modern notion that the primary test of a regime's legitimacy is acceptance by its own people. That test is also consistent with Rawls's demand that a law of peoples must tolerate different forms of society: if we regard each people as free and equal, we seem obliged to respect the form of society that each people approves for itself.

If it is popular endorsement that is supposed to ensure that a well-ordered society will recognize and respect a set of basic rights, Rawls's claim has to be an empirical one: that, as a matter of fact, no population would endorse a society that failed to accord those rights to all its members. Yet we know that there have been societies whose cultures have been embraced by entire populations, even though those cultures have not accorded basic rights to all whom they encompass. Indeed, the notion of rights has been absent from many cultures. Rawls himself observes that a political culture may be "distorted and corrupt" (*LP* p. 229) and holds that a regime may be morally inadequate because of "the nature of the public political culture and the religious and philosophical traditions that underlie its institutions" (*LP* p. 77; also pp. 74–5). He also comments that "unreasonable religion" may abet the subjection of women (*LP* p. 77).

These remarks imply that popular endorsement of a society's culture and institutions is not enough to guarantee recognition and respect for basic human rights. Moreover, while a people's belief in the justice of their society's basic structure is central to Rawls's conception of a well-ordered liberal society, he seems ready to dispense with full popular endorsement as a necessary condition of good order in a nonliberal society. In his model of a well-ordered hierarchical society, he adopts and adapts an idea from Philip Soper's *Theory of Law* and holds that the relevant judges of whether the regime is just are its rulers and officials rather than the population at large.[12] Ordinary members of the society need be persuaded only that their rulers sincerely believe the political system to be just; they do not themselves have to accept that the system is indeed just. That relaxation in the approval required for a regime's legitimacy makes internal endorsement even less satisfactory as a guarantor of human rights.

It seems then that we must turn to another, more objective and determinate, component of Rawls's conception of a well-ordered society to discover the link with human rights: his notion of a common good conception of justice. That notion could turn out to be little more objective and demanding than the standard of internal approval. Who is to decide whether the conception of justice pursued in a society is a common good conception? Given the role that Rawls's assigns to officials and their "sincere beliefs", he might have nominated them as the relevant judges. However, while his remarks on this issue are often ambiguous,[13] Rawls apparently means to give considerable independent content to the idea of a common good conception of justice.[14]

For one thing, he incorporates a significant measure of egalitarianism in that notion. He explains that he means by it,

a conception that takes impartially into account what it sees not unreasonably
as the fundamental interests of all members of society. It is not the case that
the interests of some are arbitrarily privileged, while the interests of others go
for naught. . . . It takes into account people's essential interests and imposes
moral duties and obligations on all members of society. (*LP* p. 61)

So, to be well-ordered, the institutions of a hierarchical society must "look after
the important interests of all elements of society". Although individuals in that
society are not regarded as free and equal citizens, they are nevertheless "seen
as responsible members of society who can recognise their moral duties and
obligations and play their part in social life" (*LP* p. 62). Rawls also insists that
a well-ordered hierarchical society will have a system of popular consultation
so that it is not a purely paternalistic regime and it must extend a range of freedoms, including religious freedoms, to its members (*LP* pp. 62–3).

Thus, Rawls injects a considerable degree of objective substance into the
conception of justice that a society must possess if it is to be well-ordered, and it
is that objective substance that generates or incorporates basic rights. An element of subjectivity remains since a variety of specific conceptions can qualify
as common good conceptions, and, presumably, a society qualifies as well-
ordered only if it embraces the specific conception of justice that structures its
political system. (Although, as I have already noticed, in a hierarchical society
that endorsement may be provided by the "sincere and not unreasonable"
beliefs of judges and officials (*LP* pp. 61, 63) rather than by the ordinary population.) Even so, Rawls seems able to link the idea of good order to respect for
basic rights only by way of a conception of justice that has already built into it a
decent minimum of concern and respect for all members of the society that it
structures.

Rawls therefore confronts a commonplace dilemma. He is understandably
anxious to develop a conception of international justice that respects each society's own values. Indeed, he claims to work from ideas that are the common
currency of the international community. Yet if he accepts the legitimacy of
every practice and institution that a culture might sanction or a people endorse,
he risks tolerating too much. If, on the other hand, he limits the forms of society that are tolerable, he can be accused of imposing values upon peoples which
conflict with their own self-understandings. That goes against the very nature
of his project. Part of his purpose in developing a political law of peoples is to
develop a conception of human rights that cannot be dismissed as ethnocentri-
cally Western.

Yet his notion of a well-ordered society clearly limits, and is intended to
limit, the forms of society that we should tolerate. His claim that only well-
ordered societies should be accepted as "members in good standing of a reasonable society of peoples", along with his conception of what constitutes a well-
ordered society, functions as a fourth "fundamental idea" underlying his law of

peoples and one that is crucial to his theory of human rights.[15] It is only by excluding what he deems "badly ordered" societies from his hypothetical contract that he is able to argue that all of his contracting peoples will agree to recognize and sustain the rights he calls human rights. Respect for basic rights is therefore built into the very foundations of his argument; it is not delivered by that argument.

One difficulty in all this is that the idea of a well-ordered society seems a movable feast. We may all agree that societies should be well-ordered; but that does not mean that we all agree on what it is for a society to be well-ordered. Rawls holds that, when we move from constructing a conception of justice for a liberal society to devising one for the community of nations, we rightly extend the scope of toleration and relax our criteria of "reasonableness" in setting the range of societies that we should tolerate (*LP* p. 78). But just how tolerant should we be? The more we seek to embrace a diversity of societies and cultures in a consensual international society of peoples, the more it seems we have to dilute the content of a political theory of human rights. That opens up a continuum of possibilities, and it is not clear how a Rawlsian "political" approach can tell us just what balance we should strike between these competing considerations. For example, it is not difficult to imagine a Rawlsian hierarchical society that (like Rawls's own model) is committed to a religious faith, and that is genuinely committed to promoting the common good of all its members, but which for that very reason does not allow individuals the sort of religious liberties that Rawls regards as human rights. What enables us to place that society beyond the pale of toleration? Rawls's frequent appeal to the "reasonable" or the "not unreasonable" to intimate answers to that question leaves everything still to be argued.

That problem is allied to another. If the idea of good order is subject to "political" disagreement, we cannot resolve these issues by reference to purely "political" conceptions. A political conception for Rawls is one that derives from a shared political culture rather than from a comprehensive doctrine. But, if the culture that characterizes our world is insufficiently substantial and shared to generate a consensus on what counts as a well-ordered society, we have to look elsewhere—perhaps to standards that Rawls would describe as "doctrinal"—for our criteria of good order. Thus, even if we accept the ideal of a political conception of human rights, the consensual materials necessary to construct that ideal may not be available in our world.

Human Rights and International Obligations

Suppose we set these difficulties aside and work only with societies that we agree are well-ordered and that recognize a common core of rights. The next question we confront is why those societies should wish to make rights matters of international concern. Since, for Rawls, human rights have a role only in international relations, his case for human rights depends crucially on his being able to give a convincing explanation for that role.

Rawls's approach does not readily yield that explanation. His international original position is set up so that the parties seek only to promote the interests of peoples *qua* peoples. The constraints imposed by the original position aim to ensure that those interests are provided for fairly, but the interests that the parties promote fairly remain those of societies as collectivities. Rawls explicitly rejects a global original position in which the contracting parties represent individuals rather than peoples (*LP* pp. 50, 65–6). Rather, in his model the members of different societies relate to one another only as peoples. There is nothing in all this that readily explains why societies should be concerned about the justice or legitimacy of one another's internal arrangements.[16]

Perhaps the explanation lies in the principles to which those societies are already committed. In the procedure that Rawls uses to construct a conception of justice for a single society, he is keen to insist that the ends of individuals or groups that the parties in the original position seek to promote include conceptions of the good derived from their comprehensive doctrines and not merely their selfish ends. We can presume that the same applies to peoples: their interests or ends should be taken to include the ideals and moral beliefs to which they are committed *qua* peoples and not only their self-interests narrowly understood. Thus, the argument might be that, since each well-ordered society is committed to a common core of rights, all well-ordered societies will wish to promote that common core. They will therefore accept a shared obligation to promote those rights internationally.

Yet Rawls's argument is not well calculated to deliver that conclusion. As I have explained, he understands the rights that individuals hold within their own societies as rights they hold only as members of those societies. He does not understand the rights so held as human rights. If a society did regard the rights of its individual members as rights they possessed just as human beings, it would seem committed to some sort of concern for the rights of human individuals beyond its own borders. But, if it regards its own members' rights not as local expressions of a universal principle, but only as rights appropriate to its own kind of society, and if morally it confronts individuals in other societies only through the medium of collective entities, it is hard to see what reason it has to concern itself with the internal arrangements of those entities.

These problems relate to more than just the technicalities of Rawls's constructivist method. They relate also to the entire moral structure of his argument. The curious thing about that argument is that it tries to generate human rights out of the moral relations that obtain between peoples, rather than out of those that obtain between peoples and individuals or between individuals and individuals. For Rawls, the international obligation to respect human rights derives primarily from the deference that peoples owe to peoples and only secondarily and consequentially from the concern and respect that peoples owe to the individual members of other societies.

Privileging the Political

Finally, let me return to the "political" character of Rawls's argument. Philosophically, Rawls does not intend his political conception of human rights to rival and displace theories of human rights that rely upon comprehensive doctrines. The point of a political conception is that it functions on a different plane from the diversity with which it deals. Thus, in the domestic political arena, a political conception of justice does not take issue with individuals' comprehensive doctrines. Rather, it withdraws from the arena of doctrinal conflict and attempts instead to establish fair arrangements among free and equal citizens who happen to assert different and conflicting doctrines. It makes no attempt to assess the truth or falsity of their doctrines, nor does its even-handed approach entail an implicit assertion that no doctrine is better or truer than any other. The truth of doctrines is simply beside the point for a political conception of justice, and the virtue that that conception claims for itself is not "truth" but "reasonableness".

Assuming that Rawls is committed to the same logic in the international arena, his political conception of human rights is not intended to rival comprehensive doctrines, including doctrinal theories of human rights. Rather, it too ignores questions of truth and tries to establish a reasonable set of rights for peoples and individuals independently of any doctrinal claim. Rawls even abjures such minimal philosophical notions as that "human beings are moral persons and have equal worth, or that they have certain particular moral and intellectual powers that entitle them to these rights" (*LP* p. 68).

Because of its free-standing character, Rawls's political conception is supposed to be one that people can hold *as well as* rather than *instead of* a comprehensive doctrine. Thus, if it lives up to its promise, his political conception of human rights should be one that people can embrace and act on whatever other moral beliefs they hold, including whatever other moral beliefs they hold about human rights.

It is hard to see how Rawls can honour that promise. Any theory of human rights is a practical theory: it is a theory of how human beings ought or ought not to be treated, it is a theory about what you or I or others ought to do. It must therefore contradict and conflict with other theories that assert different imperatives. Indeed, Rawls seems committed to condemning theories of human rights, other than his own, in the strongest terms. Any attempt to implement a conception of human rights grounded in a comprehensive doctrine would be unjust. It would be no different from, and no better than, any other use of political power to impose a comprehensive doctrine upon people. Thus, while Rawls apparently allows that it can be reasonable to entertain theories of human rights grounded in comprehensive doctrines, and even to assert their truth, he (implicitly) denies that it would be reasonable to act on them. Practically, therefore, his political conception of human rights cannot claim to function on a different plane from "philosophical" conceptions of human rights.

But perhaps we have moved to that conclusion too quickly. It is one thing to believe that a particular theory of human rights is morally the most compelling. It is another to consider what can reasonably be done in the name of human rights when people have different and conflicting beliefs about their ground and content. If we allow that the peoples that form the international community are reasonable, and also that a people's conception of justice can be reasonable even though it differs from our own, we can accept that we would act unreasonably if we imposed our theory of human rights upon a people, even though we reasonably continued to believe that ours was the best theory. Rawls's political conception is designed to furnish us with a conception of human rights that most reasonably guides our political conduct in a context of international philosophical and moral disagreement.

Yet even when we recognize that that is its inspiration and purpose, it is hard to see how Rawls's political theory of human rights can claim not to compete for the same moral space as philosophical theories. If his political theory were constructed for second-best circumstances, we could intelligibly accept it while also subscribing to a different theory about the rights that human beings would ideally enjoy. But Rawls's political conception is not a concession to non-ideal conditions: it is an exercise in ideal theory. He has no fault to find with the priority that peoples have over persons, or with the variety of principles and institutions that well-ordered societies—liberal and nonliberal—have adopted. Just as he holds that the plurality of incompatible doctrines that we find in liberal democratic societies is not a matter for regret but "the normal result of the exercise of human reason within the framework of the free institutions of a constitutional democratic regime" (*PL* p. xvi), so he holds that the diversity of social norms that we see across the globe is, for the most part, entirely acceptable. Consequently, the constraints imposed by that international diversity do not require us to substitute pragmatism for principle. On the contrary, those constraints are part of a normal and acceptable state of affairs, and a conception of human rights that is adjusted to them remains morally uncompromised in both its content and foundation. It is very difficult to see, therefore, how we could embrace Rawls's political conception of human rights while continuing to subscribe to a philosophical theory that took a different view of the ground and content of human rights.[17]

If, in spite of Rawls's own claim to the contrary, we have to choose between these conceptions of human rights, and if a political conception of human rights is available to us (which, I have suggested, it may not be), why should we prefer that political conception to a philosophical conception of human rights?

Quite what gives Rawls's political conceptions their moral force is something of a puzzle.[18] For the most part, he seems to suppose that, because those conceptions are derived from fundamental ideas implicit in a public culture—a culture in which "you and I" share—we will, as a matter of fact, wish to give them overriding significance. Rawls uses our settled convictions as fixed points for his argument and supposes that we will dismiss as unreasonable anything that contradicts those convictions. Thus, his proposal that we should privilege the political over the philosophical seems to rest upon his belief that that conforms with what we ("you and I") already accept.

Rawls says nothing about the peculiar value of cultures which would explain why we should give them more significance than, say, ideologies or doctrines. Nor would it be plausible to find an answer in the distinctive contents of cultures and doctrines since cultures, including political cultures, are often shaped by and heavily infused with doctrinal beliefs. What seems to distinguish cultures or "fundamental political ideas" for Rawls is their providing a shared foundation from which we can cope with our diversity. If that shared foundation does not exist, or if it does for some people but not for us, or if we question or challenge the assumptions of a political culture in which we allegedly share, Rawls it seems is left with little to say to us.

Conclusion

Although there is ample reason to be sceptical about Rawls's political approach to human rights, his notion that conceptions of justice can be political rather than doctrinal has some plausibility. In our world, people's beliefs about the proper conduct of political life often seem detached from their doctrinal beliefs, so that, in spite of their doctrinal differences, they can agree on the basic principles that should govern their political life. For example, that, in general, the independence of nation-states should be accepted and respected is a widely shared belief; for most people it seems to be a "free-standing" belief rather than one yielded by a general doctrine—philosophical, religious or moral—to which they are committed.

Perhaps we can go some way in claiming the same for human rights. The idea of human rights is now widely accepted; some specific rights are also widely accepted, for example rights not to be tortured or enslaved. Of course, governments sometimes violate these rights, but those violations are not necessarily expressions of moral disagreement, just as criminal acts are not typically exercises in conscientious objection. The problem is that, as we add to the substance of human rights, so we run increasingly into genuine dissensus. Rawls proposes that we should keep the content of human rights modest for just that reason (*LP* pp. 68–9). But even he does not propose an unameliorated "lowest common denominator" approach in which rights can be human rights only if they are acceptable to all cultures.[19] His conception of a well-ordered society limits the rights that cultures or peoples can veto. Within the limits of good order, peoples have priority over persons; beyond those limits, persons have priority over peoples. But not everyone would set the boundary between national self-determination and individual rights where Rawls locates it; nor would everyone agree with his catalogue of human rights.[20] In addition, Rawls's use of the term "peoples", with its overtones of equality, homogeneity and consensus, helps him to glide over divisions between majorities and minorities and questions concerning whose voice should count as the voice of a people.

Rawls may protest that dissensus about human rights does not show that we must abandon the political for the doctrinal. If people have different beliefs about the content of human rights or about the balance that should be struck between the authority of peoples and the rights of persons, those differences may express differences in people's free-standing political commitments rather than in their doctrinal beliefs. Hence, contrary to my earlier suggestion that no political conception of human rights may be possible in the current world, it may be that several such conceptions are available, each competing for our allegiance. But, if that is so, Rawls's approach loses much of its appeal, for, instead of showing us how to achieve harmony amidst diversity, he simply presents us with a new form of diversity.[21]

Notes

1. Throughout this chapter, I use the following abbreviations in referring to Rawls's writings:

LP—"The Law of Peoples", in S. Shute and S. Hurley, eds, *On Human Rights: The Oxford Amnesty Lectures, 1993* (New York: Basic Books, 1993);

PL—*Political Liberalism* (New York: Columbia University Press, 1993);

TJ—*A Theory of Justice* (Oxford: Oxford University Press, 1972).

2. In *LP* Rawls formulates this clause as "certain fundamental ideas seen as implicit in the public political culture of a *liberal* society" (p. 221, n. 2, my emphasis; also p. 65). However, that difference in wording seems insignificant since in both cases the public culture to which Rawls refers is that characteristic of modern liberal democratic societies. He uses the adjectives "liberal" and "democratic" interchangeably to describe those societies.

3. Rawls is strangely coy and unsystematic in his statement of these. The sources of my interpretation are: on international society as a fair scheme of co-operation, *LP* pp. 54, 65, 74; on peoples as free and equal, *LP* pp. 54, 56, 57; on the international community as forming a well-ordered society, *LP* pp. 52, 57–58, 60. Later I argue that Rawls adds to these a fourth "fundamental idea": that only well-ordered societies should be treated as members in good standing of the society of peoples.

4. For ease of expression, I use the phrase "political conception of justice" to describe only the conception of justice that Rawls develops in *PL* for pluralistic democratic societies. However, I should note that Rawls's account of the law of peoples is also intended, and is equally describable, as a "political conception of justice".

5. Rawls himself develops the international original position and the law of peoples in two stages. At the first stage, he includes in the original position only parties representing liberal democratic societies and elaborates the law of peoples upon which they would agree. He then broadens the original position to include representatives of well-ordered hierarchical societies and discovers that they would agree upon the same law of peoples. Thus, it would seem that the parties in the original position would arrive at the same principles of international justice whether they represented liberal democratic societies only or well-ordered nonliberal societies only or a mixture of the two. The condition that each party in the original position should not know whether he is acting on behalf of a liberal or a hierarchical society and, if a hierarchical society, to what comprehensive doctrine that society is committed, is analogous to his not knowing in the domestic case the comprehensive doctrine of the citizens for whom he acts.

6. I include domestic conceptions of justice here as well as comprehensive doctrines, since a society that subscribed to Rawls's political conception of justice would not, *qua* society, be committed to a comprehensive doctrine. Nevertheless, Rawls implies that a society that sought to impose that political conception upon a nonliberal society would be guilty of the same sort of wrong as a society that sought to impose a comprehensive doctrine upon another.

The interpretation of Rawls's political liberalism is a no easy matter (on which, see P. Jones, "Two Conceptions of Liberalism, Two Conceptions of Justice", *British Journal of Political Science*, Vol. 25, No. 4 (October 1995), pp. 515–550), but Rawls's approach to the law of peoples suggests that he does not regard his political conceptions of liberalism and justice as intrinsically or uniquely right. They are merely the most reasonable conceptions for modern democratic societies, given the diversity of doctrinal commitments that tend to arise in those societies. In nondemocratic societies, not characterized by that diversity, there may be nothing to recommend them.

7. Some philosophers have suggested (in my view, without adequate reason) that human rights should be thought of only as rights held by individuals against states, but even they have not limited the role of human rights to international relations. See, e.g. B. Mayo, "What Are Human Rights?" in D.D. Raphael, ed., *Political Theory and the Rights of Man* (London: Macmillan, 1967), pp. 77–78; R. Martin, "Human Rights and Civil Rights", *Philosophical Studies*, Vol. 37 (1980), pp. 391–403; C. Wellman, "A New Conception of Human Rights", in E. Kamenka and A. Tay, eds, *Human Rights* (London: Edward Arnold, 1978), pp. 55–56.

8. Rawls's portrait of a well-ordered hierarchical society based upon a comprehensive doctrine seems at odds with what he describes in *Political Liberalism* as "the fact of oppression": "a continuing shared understanding on one comprehensive religious, philosophical, or moral doctrine can be maintained only by the oppressive use of state power. If we think of political society as a community united in affirming one and the same comprehensive doctrine, then the oppressive use of state power is necessary for political community." Rawls apparently claims that such oppression must be used to

secure doctrinal uniformity in *any* society, not just a modern democratic society. He goes on: "In the society of the Middle Ages, more or less united in affirming the Catholic faith, the Inquisition was not an accident; its suppression of heresy was needed to preserve that shared religious belief" (*PL* p. 37).

9. Rawls also includes among the requirements for a well-ordered hierarchical society that "it must be peaceful and gain its legitimate aims through diplomacy and trade, and other ways of peace". If it is committed to a religious doctrine, it must not be expansionist but must respect "the civic order and integrity of other societies" (*LP* p. 61). That looks more like a condition for a society's being a member of a well-ordered international community than a condition of its being itself a well-ordered society. However, Derek Bell has suggested to me that "well-ordered" applied to societies in the international case functions much as "reasonable" applied to comprehensive doctrines in the domestic (liberal democratic) case. A democratic society need accommodate only those comprehensive doctrines that are "reasonable"—those that are compatible with the essentials of a democratic regime (though Rawls sometimes describes doctrines as "reasonable" or "unreasonable" in other senses); it would be unreasonable to require a democratic society to accommodate doctrines that were at odds with its own foundations. Similarly, international society need accommodate only "well-ordered" societies—societies that, among other things, are peaceful and respect the civic order and integrity of other societies; aggressive and expansionist societies are at odds with the very project of establishing a just political society of peoples.

10. "[a well-ordered society's] legal system satisfies certain requisite conditions of legitimacy in the eyes of its own people; and, *as a consequence of this*, it honours basic human rights"; "a well ordered hierarchical society also meets a third requirement: it respects basic human rights. *The argument for this conclusion* is that the second requirement [concerning a common good conception of justice, a reasonable consultation hierarchy, etc.] rules out violations of these rights" (*LP* pp. 43, 62–63, my emphases). For similar statements, see *LP* pp. 62, 67, 68.

11. Though, in one place, Rawls does describe all well-ordered societies as "just" and the international community that they form as "a well-ordered society of the just peoples of the world" (*LP* p. 52). Perhaps that is because all of them comply with his notion of a common good conception of justice.

12. P. Soper, *A Theory of Law* (Cambridge, Mass.: Harvard University Press, 1984); *LP* pp. 61–64, 224–225; *PL* pp. 109–110.

13. Sometimes Rawls implies that the relevant test is that judges and other officials believe "sincerely and not unreasonably" (*LP* p. 61) that the law of their society is informed by a common good conception of justice. Thus, those officials must be willing to justify the legal system in terms of that conception to their own population (*LP* p. 62). At other times, his words suggest that we need refer to the "sincere and not unreasonable" beliefs of officials only when we test whether a regime is really guided by, and actually implements, the common good conception of justice that it professes. The first of these two possible understandings seems more consistent with all that Rawls says. However, even on that understanding, his condition that the beliefs of officials must be "not unreasonable" limits the authority that he gives to their merely sincere beliefs. Rawls observes that "not unreasonable" is a weaker standard than

"reasonable" (*LP* p. 225, n. 28), yet in this context he sometimes uses the two terms interchangeably (e.g. *LP* p. 63).

14. To Soper's requirement that the beliefs of officials must be "sincere", Rawls adds that they must also be "reasonable" or "not unreasonable". It is not surprising that Rawls should want a more substantial test than Soper's. Soper aims only to lay down the minimum conditions a system must meet to qualify as a legal (rather than a merely coercive) system and for those within its jurisdiction to have some obligation to obey it. However, that obligation is only a *prima facie* obligation and can be easily outweighed by countervailing considerations, including the actual injustices of the system. Rawls, by contrast, is trying to give full criteria for regimes' having "the moral status required to be members in good standing in a reasonable society of well-ordered peoples" (*LP* p. 64). Like Rawls, Soper argues that his criteria for a legal system imply a number of individual rights, but Soper's rights are more modest in nature than Rawls's human rights; cf. Soper, *Theory of Law*, pp. 125–143.

15. Rawls very frequently states this idea; see *LP* pp. 42, 52, 64, 68, 71, 74, 76, 78, 79, 80, 224, 226. I describe it as a "fourth fundamental idea" because it seems to have the same foundational status in his constructivist argument for the law of peoples as the three ideas of international society as itself a well-ordered society, of that society as a fair system of co-operation, and of peoples conceived as free and equal.

16. An argument that Rawls might have used, but does not, is that peoples have reason to protect themselves from internal oppression by agreeing with one another to take collective international action against a regime that oppresses any of their number.

17. Ultimately, Rawls's political conception of justice for the domestic arrangements of liberal democratic societies runs up against the same issue. Rawls usually describes the competing comprehensive doctrines, whose pursuit his political conception of justice regulates, as "philosophical, religious and moral doctrines", which suggests that their concerns are quite different from those of the political conception itself. Yet these are supposed to be *comprehensive* doctrines, which means that they will encompass political as well as other matters. Thus, Rawls seems committed to claiming that people can intelligibly hold his political conception while also holding a political doctrine that may have a different and conflicting content. Perhaps that is one reason why he suggests, optimistically, that conflicting comprehensive doctrines will converge politically and produce an "overlapping consensus" in support of his political conception of justice. In that case, people will be spared the embarrassment of holding conflicting political beliefs.

18. See Jones, "Two Conceptions of Liberalism, Two Conceptions of Justice", pp 528–532.

19. For examples of the lowest common denominator approach, see A. J .M. Milne, *Human Rights and Human Diversity* (Basingstoke: Macmillan, 1986), and A. D. Renteln, *International Human Rights: Universalism versus Relativism* (Newbury Park, Cal.: Sage, 1990).

20. One example of a human right in Rawls's brief list that is not merely controversial but *politically* controversial is the right to subsistence; that right, as he understands it, entails international obligations of assistance (cf. *LP* pp. 56, 62, 64, 75–77, 223, 225, 228–230). While there does seem to be a reasonably widespread sentiment that countries "ought" to do something to relieve the economic distress of the popula-

tions of other countries, there is much less general acceptance that that "ought" should be cast in the language of human rights: do "they" have a right to "our" resources? Even Rawls seems more inclined to deal with this issue by encouraging each society to put its own house in order than by advocating international redistribution (*LP* p. 77). The same ambivalence is present in the UN's International Covenant on Economic, Social and Cultural Rights (1966). Article 11 of the Covenant, "recognising the fundamental right of everyone to be free from hunger", commits the state parties to taking measures "to ensure an equitable distribution of world food supplies in relation to need". On the other hand, article 2 states that "All peoples may, for their own ends, freely dispose of their natural wealth and resources without prejudice to any obligations arising out of international economic co-operation . . ."; and article 25 provides that "Nothing in the present Covenant shall be interpreted as impairing the inherent right of all peoples to enjoy and utilise fully and freely their natural wealth and resources". See further P. Jones, *Rights* (Basingstoke: Macmillan, 1994), pp. 157–171.

21. I am grateful to the other contributors to this volume for helpful discussion of an earlier version of this chapter and to Derek Bell, Simon Caney and Susan Mendus for their detailed and incisive comments on my reading of Rawls.

Index

About the Book

Nationalism is once again rising and spreading. Nationalist movements are active throughout the world, demanding political recognition of their nations' identity. Yet the current revival of nationalism has taken place alongside claims that nation-states are becoming obsolete in an increasingly globalized world. In addition, now perhaps more than ever, people are conscious of humanity as a whole and are ready to take seriously the international dimensions of morality.

In this collection of timely essays, distinguished moral and political philosophers examine issues raised by the competing claims of nationhood and internationalism from a variety of perspectives and defend a variety of answers. Questions discussed include: Is humanity really divided into nations or are nations invented by nationalists? Does a nation have the right to be self-determining? If so, must each nation form a separate and sovereign state? Do our obligations stop at national boundaries? Do we not have obligations to human beings as such? Why then should we be less concerned about "foreigners" than about our compatriots? Can we be concerned for social justice within societies yet not across the world as a whole? If we embrace ideas of human rights and global obligations, how do we establish what those rights and obligations actually are? Is it proper, plausible, or practical to aspire to such universal moral principles in a world characterized by national diversity and cultural difference?